Hands-On Automated Testing with Playwright

Create fast, reliable, and scalable tests for modern web apps with Microsoft's automation framework

Faraz K. Kelhini

Butch Mayhew

<packt>

Hands-On Automated Testing with Playwright

Portfolio Director: Ashwin Nair
Relationship Lead: Aaron Lazar
Project Manager: Vishnu Priya R
Content Engineer: Adrija Mitra
Technical Editor: Arjun Varma
Copy Editor: Safis Editing
Indexer: Tejal Soni
Proofreader: Adrija Mitra
Production Designer: Shantanu Zagade
Growth Lead: Anamika Singh

First published: January 2026

Production reference: 1070126

Published by Packt Publishing Ltd.
Grosvenor House
11 St Paul's Square
Birmingham
B3 1RB, UK.

978-1-80610-647-9

www.packtpub.com

Foreword

I've had the pleasure of knowing Butch for the last few years and meeting Faraz a handful of times. Each interaction has left me impressed, not only by their technical mastery but by their thoughtfulness, humility, and generosity. In a field that moves as fast as ours, those qualities are rare and valuable. Real expertise isn't just about knowing the tools; it's about understanding how to think about them, how to teach them, and how to make them accessible to others.

Playwright sits at the crossroads of many of the changes reshaping modern software engineering. It's not just another testing tool; it represents a shift in how we approach automation, reliability, and the developer experience. It combines speed with expressiveness and power with accessibility. Yet, as with any technology that evolves quickly, its true potential is unlocked not by the code itself but by the community and knowledge that forms around it. That's where Butch and Faraz come in.

This book is more than a technical manual. It's a map drawn by two people who have lived the journey, faced the pitfalls, and found elegant solutions to the real-world problems teams encounter every day. They've distilled not just what Playwright does, but how to use it well. They illuminate a mindset of quality engineering rooted in curiosity, clarity, and respect for both the craft and the process.

We live in a time when AI, automation, and relentless innovation are constantly redefining what's possible in software. Frameworks rise and fall with dizzying speed. Teams are asked to move faster, test smarter, and release more confidently, often with fewer people and tighter timelines. Amid all this, books such as this serve as grounding points. They remind us that while technology changes, sound engineering principles endure.

In the age of AI-assisted development, it's tempting to let tools do more of the thinking for us. But Butch and Faraz show that understanding still matters. The best engineers aren't just automating tasks; they're building systems that express intent, create confidence, and help teams move forward safely. Playwright, used thoughtfully, is one of the rare tools that makes this possible, and this book shows you how.

Over time, I've come to view every interaction with Butch and Faraz as an opportunity to learn. They bring an energy that is both deeply technical and profoundly human. They care about details, not out of pedantry, but because they know that craft lives in the details. And they care about people: their teammates, their communities, and the next generation of engineers who will inherit the systems we are building today.

That spirit runs through every page. The book is practical, insightful, and full of lessons that reach beyond Playwright itself. It encourages testing as exploration, automation as communication, and engineering as craftsmanship. It acknowledges the chaos of modern development, the shifting libraries, the endless updates, and the growing influence of AI, and offers a steady hand to help navigate through it.

What makes this work so valuable isn't just that it teaches you to write better tests. It teaches you to think better about testing, about systems, and about your role as a builder of reliable software in an unpredictable world.

Whether you're picking up Playwright for the first time or leading a team through its next evolution, take your time with this book. Let it guide you. Let it reaffirm that excellence doesn't come from chasing every new trend, but from mastering the fundamentals and applying them with curiosity, empathy, and discipline.

Butch and Faraz embody that philosophy. Their work is a gift to anyone who believes that quality matters, clarity counts, and that learning, in all its messy, joyful, human forms, remains at the heart of great engineering.

Ben Fellows

– CEO, Loop Software & Testing Services, Inc

Playwright Ambassador

Contributors

About the authors

Faraz K. Kelhini is a test automation engineer, full-stack JavaScript expert, and author with a decade of experience turning complex web problems into elegant solutions. He has written three highly regarded books: *Modern Asynchronous JavaScript*, *Text Processing with JavaScript*, and *JavaScript Brain Teasers*. Beyond books, Faraz creates interactive courses for Educative.io, pens in-depth tutorials for LogRocket, and polishes manuscripts as a technical editor for Pearson and Packt. Whether he's architecting enterprise-grade applications, developing essential tooling, or guiding emerging talent, Faraz's mission remains the same: empower developers to write smarter code and have fun doing it.

Writing this book has been a rewarding collaboration. I'm grateful to Butch Mayhew for building and refining this vision with me, to our editor Adrija Mitra for thoughtful guidance, and to Aaron Lazar for championing this project. And thank you, reader, for joining us. I hope these practices help you ship better software and maybe even enjoy testing a bit more.

Butch Mayhew is a Playwright Ambassador and quality consultant focused on enabling quality across organizations through modern testing practices and pragmatic automation. With 10+ years in test automation and deep exploratory testing, he helps teams build confidence in their software by improving how they test, what they test, and how quickly they can learn from results. He is the founder of Howdy QA, a consultancy that supports companies with Playwright adoption, framework design, CI/CD integration, accessibility testing, and hands-on training. His approach blends strong technical execution with a culture-first mindset: quality isn't a phase, it's a habit teams build together. He has also created LinkedIn Learning courses on Playwright, giving engineers and testers a structured, hands-on path to leveling up their automation skills.

I would like to extend my thanks to my wife and family for all the support they have provided me this year and throughout the years. I would like to thank Faraz Kelhini for all the hard work and effort he has put into this book. Special thanks to Sergei Gapanovich for his friendship and for raising the bar on my craft through honest challenge, sharp feedback, and relentless curiosity. Finally, thanks to the entire Packt team for their support during the course of writing this book.

About the reviewers

Carlos Gauto, better known in tech circles as **Charly Automatiza**, is a dedicated IT project leader with more than 19 years of practical experience in software development, test automation, and performance engineering. His career has been marked by hands-on roles that blend technical expertise with a genuine passion for mentoring and community building.

A Microsoft MVP and tool ambassador (Playwright, Grafana k6, SelectorsHub), he is an AI advocate, participating in major events in Spain and Latin America, with talks delivered in Spanish, Portuguese, and English.

Deepak Kamboj is a senior software engineer at Microsoft with 24+ years of experience, including 8 years in architecture. He leads critical projects focusing on AI agent workflows, test automation, and infrastructure, and developed a large-scale Playwright test setup that executes over 14,000 tests for 50+ internal teams. His work is directly focused on driving efficiency and reliability across the enterprise.

He is deeply passionate about blending AI, productivity, and automation to make development work smoother and smarter. His core expertise spans AI agents, generative testing, Copilot Studio, RAG, and MCP-based automation and AI-driven solutions.

As a trusted advisor, coach, and conference speaker, he guides teams in adopting next-gen AI, ensuring test reliability, and optimizing DevOps. He shares practical, real-world solutions and explores innovative AI uses for tangible impact, advancing AI automation, workflow orchestration, and constructing modern, goal-oriented agent ecosystems for the cloud age. Deepak welcomes discussions on next-gen software testing and practical solutions that drive success in technology.

Table of Contents

Chapter 3: Browser-Agnostic Testing Across Chromium, Firefox, and WebKit 43

Chapter 7: Integrating Workflows with CI/CD Pipelines 135

Chapter 8: Headless Testing and Debugging 159

Chapter 15: Best Practices for Test Maintainability 305

Chapter 16: Real-World Project – Testing an E-Commerce Website 323

Preface

This book is your hands-on guide to mastering **Playwright**, Microsoft's modern automation framework for end-to-end testing. Throughout these chapters, we'll walk through everything from getting started with Playwright's core features, such as browser automation, selectors, and locators, to building robust test suites with fixtures, page objects, and test data management. You'll learn how to run tests in parallel, integrate them into CI/CD pipelines, use Playwright Test for reporting and debugging, and even scale your tests for complex web applications.

When I first started working with automated testing, I remember how it felt like juggling too many things at once: browser versions, test runners, CI pipelines, and that mysterious "timeout error" that always showed up right before a release. Automation promised speed and confidence, but too often it delivered frustration and endless debugging sessions. I wanted to change that.

Then I discovered Playwright, and it felt like someone finally read every tester's wish list and decided to build the tool we'd all been waiting for. Fast, reliable, cross-browser testing that actually works across modern web apps? But even with such a powerful tool, there's still a learning curve: how to use it effectively, how to structure tests, and how to keep them fast, readable, and maintainable.

While digging deeper into the Playwright ecosystem, I came across Butch Mayhew's blog, which was full of insightful, practical advice that immediately resonated with me. Butch, a Playwright Ambassador, has a real gift for making testing feel approachable and for breaking down complex concepts into clear explanations. One conversation led to another, and before long, we decided to join forces to write this book.

This book is the result of that collaboration: our shared experience, our lessons learned (sometimes the hard way), and our excitement about what Playwright makes possible. It's packed with hands-on examples, real-world scenarios, and actionable guidance to help you build fast, reliable, and scalable tests for modern web applications.

Whether you're a developer dipping your toes into test automation, a QA engineer looking to upgrade your toolkit, or a tech lead aiming to bring stability and confidence to your releases, we wrote this book with you in mind.

Who this book is for

This book is for anyone who believes that automated testing should make your life easier, not harder.

If you're a **developer** looking to integrate end-to-end testing into your development process, you'll find plenty of practical guidance on writing clean, maintainable test code, and building tests that run seamlessly alongside your applications.

If you're a **software tester**, **QA engineer**, or **SDET** who's tired of chasing flaky tests and fighting inconsistent results across browsers, this book will show you how Playwright can simplify your workflow.

If you're a **team lead** or **engineering manager**, this book will help you understand how to structure a Playwright test framework that scales with your team, so you can standardize test practices, reduce maintenance overhead, and speed up delivery cycles without sacrificing quality.

If you already have some experience with Selenium, Cypress, or Puppeteer, you'll quickly see how Playwright takes familiar concepts and pushes them further with powerful features such as auto-waiting, cross-browser execution, and robust parallelization. You'll also pick up techniques to make your existing testing practices more efficient and scalable.

What this book covers

Chapter 1, *Quick Setup Refresher*, serves as an entry point for you and offers a concise refresher on setting up Playwright and writing basic tests. It ensures you can quickly get a testing environment running and understand Playwright's core structure.

Chapter 2, *Advanced Selectors and Handling Dynamic Content*, explores techniques for interacting with complex web elements using Playwright's selector engine. It covers dynamic content, waits, and advanced DOM structures such as iframes and shadow DOM.

Chapter 3, *Browser-Agnostic Testing Across Chromium, Firefox, and WebKit*, introduces you to Playwright's browser-agnostic testing capabilities. We'll dive into all the ways you can tweak your browser contexts: adjusting viewport sizes and user agents, emulating various devices, and even setting permissions.

Chapter 4, *AI-Powered Test Generation*, explores how AI tools can improve Playwright test creation by generating scripts from natural language and refining tests for reliability.

Chapter 5, *Crafting Scalable Tests with the Fixture System*, shows you how to use Playwright's fixture system to its full potential. We'll start with the built-in fixtures, then move on to creating your own and understanding how fixture scope and lifecycle affect your tests.

Chapter 6, *Test Parallelization and Performance Optimization*, focuses on scaling tests efficiently by running them in parallel and optimizing performance. It includes using the Chrome DevTools Protocol to measure and improve web app metrics.

Chapter 7, *Integrating Workflows with CI/CD Pipelines*, details incorporating Playwright tests into CI/CD workflows using GitHub Actions. It covers environment setup and reporting for automated pipelines.

Chapter 8, *Headless Testing and Debugging*, explains running tests in headless mode for efficiency and debugging failed tests with Playwright's tools. It includes capturing media for diagnostics.

Chapter 9, *Accessibility Testing with Playwright and Axe-core*, covers testing for web accessibility using Playwright and libraries such as axe-core. It emphasizes best practices to ensure inclusive applications.

Chapter 10, *Setting up Visual Regression Testing*, involves setting up tests to compare screenshots, handling differences and ensuring visual consistency.

Chapter 11, Testing Mobile Web Experiences, focuses on testing mobile web experiences by simulating devices and handling. It addresses mobile-specific challenges.

Chapter 12, Testing Forms, explores testing form interactions, including inputs, validations, and specialized fields. It ensures robust handling of user inputs.

Chapter 13, Handling File Uploads and Downloads, addresses uploading files, downloading and verifying content, and managing different file types.

Chapter 14, Security and Authentication, focuses on login management, testing user roles, and securely storing credentials.

Chapter 15, Best Practices for Test Maintainability, explores how to structure your tests, leverage the **Page Object Model (POM)** to keep things tidy, and manage test data to avoid frustrating failures.

Chapter 16, Real-World Project – Testing an E-commerce Website, walks you through creating a solid and adaptable end-to-end testing framework for an e-commerce website.

Appendix A, Streamlining Playwright in Modern Development Workflows, dives into how Playwright can seamlessly fit into today's development practices, such as Agile, DevOps, and different CI/CD pipelines.

Appendix B, References & Resources, provides a curated list to guide your further exploration.

To get the most out of this book

- You don't need to be a testing guru or a JavaScript wizard to follow along, but having a little bit of programming experience will help. If you've written code in JavaScript, TypeScript, or even Python, you'll feel comfortable pretty quickly. The examples in this book primarily use TypeScript, since it's Playwright's native language and helps catch errors early, but you can easily adapt the concepts to any supported language. Everything else, we'll walk through together, step by step, with plenty of real-world examples and practical exercises.

- As you work through the chapters, you'll find plenty of hands-on exercises. Don't just read them: try them out! The best way to learn Playwright is by doing. Break things, tweak things, and experiment. You'll learn far more from watching your tests run (and sometimes fail) than from just reading code snippets.
- Each chapter builds on the previous one, but feel free to skip around if you're already familiar with certain topics. You can use this book as a guided tutorial from start to finish or as a reference when you're solving specific testing challenges.

Download the example code files

The code bundle for the book is hosted on GitHub at `https://github.com/PacktPublishing/Hands-On-Automated-Testing-with-Playwright`.

We also have other code bundles from our rich catalog of books and videos available at `https://github.com/PacktPublishing`. Check them out!

Conventions used

There are a number of text conventions used throughout this book.

`CodeInText`: Indicates code words in text, database table names, folder names, filenames, file extensions, pathnames, dummy URLs, user input, and Twitter handles. For example: "By wrapping the base test with `base.extend()`, we are introducing a new fixture (`noConsoleErrors`) that integrates automatically into the test life cycle."

A block of code is set as follows:

```
{
  name: 'webkit-ipad',
  use: {
    ...devices['Desktop Safari'],
    userAgent: 'Mozilla/5.0 (Windows NT 10.0; Win64; x64; rv:138.0)
Gecko/20100101 Firefox/138.0',
  },
},
```

Any command-line input or output is written as follows:

```
git add .github/workflows/playwright.yml
git commit -m "Add Playwright tests GitHub Actions workflow"
git push
```

Bold: Indicates a new term, an important word, or words that you see on the screen. For instance, words in menus or dialog boxes appear in the text like this. For example: "Playwright offers two fixture scopes, **test** and **worker**, each designed for different scenarios."

Warnings or important notes appear like this.

Tips and tricks appear like this.

Get in touch

Feedback from our readers is always welcome.

General feedback: If you have questions about any aspect of this book or have any general feedback, please email us at `customercare@packt.com` and mention the book's title in the subject of your message.

Errata: Although we have taken every care to ensure the accuracy of our content, mistakes do happen. If you have found a mistake in this book, we would be grateful if you reported this to us. Please visit `http://www.packt.com/submit-errata`, click **Submit Errata**, and fill in the form.

Piracy: If you come across any illegal copies of our works in any form on the internet, we would be grateful if you would provide us with the location address or website name. Please contact us at `copyright@packt.com` with a link to the material.

If you are interested in becoming an author: If there is a topic that you have expertise in and you are interested in either writing or contributing to a book, please visit `http://authors.packt.com/`.

Share your thoughts

Once you've read *Hands-On Automated Testing with Playwright*, we'd love to hear your thoughts! Scan the QR code below to go straight to the Amazon review page for this book and share your feedback.

https://packt.link/r/1806106477

Your review is important to us and the tech community and will help us make sure we're delivering excellent quality content.

Playwright Events

If you're looking to put your learning into practice and discover hidden tips and tricks to make the most of Playwright, you might want to check out our events. Scan the QR code to register your interest via the landing page and be among the first to hear about upcoming events, including exclusive related offers.

https://landing.packtpub.com/automated-testing-with-playwright/

Free Benefits with Your Book

This book comes with free benefits to support your learning. Activate them now for instant access (see the *"How to Unlock"* section for instructions).

Here's a quick overview of what you can instantly unlock with your purchase:

PDF and ePub Copies

- Access a DRM-free PDF copy of this book to read anywhere, on any device.
- Use a DRM-free ePub version with your favorite e-reader.

Next-Gen Web-Based Reader

- **Multi-device progress sync**: Pick up where you left off, on any device.
- **Highlighting and notetaking**: Capture ideas and turn reading into lasting knowledge.
- **Bookmarking**: Save and revisit key sections whenever you need them.
- **Dark mode**: Reduce eye strain by switching to dark or sepia themes.

How to Unlock

UNLOCK NOW

Scan the QR code (or go to `packtpub.com/unlock`). Search for this book by name, confirm the edition, and then follow the steps on the page.

***Note:** Keep your invoice handy. Purchases made directly from Packt don't require one.*

1

Quick Setup Refresher

Welcome to your journey with Playwright! This book will guide you through mastering this versatile tool for web testing and automation.

One of Playwright's biggest strengths is its ability to automate browsers such as Chromium, Firefox, and WebKit with a single API, which means you can test across multiple browsers effortlessly. Another standout feature is its auto-wait mechanism, which helps reduce flaky tests by waiting for elements to be ready before interacting with them. Plus, it supports multiple languages, such as JavaScript, Python, and C#, so teams can use it in their preferred tech stack.

Before we dive into the exciting features, let's take a few minutes to get everything set up properly. Even if you've used Playwright before, this chapter will make sure we're all starting on the same page.

In this chapter, we'll begin by installing Playwright and its dependencies to set up our development environment. Then, we'll explore the difference between Playwright Test and the Playwright Library, which will help you understand when to use each.

Next, you'll get hands-on experience by writing and running your first test. We'll also cover how to configure your test environments for optimal productivity and delve into the basics of Playwright's test runner to give you a solid foundation.

By the end of this chapter, you'll have a fully functional Playwright setup, understand the key components, and be ready to start writing and running tests with confidence.

These are the key topics we'll explore:

- Installing Playwright and dependencies
- Understanding the difference between Playwright Test and Playwright Library
- Writing and running your first test
- Configuring test environments
- Understanding Playwright test runner basics

Let's get started!

> **Free Benefits with Your Book**
>
> Your purchase includes a free PDF copy of this book along with other exclusive benefits. Check the *Free Benefits with Your Book* section in the *Preface* to unlock them instantly and maximize your learning experience.

Technical requirements

The source code for this chapter is available at `https://github.com/PacktPublishing/Hands-On-Automated-Testing-with-Playwright/tree/main/Chapter01`.

Understanding the difference between Playwright Test and Playwright Library

A common question among newcomers is: *What is the difference between Playwright Test and the Playwright Library?* Although they have the same capabilities, each is suitable for different use cases.

Imagine you're building a data extraction pipeline that scrapes content from multiple sites every night. You don't need full test reports or assertions. You just want reliable browser automation. In that case, the Playwright Library fits perfectly. You can plug it into your existing Node.js workflow, schedule it with `cron`, and keep things lightweight.

Now, suppose you're developing a web application and want to ensure your login, checkout, and dashboard workflows remain reliable across Chrome, Firefox, and Safari. Playwright Test handles the orchestration: running tests, generating reports, and making debugging easier without additional setup.

To be more exact, the **Playwright Library** gives you a set of APIs to automate browser tasks. You can use it to do the following:

- Launch browsers in *headless* or *headed* mode. That means you can run automated tests either without a visible browser window (headless), which is faster and ideal for CI pipelines, or with a visible window (headed), which is helpful for debugging and development.
- Interact with web pages by clicking, filling in forms, and capturing screenshots.
- Execute JavaScript in the browser's context.

This API can be combined with any test runners, such as Jest or Mocha, or even used in custom scripts. The design focuses on browser automation and leaves test orchestration and reporting up to you.

On the other hand, **Playwright Test** builds on top of the core library but adds features for making writing tests easier. It has features such as the following:

- Built-in test runner to recognize test files automatically, run them in parallel, and support multiple browsers
- Generate visual reports and debug test failures via the CLI
- Command-line options to run tests, record videos for debugging failures, and more

So, use the Playwright Library if you already work within another test framework that you trust or need to integrate browser automation into a larger process. If your focus is on quickly writing tests and using an all in one solution, Playwright Test is a better option.

In the next section, we'll look at how to get each one installed on your system.

Installing Playwright and dependencies

Before anything else, you must ensure your system is prepared to run Playwright. Playwright is built on top of Node.js, so verifying that Node and `npm` (or `yarn`) are available is the first step.

Installing Node.js

Most modern development systems already have Node installed, but if not, download it from `nodejs.org`. We recommend using the **Long-Term Support** (**LTS**) version. You can verify your installation with the following:

```
node -v
npm -v
```

These commands should return version numbers that confirm Node.js and `npm` are installed. If you're managing multiple Node versions, consider using `nvm` or a similar version manager.

Initializing your project

Create a new project directory and initialize it as an `npm` project:

```
mkdir playwright-quick-setup
cd playwright-quick-setup
npm init -y
```

This command creates a `package.json` file, which is needed to manage your project's dependencies.

Installing Playwright

As we discussed earlier in this chapter, there are two main ways to install Playwright: Playwright Library and Playwright Test.

To install the Playwright Library, you can use the following command:

```
npm install playwright
```

This installs the core Playwright library, which gives you the browser automation API. It's suitable if you want to use Playwright's automation capabilities programmatically or integrate it with other testing frameworks.

If you prefer an integrated testing solution, install the following:

```
npm install --save-dev @playwright/test
```

This installs the Playwright Test package, which includes a built-in test runner, assertions, and features like *parallel execution.*

> Note that the preceding command only installs the `@playwright/test` package as a dev dependency in your existing project. It does not create configuration files or example tests or initialize any project structure. Also, it does not install browser binaries automatically (you need to run `npx playwright install` separately).

Use this approach when you're adding Playwright Test to an existing project that already has a testing setup or if you prefer to configure Playwright manually. You will also need to set up the `playwright.config.ts` file and organize the test structure on your own.

If you want a guided setup with configuration and examples, or want to save time by letting Playwright scaffold the project for you, use the following:

```
npm init playwright@latest
```

This command initializes a new Playwright project with the Playwright Test framework. It sets up a complete testing environment, including the following:

- Installing `@playwright/test` as a dev dependency
- Creating a sample configuration file (`playwright.config.ts`)
- Generating example test files (such as `tests/example.spec.ts`)
- Optionally installing browser binaries (if you choose to do so during the setup prompts)

So, if you need to build tests using the bundled test runner, go with Playwright Test; otherwise, if you're integrating into a different test framework, the core API is often enough. Now that your environment is set up, we can move on to building and running your first Playwright test.

Writing and running your first test

So, ready to run your first test? Great! By the end of this section, you will have a functional test that visits a website, checks its title, and lays the groundwork for more advanced testing strategies.

Setting up a simple test file

Create a new file in your `tests` directory named `example.spec.ts`. Then, add the following code:

```
import { test, expect } from '@playwright/test';

test('homepage has Playwright in title', async ({ page }) => {
  // Navigate to the Playwright homepage
  await page.goto('https://playwright.dev');

  // Fetch the title of the page
  const title = await page.title();

  // Assert that the title contains 'Playwright'
  expect(title).toContain('Playwright');
});
```

This simple test uses Playwright Test's API to define a new test, then launches a browser page and navigates to the Playwright home page. Next, it retrieves the page title and asserts that it contains the `Playwright` keyword.

Running the test

To run your test, execute the following command in your terminal:

```
npx playwright test
```

The test runner will scan your project directory, find your test file, launch the appropriate browser, execute the test, and then output a report.

You can also tell Playwright to run a specific test like this:

```
npx playwright test tests/example.spec.ts
```

In addition, you can enable debugging mode with the following:

```
npx playwright test --debug
```

This command opens an interactive inspector to help you troubleshoot any issues that might arise during test execution.

> We'll dive deeper into debugging in *Chapter 8, Headless Testing and Debugging.*

By default, Playwright runs tests in headless mode, meaning the browser UI is not shown. In headed mode, the browser UI is displayed during test execution. This is useful for debugging or when visual confirmation is necessary.

You can enable it with the following:

```
npx playwright test --headed
```

You can also do so by modifying the test config (`playwright.config.ts`):

```
use: {
  headless: false,
}
```

Playwright supports multiple browser engines:

- **Chromium** (used in Chrome and Edge)
- **Firefox**
- **WebKit** (used in Safari)

To run tests in a specific browser, you can use CLI flags like this:

```
npx playwright test --project=chromium
npx playwright test --project=firefox
npx playwright test --project=webkit
```

Alternatively, you can define projects in `playwright.config.ts`:

```
projects: [
  { name: 'chromium', use: { browserName: 'chromium' } },
],
```

This code tells Playwright to run the test on Chromium only.

Interpreting test results

After running the tests, you will be able to see an informative summary by running the `npx playwright show-report` command. This summary includes the total number of tests executed, the browser(s) used for testing, and the execution time, which helps you determine whether parallelization or test optimization is needed (we'll dive deeper into this in *Chapter 6*, *Test Parallelization and Performance Optimization*).

You've just gone from zero to executing an end to end test in just a few commands! Now, let's take things further by configuring your test environments, which is an important step in building reliable end-to-end tests.

Configuring test environments

In this part, we look at configuring the Node.js environment and your **Integrated Development Environment** (**IDE**) for an effective Playwright development experience.

Setting up the Node.js environment

Make sure you're using a stable version of Node.js, ideally the LTS version, and consider using tools such as `nvm` to manage different Node versions, which can be helpful when working on multiple projects.

It's also important to keep your project structure organized so everything stays clear and easy to navigate. While there isn't one perfect way to organize a Playwright project, here's an example layout to give you some inspiration:

```
my-playwright-project/
├── tests/
│   ├── example.spec.ts         // Test files for different scenarios
│   ├── logged-in/
│   │   ├── api.spec.ts
│   │   ├── login.setup.ts
│   │   └── ...
│   └── logged-out/
│       ├── api.spec.ts
│       ├── auth.spec.ts
│       └── ...
│
├── src/
│   ├── pages/
│   │   ├── BasePage.ts       // Common page functions and elements
│   │   ├── DashboardPage.ts  // Page Object Model for the dashboard
│   │   └── ...
│   └── utils/
│       ├── apiHelper.ts      // Utility functions for API calls
│       ├── stringUtils.ts    // Additional helpers
│       └── ...
│
├── fixtures/
│   ├── testData.json         // Sample data used for tests
│   └── ...
│
├── auth/
│   └── credentials.json      // Holds credentials and session details
│   └── ...
│
```

```
├── helpers/
│   ├── list-test.ts           // Helper functions
│   └── ...
│
├── test-results/              // Stores test execution results
├── playwright-report/         // Directory for Playwright test reports
├── playwright.config.ts       // Playwright configuration settings
├── package.json               // NPM package manifest
├── tsconfig.json              // TypeScript configuration
├── .gitignore:                // files to exclude from version control
└── README.md                  // Project overview and documentation
```

Let's dive a bit deeper:

- Configuration lives in `Root`: your TS compiler options, `playwright.config.ts`, environment variables, plus your `package.json` and `.gitignore`. Docs and top-level scripts belong here too.
- In `tests/`, we've grouped `logged-in` and `logged-out` scenarios into subfolders so you can share setup logic (such as `login.setup.ts`) and keep related specs together.
- `src/` is the heart of your **Page Object Model** (**POM**). `pages/` holds individual page classes, while `utils/` is home to low-level helpers and shared API logic.
- `fixtures/` holds static or semi-static test data (JSON, CSV, etc.) that your tests can load.
- `auth/` contains credentials, session dumps, tokens, or anything sensitive or environment-specific you don't want scattered through your code.
- `helpers/` holds one-off or cross-cutting functions that don't fit neatly in `utils/`, such as list generators or custom matchers.
- Finally, auto-generated output, such as raw JSON logs, HTML reports, screenshots, and videos, is stored in `test-results/` and `playwright-report/`.

This organization keeps your test code, helpers, and configuration clearly separated, so when the project grows, you always know where to look, and more importantly, where to add new files.

Setting up your IDE

Using a modern IDE such as **Visual Studio Code (VS Code)** can improve your coding experience. Start by installing helpful extensions such as the official Playwright Test extension, which provides syntax highlighting, code completion, and inline test results:

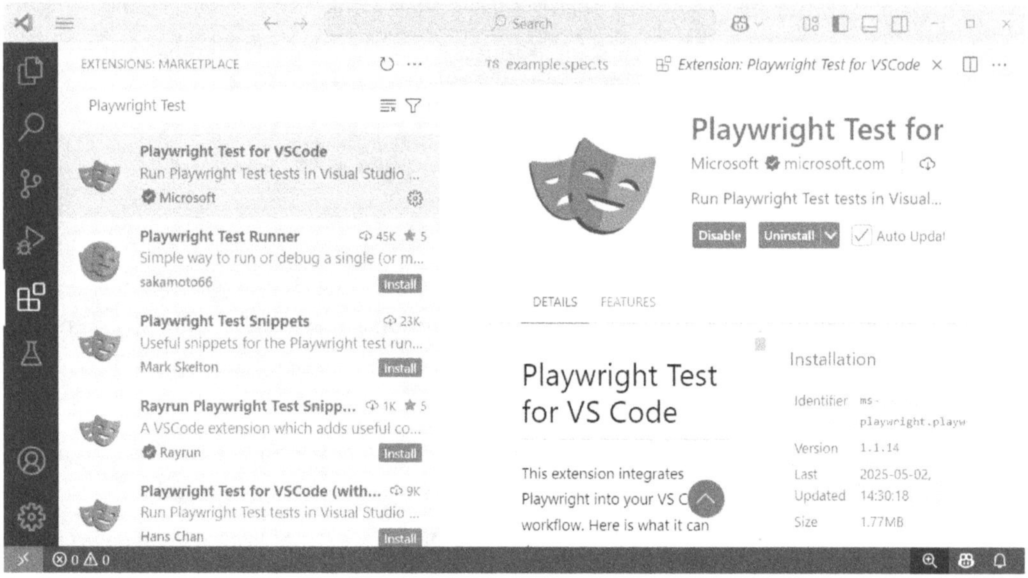

Figure 1.1: Extensions view in VS Code

To install the extension in VS Code, follow these steps:

1. Go to the Extensions view by clicking the extensions icon in the Activity Bar on the side (or press *Ctrl* + *Shift* + *X*).
2. In the search bar, type `Playwright Test`.
3. Find the extension by Microsoft named Playwright Test for VS Code and click **Install**.

You can also add **ESLint** and **Prettier** for code formatting, which help keep your code consistent. Setting them up is pretty similar to how you installed Playwright Test for VS Code.

Configuring Playwright settings

Playwright allows you to customize how your tests run by using the `playwright.config.ts` file. In this file, you can set global preferences, tweak browser behavior, and fine-tune how your tests are executed. This section will guide you through the key settings to help you get started.

First, go to your project directory. If you don't have a `playwright.config.ts` file yet (maybe you're working with an existing project), you can create the config file manually.

The following is an example of a minimal configuration:

```
import { defineConfig } from '@playwright/test';

export default defineConfig({
  testDir: './tests', // Directory where tests are located
  timeout: 30000, // Test timeout in milliseconds
  use: {
    browserName: 'chromium', // Default browser
    headless: true, // Run tests in headless mode
    viewport: { width: 1280, height: 720 }, // Default viewport size
  },
});
```

Once the initial configuration is in place, you can begin customizing it to better suit your project's specific testing needs.

The configuration file supports a variety of options to customize test execution. When you're setting things up, it's best to keep it simple at first. Start with the basic settings, and only add complexity if you need it later. Also, make sure to document your choices by adding comments in the config file. This way, you can easily remember why certain settings were made, and it'll be clearer for anyone else who works on it later.

The following are the most commonly used settings. We'll come back to many of these in later chapters, so no worries if you're not totally sure how they work just yet.

Test directory and file matching

Use these options to control which files Playwright includes or excludes when discovering tests:

- `testDir`: Specifies the directory containing your test files. By default, Playwright looks for tests in the `./tests` folder.
- `testMatch`: Defines a pattern to match test files (such as `*.spec.ts` or `/*.test.ts`).
- `testIgnore`: Excludes files or directories from test discovery (such as `/*.setup.ts`).

The following is an example:

```
export default defineConfig({
  testDir: './tests',
  testMatch: '/*.spec.ts',
  testIgnore: '/*.unit.ts',
});
```

Timeouts

These settings define how long Playwright should wait before timing out at different stages of the test run:

- `timeout`: Maximum time (in milliseconds) for a test to complete
- `globalTimeout`: Maximum time for the entire test suite to run
- `actionTimeout`: Timeout for individual Playwright actions (such as `page.click()`)

The following is an example:

```
export default defineConfig({
  timeout: 30000, // 30 seconds per test
  globalTimeout: 1800000, // 30 minutes for the entire suite
  use: {
    actionTimeout: 10000, // 10 seconds per action
  },
});
```

Browser and context options

The `use` property defines default browser and context settings for all tests:

- `browserName`: Specifies the browser (Chromium, Firefox, or WebKit)
- `headless`: Runs browsers in headless (`true`) or headed (`false`) mode
- `viewport`: Sets the default viewport size
- `locale`: Configures the browser's language (such as `en-US`)
- `timezoneId`: Sets the browser's timezone (such as `America/New_York`)
- `device`: Emulates a specific device from Playwright's device list (such as `iPhone 16`)

The following is an example:

```
export default defineConfig({
  use: {
    browserName: 'firefox',
    headless: false,
    viewport: { width: 1920, height: 1080 },
    locale: 'en-GB',
    timezoneId: 'Europe/London',
    device: 'Desktop Firefox',
  },
});
```

Parallelism and workers

These options manage how tests are executed in parallel and across CPU resources:

- `workers`: Number of parallel test workers. Set to a number (such as 4) or `'50%'` to use half the CPU cores
- `fullyParallel`: Enables (`true`) or disables (`false`) running tests in parallel within a single file

The following is an example:

```
export default defineConfig({
  workers: 3, // Run 3 tests in parallel
  fullyParallel: true,
});
```

Retries and failure handling

These settings help control test retries and when the test run should stop after failures:

- `retries`: Controls how many times a failed test will be retried before it's marked as failed
- `maxFailures`: Sets a global threshold for how many test failures are allowed before Playwright stops the entire test run

The following is an example:

```
export default defineConfig({
  retries: 2, // Retry failed tests twice
  maxFailures: 10, // Stop after 10 failures
});
```

Reporters

Now we come to `reporter`. Playwright supports multiple reporters for test output. Options include `list`, `dot`, `line`, `json`, `junit`, `html`, or custom reporters.

The following is an example:

```
export default defineConfig({
  reporter: [
    ['list'], // Console output
    ['html', { outputFolder: 'playwright-report' }], // HTML report
    ['json', { outputFile: 'test-results.json' }], // JSON report
  ],
});
```

To view the HTML report, run the following:

```
npx playwright show-report
```

When Playwright runs in a CI/CD pipeline (which is usually headless), the command to open a browser may hang, which causes the entire pipeline job to get stuck and eventually time out. When running in CI/CD, explicitly set the open option to `'never'` for the HTML reporter in the configuration file:

```
export default defineConfig({
  reporter: [
    ['list'],
    ['html', { outputFolder: 'playwright-report', open: 'never' }],
    ['json', { outputFile: 'test-results.json' }],
  ],
});
```

Projects for multi-browser testing

The `projects` property allows you to define multiple test configurations (such as for different browsers or devices). Each project inherits global settings but can override them.

The following is an example:

```
export default defineConfig({
  projects: [
    {
      name: 'Chromium',
```

```
      use: { browserName: 'chromium' },
    },
    {
      name: 'Firefox',
      use: { browserName: 'firefox' },
    },
    {
      name: 'Mobile Safari',
      use: { device: 'iPhone 16' },
    },
  ],
});
```

Run tests for a specific project:

```
npx playwright test --project=Chromium
```

Debugging configuration issues

If your tests fail because of a configuration issue. Start by checking the syntax to make sure your configuration file is correct in TypeScript. Next, check the logs by running the tests with the `--debug` flag using the `npx playwright test --debug` command to get a closer look at Playwright's behavior. If you're still stuck, try temporarily reverting to the default settings to help isolate the problem. Lastly, make sure you're using the latest version of Playwright by running `npm install @playwright/test@latest` to stay up to date.

With your development and testing environments properly configured, you're now ready to dive into the core functionality of Playwright.

Understanding Playwright's test runner basics

The Playwright test runner manages your tests, provides diagnostic utilities, and ensures that your testing script runs in various environments.

Playwright automatically detects files that follow its naming conventions (such as `*.spec.js` or `*.test.ts`). This means that once your tests are in place, running the test runner will automatically aggregate them.

In this section, we'll briefly explore key features of the test runner, such as built-in hooks, fixtures, and support for parallel execution.

Using parallel execution and test isolation

Out of the box, Playwright's test runner distributes your test files across multiple worker processes (typically one per CPU core) to take advantage of the full power of modern multicore systems. This concurrency cuts down the overall testing time, especially for large projects, by running several tests at the same time instead of waiting for one test to finish before starting the next.

Playwright lets you control the number of workers through configuration in your `playwright.config.ts`:

```
import { defineConfig } from '@playwright/test';
export default defineConfig({
  workers: 4,
  // ... other settings
});
```

Test isolation is important to ensure that the outcome of one test never affects another. In Playwright, isolation is achieved by using a fresh browser context for each test. Because each test gets its own browser context, any state (such as cookies, session data, or local storage) that is set by one test remains confined to that test alone.

This separation is done automatically by Playwright's test runner. Even if one test logs in to an application, manipulates local storage, or alters cookies, these changes are within that specific context, which is important for avoiding flaky test outcomes.

Using built-in hooks and fixtures

Playwright's built-in *hooks* and *fixtures* are two features that make writing isolated tests much easier. Let's explore them!

Hooks

Hooks are functions that run at specific moments during your test process. You can use them to initialize resources such as opening a database connection or getting your test data ready before your tests begin. When the tests are finished, hooks help you wrap things up: closing connections, cleaning up data, or logging useful info for next time.

Common hooks include the following:

- `test.beforeAll`: Runs once before all tests in a file or a group. This is the place for expensive setup tasks that need to happen only once.

- `test.beforeEach`: Executes before each individual test. Perfect for things such as navigating to a starting page or ensuring a fresh state.
- `test.afterEach`: Runs after every test and allows you to clean up resources or reset certain configurations.
- `test.afterAll`: Runs once after all tests in a file or group, typically used for final cleanup.

For example, let's say you want a script that logs in to a site and then runs two tests: one to confirm the inventory page's title, and another to confirm that the shopping cart link is visible. Here's how you can use the `beforeEach` hook to write this script:

```
import { test, expect } from '@playwright/test';

test.beforeEach(async ({ page }) => {
  await page.goto('https://www.saucedemo.com/');
  await page.getByPlaceholder('Username').fill('standard_user');
  await page.getByPlaceholder('Password').fill('secret_sauce');
  await page.getByRole('button', { name: 'Login' }).click();
  await expect(page).toHaveURL(/inventory.html/);
});

test('Check inventory page title', async ({ page }) => {
  await expect(page).toHaveTitle('Swag Labs');
});

test('Check shopping cart link is visible', async ({ page }) => {
  const cartLink = page.locator('.shopping_cart_link');
  await expect(cartLink).toBeVisible();
});
```

This script begins by importing the `test` and `expect` functions from the `@playwright/test` module. These are part of the Playwright testing framework, where `test` is used to define a test case and `expect` is used for assertions.

The `test.beforeEach` hook is defined to run before each test. It opens a new browser page and navigates to `https://www.saucedemo.com/`, which is a demo e-commerce site that's useful for testing.

The first actual test verifies that after the login, the page title is exactly *Swag Labs*. This is a quick way to confirm that the app has loaded the right page.

The second test checks whether the shopping cart link (in the top-right corner of the application) is visible on the page. It uses a CSS class selector, `.shopping_cart_link`, to locate the element and then checks whether it is visible to the user.

No worries if you don't completely get how this code works just yet. What really matters for now is knowing that the `beforeEach` hook gets everything ready so each test runs with an authenticated session.

Fixtures

A **fixture**, on the other hand, is a pre-configured helper that sets up everything you need for your tests. It takes care of creating, configuring, and cleaning up resources. This means you don't have to write the same setup code over and over.

When you define a test, you can specify the resources you need (such as page, `browser`, or custom ones), and Playwright will automatically provide them by running the necessary fixture functions.

For example, the `request` fixture gives you an `APIRequestContext` instance, which makes it easy to make HTTP requests and do API testing alongside your web interactions in the same test suite. You can use methods such as `request.get()`, `request.post()`, and `request.fetch()` to interact with APIs. It's isolated for each test, so there's no worry about shared state.

Here's an example using the `request` fixture in Playwright:

```
import { test, expect } from '@playwright/test';

test('check API response', async ({ request }) => {
  const response = await request.get('https://api.github.com');
  expect(response.status()).toBe(200);
});
```

This code uses the `request` fixture to make a `GET` request to a public API endpoint. It then checks whether the response status is `200`, which means the request was successful.

For a web app with a backend API, you might use the `request` fixture to authenticate a user via an API call, then use the page fixture to verify that the UI reflects the logged-in state.

We'll dive deeper into fixtures in *Chapter 5, Crafting Scalable Tests with the Fixture System.*

So, hooks help you handle setup and cleanup without repeating yourself, and fixtures let you share common test data or browser contexts in an organized way. Once you get the hang of them, you'll find your tests much easier to manage.

Summary

In this chapter, we've laid the groundwork for using Playwright by walking through the setup process and exploring key aspects of testing. We began by installing Node.js and Playwright, then distinguished between the core automation library and the testing framework. We wrote a simple *first test*, configured our test environment with best practices in Node.js and IDE integration, and finally, dove into the inner workings of Playwright's test runner.

By now, you should feel confident in setting up Playwright for your projects. In the next chapter, we will build upon these fundamentals by exploring techniques for interacting with complex web elements using Playwright's selector engine.

2

Advanced Selectors and Handling Dynamic Content

Welcome to *Chapter 2*! In modern web applications, the interface is rarely static. Pages update dynamically, content changes on the fly, and even the layout can change depending on user interaction. In this chapter, we dive into the advanced techniques offered by Playwright for dealing with such complexity.

We'll start by exploring Playwright's recommended way of finding elements: the `getBy*` locators. You'll also learn when it makes sense to switch to more traditional selectors instead. Next, we'll take a look at how Playwright handles waiting for elements, so your tests stay smooth even when dealing with dynamic content. We'll also cover how to work with browser alerts, confirms, and prompts.

You'll get comfortable testing content inside iframes and learn how to reach into shadow DOMs to test web components that live in those hidden layers. By the end of this chapter, you'll be ready to write tests that are resilient even when your app's UI keeps changing.

The chapter is structured into these parts:

- Prioritizing Playwright's `getBy*` locators for accessible tests
- Using fallback selectors (**CSS**, **XPath**, text-based) for complex or unsupported cases
- Managing dynamic elements with auto-wait and custom waits
- Handling alerts and confirmation dialogs
- Interacting with iframes and nested frames
- Handling shadow DOM components

Technical requirements

The source code for this chapter is available at `https://github.com/PacktPublishing/Hands-On-Automated-Testing-with-Playwright/tree/main/Chapter02`.

Prioritizing Playwright's getBy* locators for accessible tests

When you're writing end-to-end tests with Playwright, the locators you choose can make a big difference: not just to how reliable your tests are, but also to how accessible your app is. Playwright's `getBy*` locators are designed to reflect how real users, including those using assistive tech, interact with your site. By leaning on these locators, you're not only making your tests easier to maintain but you're also building a more inclusive experience. Let's dive into why these locators are preferred.

Why getBy* locators beat CSS and XPath

Playwright makes it easier to work with web elements by offering a handy set of locators such as `getByRole`, `getByLabel`, `getByPlaceholder`, and more. These are designed with accessibility in mind and are a modern alternative to the old-school CSS or XPath selectors (we'll explore these in more detail shortly).

One of the biggest advantages of using these **getBy*** locators is their ability to handle changes in the DOM gracefully. Unlike CSS or XPath, which rely on the layout or style of the page, these locators target the meaning behind the elements (things such as roles, labels, and visible text). That means even if the HTML or styling gets reworked, your tests are more likely to keep running as long as those accessibility attributes stay the same.

For example, instead of writing a complicated CSS selector to target a button, you can just use the following:

```
test('Submits the form on button click', async ({ page }) => {
  const submitButton = await page.getByRole('button',
    { name: /submit/i });
  await submitButton.click();
});
```

Here, `getByRole('button', { name: /submit/i })` tells Playwright to find a button element whose accessible name (such as its visible label or `aria-label`) matches the case-insensitive regular expression `/submit/i`.

`/submit/` is the pattern itself: it matches the exact word *submit*. `i` is a flag that makes the match case-insensitive, so it will match *Submit*, *submit*, *SUBMIT*, and so on.

While `getBy*` locators aren't a complete replacement for full accessibility audits (like those done with tools such as Axe), they can help catch potential issues early on. For example, if a `getByRole` locator can't find a button, it might mean the element is missing a proper ARIA role or accessible name. Catching things like this early gives you a chance to fix them before anything goes live.

> **What Is ARIA?**
>
> **ARIA** (short for **Accessible Rich Internet Applications**) plays an important role in making websites more inclusive and user-friendly for people who use assistive technologies such as screen readers. It helps by adding extra information to elements on a page (especially custom buttons, pop-ups, sliders, or anything built with JavaScript) that might not be easily understood by default. ARIA roles, states, and properties tell assistive tools what each part of the page is for and how it behaves, so users can navigate and interact with it more easily.

The available `getBy*` locators include the following:

- **getByLabel**: Targets elements by their associated label, such as form inputs linked to `<label>` tags
- **getByRole**: Finds elements by their ARIA role, such as `button` or `dialog`, with optional name filtering
- **getByPlaceholder**: Locates inputs by their placeholder text
- **getByText**: Matches elements by their visible text content
- **getByAltText**: Targets images by their alt text
- **getByTitle**: Finds elements by their title attribute
- **getByTestId**: Locates elements by a custom test ID attribute

Revisiting our script with accessibility in mind

Let's take another look at the script we used in *Chapter 1, Quick Setup Refresher*, to log into an e-commerce website and then run two tests:

```
import { test, expect } from '@playwright/test';

test.beforeEach(async ({ page }) => {
  await page.goto('https://www.saucedemo.com/');
  await page.getByPlaceholder('Username').fill('standard_user');
  await page.getByPlaceholder('Password').fill('secret_sauce');
  await page.getByRole('button', { name: 'Login' }).click();
  await expect(page).toHaveURL(/inventory.html/);
});

test('Check inventory page title', async ({ page }) => {
  await expect(page).toHaveTitle('Swag Labs');
});

test('Check shopping cart link is visible', async ({ page }) => {
  const cartLink = page.locator('.shopping_cart_link');
  await expect(cartLink).toBeVisible();
});
```

This test is not only functional but also accessibility-focused, as it relies on user-facing attributes that are critical for assistive technology users. If the test fails, it may indicate an accessibility issue, such as a missing label or incorrect role, which can be addressed before the application is deployed.

> In complex scenarios, you may need to narrow down the selection by combining locators. For example, to target a specific button within a form, you can use `page.locator('form').getByRole('button', { name: 'Submit' })`.

The second test in the script uses `page.locator('.shopping_cart_link')` instead of a `getBy*` method, such as `getByRole` or `getByTestId`, because of how the element is defined in the HTML of the page.

The target element is as follows:

```
<a class="shopping_cart_link" data-test="shopping-cart-link"></a>
```

This <a> tag has no inner text, no accessible role override, and no ARIA label. Playwright's getByRole() or getByText() cannot match it without those. Similarly, getByLabel(), getByPlaceholder(), and so on all depend on accessible attributes or labels, which this element lacks.

When accessible labels or roles aren't available, it's important to fall back on more general selectors. This leads us to the next section.

Using fallback selectors (CSS, XPath, text-based) for complex or unsupported cases

While they might not be the most reliable for long-term use, CSS and XPath selectors can be very helpful when dealing with legacy code or third-party components. Sometimes, you just don't have control over an element's accessible attributes. If an element doesn't have ARIA roles, labels, or other accessibility features, locators may not work as expected.

That's where **fallback selectors** come in. They can get the job done when HTML is poorly structured or you're working with external components. Just keep in mind that these selectors often depend on the page's structure or internal implementation details, which means they can break more easily if the page changes. So, while fallback selectors are useful in certain situations, it's best to stick with getBy* locators or **test IDs** (we'll discuss test IDs in a bit) whenever you can.

CSS selectors

In Playwright, you can use **CSS selectors** with the page.locator() method. Playwright automatically assumes you're using a CSS selector unless you specify otherwise with something such as xpath= at the start.

For example, if you want to click the first button on a page, you can simply write the following:

```
await page.locator('button').click();
```

If you need something more specific you can use class names, IDs, or attributes like this:

```
// Fill in the input with ID 'login-form'
await page.locator('#login-form').fill('user@example.com');

// Fill in a password input
await page.locator('input[type="password"]').fill('secret');
```

CSS selectors are familiar to most developers and usually work well, but since they depend on the page's structure (which can change over time), overly complex or deeply nested selectors such as `#tsf > div:nth-child(2) > button` can easily break your tests. These kinds of selectors are also not great for testing accessibility since they don't focus on user-facing attributes the way `getBy*` locators do.

To make your tests more reliable, try to keep your CSS selectors straightforward. When possible, use test IDs, which can target elements without relying on fragile page structure.

XPath selectors

XPath is a query language for selecting nodes in an XML or HTML document. In Playwright, XPath selectors are also supported via `page.locator()`, with any selector starting with `//` or `..` automatically treated as an XPath expression.

To use an XPath selector, pass it to `page.locator()`. For example, here's how to click a submit button:

```
await page.locator('//button[@type="submit"]').click();
```

This XPath selects any `<button>` element on the page that has a `type="submit"` attribute. The `//` indicates a search through the entire DOM for such buttons, and `[@type="submit"]` filters to only those with that specific attribute.

XPath comes in especially handy when CSS selectors fall short, such as when you need to select elements based on their text content or how they're nested within other elements:

```
// Select a div containing specific text
await page.locator('//div[contains(text(), "Welcome")]').click();

// Select a button that is a child of a specific form
await page.locator('//form[@id="login-form"]//button').click();
```

Playwright also supports explicit XPath prefixes for clarity:

```
await page.locator('xpath=//button[@type="submit"]').click();
```

Since XPath expressions are closely tied to the structure of the page, they can break if the layout changes. They also tend to be slower than CSS selectors, especially when the expressions get complex.

Maintaining long or complicated XPath strings such as `//*[@id="tsf"]/div[2]/button` can be tricky and is best avoided when possible. It's usually best to stick with CSS or `getBy*` locators unless XPath is the only option. If you do need to use XPath, try to keep it simple and focus on selecting elements by unique attributes or specific text content.

Text-based selectors

If your target element has text content, using `page.getByText()` can be a more readable and straightforward option compared to CSS or XPath selectors. For example, if you're looking for a welcome message, you might write the following:

```
await expect(page.getByText('Welcome, John')).toBeVisible();
```

By default, `page.getByText()` matches substrings and also normalizes whitespace. This means it treats multiple spaces as one and ignores any leading or trailing spaces. If you need a more precise match, you can fine-tune your query using options such as exact matching or regular expressions.

For an exact match, you can do something like this:

```
await page.getByText('Welcome, John', { exact: true }).click();
```

Or, if you'd like to match using a regular expression (for example, if the name might change), try the following:

```
await page.getByText(/welcome, [A-Za-z]+$/i).click();
```

`/` and / denote the start and end of the regex; the `i` flag makes the match case-insensitive. The `[A-Za-z]+` pattern matches one or more letters (uppercase or lowercase), and `$` asserts that this is the end of the string. So, it would match something such as `"Welcome, John"` or `"welcome, alice"`, but not `"welcome, John123"` or `"hi, John"`.

You can also use text-based selectors to filter other locators. Suppose you want to click a button that contains the text **Submit**. Instead of searching by role alone, you can filter by text:

```
await page.getByRole('button').filter({ hasText: 'Submit' }).click();
```

Text-based selectors are not always the best fit for every situation. If the text changes frequently (as with localization or dynamic content) your tests might break more often than you'd like.

> Besides filtering by text, you can filter locators by child/descendant, not having text, or not having child/descendant.
>
> To learn more, check out `https://playwright.dev/docs/locators#filtering-locators`.

Integrating with test IDs

If you find yourself relying on fallback selectors often, it might be a sign that your application lacks sufficient accessibility attributes or stable identifiers. A great way to improve this is by adding test IDs, which give you a more dependable way to target elements. Playwright makes this easy with `page.getByTestId()`, which looks for elements with a `data-testid` attribute (or another custom attribute if you've set one up in your test config).

Here's an example:

```
// HTML: <button data-testid="submit-button">Submit</button>
await page.getByTestId('submit-button').click();
```

`data-testid` is used by default. To use a custom test ID attribute, you can configure it in the Playwright config:

```
import { defineConfig } from '@playwright/test';
export default defineConfig({
  use: {
    testIdAttribute: 'data-pw'
  }
});
```

Test IDs are usually more reliable than CSS or XPath selectors because they're designed with testing in mind and tend to stay stable even as the code changes. They should be considered a bridge between `getBy*` locators and fallback selectors.

To keep your automation running smoothly, it's a good idea to plan for elements that might not always behave exactly as expected, especially on dynamic websites where timing can affect whether something appears or can be clicked. With that in mind, let's jump into our next key topic.

Managing dynamic elements with auto-wait and custom waits

Playwright has your back with built-in auto-waiting that pauses your test just long enough for things to be ready. But sometimes, you might need a bit more control, and that's where custom waits come in handy. In this section, we'll look at how to make your tests more reliable by using Playwright's smart auto-wait features and adding custom waits when needed.

How Playwright ensures actions happen at the right time

When you're working with modern web apps, you'll often run into dynamic elements that show up, disappear, or change depending on what the user does or what's happening in the background. These changes can make automated testing tricky. If your test tries to interact with something before it's ready, it might fail or behave inconsistently.

That's where Playwright's **auto-wait** mechanism and a suite of custom wait methods come in: they ensure that each action is executed only when the application is in the expected state. Rather than depending on guesswork with timeouts, Playwright uses smart auto-waiting to pause test execution until elements are actually ready to go.

It includes handy built-in methods such as `waitForLoadState`, `waitForResponse`, and `waitForFunction`, which keep an eye on how your app behaves and reacts in real time. This makes your tests much easier to maintain.

When you perform actions such as clicking a button or filling in a text field, Playwright automatically ensures that an element is as follows:

- **Visible**: The element is rendered and visible on the page
- **Stable**: The element is not moving or resizing (no ongoing animations)
- **Enabled**: The element is not disabled and can be interacted with
- **Receivable**: The element can receive input or clicks (not obscured by other elements)

This built-in waiting eliminates the need for arbitrary pauses (such as fixed delays).

Using custom waits for specific scenarios

While Playwright's auto-waiting does a great job in most situations, there are times when you'll want more control. **Custom waits** come in handy when you need to wait for something specific.

For example, maybe you're waiting for a network response, an animation to finish, or a state change in your app that Playwright doesn't automatically catch. In these cases, custom wait logic helps keep your tests reliable.

Luckily, Playwright offers several ways to build custom waits.

page.waitForRequest(urlOrPredicate)

This method waits for a specific network request to be initiated. You can provide a URL or a predicate function to match the request.

Here's an example:

```
await page.waitForRequest('https://example.com/api/data');
```

This is particularly useful for testing API-driven applications.

page.waitForResponse(urlOrPredicate)

`waitForResponse` waits for a network response and allows you to verify the response's URL, status, or other properties.

Here's an example:

```
await page.waitForResponse(response => response.url().includes('api/
orders') && response.status() === 200);
```

This waits for a response to the `/api/orders` endpoint with a `200` status code.

> `waitForRequest` and `waitForResponse` are both used to monitor network activity, but they serve distinct purposes. `waitForRequest` waits for a specific HTTP request to be initiated by the browser, which matches criteria such as URL or request method. It's useful for verifying that a request is sent (such as an API call triggered by a user action). In contrast, `waitForResponse` waits for the server's response to a specific request, and allows you to inspect the response status, headers, or body (such as confirming a successful API response). In short, `waitForRequest` watches what's going out, and `waitForResponse` watches what's coming back. Together, they give you great control over network behavior in your tests.

page.waitForLoadState(state)

This method waits for the page to reach a specific load state.

Here's an example:

```
await page.waitForLoadState('networkidle');
```

You usually won't need to call this method yourself, since Playwright automatically waits for elements before performing actions.

page.waitForFunction(pageFunction, arg, options)

You can use this method to wait until a JavaScript function (`pageFunction`) returns a truthy value when executed in the browser context.

Here's an example:

```
await page.waitForFunction('document.querySelector(".my-element") !==
null');
```

Here, we're telling Playwright to wait until an element with class `my-element` exists.

page.waitForEvent(event, options)

Take advantage of this method when you need to wait for a specific event (such as a popup, download, or websocket) to occur on the page.

Here's an example:

```
const popup = await page.waitForEvent('popup');
```

This code waits for a new browser window/tab to open and returns the pop-up page.

page.waitForURL(url, options)

This is a method used to pause the script execution until the page's URL matches a specified value or pattern.

Here's an example:

```
await page.waitForURL('**/newpage.html');
```

This is particularly useful for handling page redirects, waiting for navigation to complete, or managing dynamic URL changes during single-page app transitions.

page.waitForTimeout(milliseconds)

This method pauses test execution for a specified number of milliseconds. This method is considered an anti-pattern because it introduces hardcoded delays, which can make tests flaky. Playwright encourages using more robust waiting mechanisms that wait for specific conditions rather than arbitrary time intervals.

Here's an example:

```
await page.waitForTimeout(3000); // Wait for 3 seconds
```

Use it only as a last resort for debugging or when no other reliable wait condition exists.

page.waitForSelector(selector, options)

This method waits for an element that matches the given selector to show up in the DOM. However, it's generally not recommended, since Playwright already takes care of waiting for elements to be ready before interacting with them. Using locator objects and web-first assertions helps your code run smoothly without needing to use `waitForSelector`.

Here's an example:

```
await page.waitForSelector('#submit-button', { state: 'visible', timeout:
5000 });
```

This waits up to 5 seconds for the `#submit-button` element to become visible. You can specify the desired state (such as `'visible'`, `'hidden'`) and a custom timeout to control how long to wait.

page.waitForNavigation(options)

You can use this method to wait for the page to navigate to a new URL, often triggered by actions such as form submissions or link clicks. You can specify the expected URL and timeout.

Here's an example:

```
await page.getByRole('link', { name: 'Dashboard' }).click();
await page.waitForNavigation({ url: 'https://example.com/dashboard',
timeout: 10000 });
```

As of Playwright's recent versions, `page.waitForNavigation` is considered outdated. Instead, Playwright recommends using `page.waitForURL` or simply relying on the promise returned by navigation methods such as `page.goto()`. For instance, when you use `await page.goto(url)`, it already waits for the navigation to finish. So, in most cases, there's no need to call `waitForNavigation` separately. If you're looking to wait for more specific navigation events, you can use something such as `page.waitForEvent('navigated')` instead.

Practical example: verifying language switch

Now that you're familiar with the different methods for creating custom waits, let's check out a real-world example. Suppose you want to write a test script that navigates to a Wikipedia article, simulates a user clicking the button to access the article in other languages, and open the German language version of the article.

Here's how we can do that:

```
import { test, expect } from '@playwright/test';

test('Change article language to Deutsch', async ({ page }) => {
  // Go to Wikipedia page
  await page.goto('https://en.wikipedia.org/wiki/Playwright_(software)');

  // Click the change language
  await page.getByRole('button', { name: 'Go to an article in another'
}).click();

  // Click the Deutsch language link
  await page.getByRole('link', { name: 'Deutsch' }).click();

  // Wait for the Deutsch Wikipedia URL
  await page.waitForURL('https://de.wikipedia.org/wiki/Playwright_
(Software)', { timeout: 5000 });

  // Assert that the URL is as expected
  expect(page.url()).toContain('de.wikipedia.org');

  console.log('Successfully navigated to German Wikipedia.');
});
```

The script starts by navigating to the Wikipedia article for *Playwright (software)* in English. Next, it simulates a user clicking the button to access the article in other languages. This is done using `page.getByRole()`, which searches for a button element with the accessible name that includes `Go to an article in another`. Once found, the `click()` method simulates the user's click.

After that, the script clicks on the link labeled `Deutsch`, to open the German version of the article. Just like before, it uses `getByRole()` to find the link by its accessible name. The script then waits for the browser to navigate to the expected German-language URL using `page.waitForURL()`, which ensures the navigation completes within a 5-second timeout. This is important to confirm that the page transition occurred successfully.

After confirming navigation, we use `expect` to verify that the page URL includes `de.wikipedia.org`, which indicates that the German Wikipedia site has been loaded.

Remember, Playwright's auto-wait feature takes care of most standard cases for you. Try using custom waits only when you're dealing with something that falls outside of the norm. It's best to avoid fixed delays such as `await page.waitForTimeout(5000)`. They can slow your tests down; instead, stick with auto-waits or smart custom waits that pause just long enough. Don't forget: all waiting methods let you set a timeout. You can tweak these to match how your app performs, so you're not waiting too long or failing too soon.

So, custom waits give you precise control over when a page or element is ready, but web apps often have components such as alerts and confirmation popups that need a different approach. Let's take a look at the best ways to handle these kinds of interactive elements.

Handling alerts and confirmation dialogs

Working with **browser dialogs** in Playwright (such as **alerts**, **confirmations**, and **prompts**) is surprisingly easy, thanks to its event-driven API. As soon as a dialog appears on the page, Playwright lets you interact with it right away.

In web applications, these dialogs usually pop up when JavaScript functions such as `window.alert()`, `window.confirm()`, or `window.prompt()` are called. These modal windows pause JavaScript execution until the user responds.

Playwright lets you handle these by listening for the `'dialog'` event on the page. When a dialog shows up, Playwright emits the event and hands you a dialog object you can use to understand what kind of dialog it is. You can use the following:

- `dialog.type()` to find out whether it's an alert, confirm, or prompt
- `dialog.message()` to read the message shown in the dialog
- `dialog.defaultValue()` to see the default input text if it's a prompt

It also allows you to interact with the dialog:

- `dialog.accept()` is like clicking **OK**. For prompts, you can pass in a string to simulate user input.
- `dialog.dismiss()` is like clicking **Cancel**, which is especially useful with confirm dialogs.

Just make sure to set up your dialog handler before triggering the action that causes the dialog; otherwise, you might miss it.

Suppose the page you are testing may show multiple dialogs. In this case, you can write the following:

```
import { test } from '@playwright/test';

test('handle all dialogs', async ({ page }) => {
  page.on('dialog', async dialog => {
    console.log(`Dialog type: ${dialog.type()},
                 message: ${dialog.message()}`);
    if (dialog.type() === 'prompt')
      await dialog.accept('some answer');
    else if (dialog.type() === 'confirm')
      await dialog.accept();      // clicks "OK"
    else
      await dialog.dismiss();     // clicks "Cancel"
  });

  await page.goto(' https://testpages.eviltester.com/styled/alerts/alert-
test.html');
  await page.getByRole('button', {name: 'Show alert box'}).click();
  await page.getByRole('button', {name: 'Show confirm box'}).click();
});
```

This test navigates to a demo alerts page and triggers two dialogs by clicking buttons labeled **Show alert box** and **Show confirm box**. The script listens for and handles all JavaScript dialog boxes (alerts, confirms, and prompts) triggered by the page.

Here we are using the `page.on()` method because multiple dialogs appear during the test run. But you can also use `page.once()` if you expect only one dialog (replace `page.on()` with `page.once()` to see the effect). This prevents handlers from unintentionally affecting unrelated parts of your test.

To make sure your dialog displays the correct message, you can grab it using `dialog.message()` and check it against the expected text. This comes in handy when you're testing things such as error messages, confirmation boxes, or instructional alerts in your app.

Also, don't forget to either accept or dismiss the dialog in your test. If you leave it hanging, the modal can block further steps and cause your test to stall indefinitely.

When testing different web pages, a hurdle you might run into is working with iframes and nested frames, which are used to display content from other sources or different parts of a site. In the next section, we'll walk through how to handle these elements smoothly in your automation tasks.

Interacting with iframes and nested frames

Playwright sees every web page as a tree made up of frames. The main document is the primary or main frame, and any `<iframe>` elements inside it are treated as child frames. Some websites use iframes or even nested frames to organize content, often for security or to keep things modular. If you want to interact with something inside one of those frames, such as clicking a button or typing in a field, you'll need to switch your focus to that specific frame so your actions happen in the right place.

Accessing an iframe

An `<iframe>` element creates an inline frame that loads another HTML document. It operates as a separate browsing context, meaning elements inside an **iframe** are isolated from the parent page.

To work with elements inside an iframe, start by finding the iframe using `frameLocator`. Just call `page.frameLocator(selector)` and pass in the iframe's CSS selector, ID, or another attribute to target it. Once you've got the iframe, you can use the `locator` method to find elements inside it and do things such as click, fill out fields, or get their text.

Here's an example:

```
import { test, expect } from '@playwright/test';

test('Interact with iframe', async ({ page }) => {
  await page.goto('https://testpages.eviltester.com/styled/iframes-test.
html');

  // Locate the iframe
  const frame = page.frameLocator('#thedynamichtml');
```

```
    // Interact with elements inside the iframe
    await expect(frame.getByRole('heading', { name: 'iFrame' }))
      .toBeVisible();
});
```

This script visits a web page that includes an iframe and checks to make sure a heading inside it is visible. Inside that iframe, it looks for a heading (identified by its ARIA role) with the text `iFrame` and confirms it's visible. This helps verify that the iframe has loaded properly and its content is ready to interact with.

Another way to work with iframes is to first get the iframe element using `locator`, then retrieve the actual `Frame` object with `contentFrame()`, and afterward interact with elements inside it:

```
import { test, expect } from '@playwright/test';

test('Interact with iframe', async ({ page }) => {
  await page.goto('https://testpages.eviltester.com/styled/iframes-test.
html');

  // Interact with elements inside the iframe
  await expect(page.locator('#thedynamichtml')
                 .contentFrame()
                 .getByRole('heading', { name: 'iFrame' })
             ).toBeVisible();
});
```

This approach gets you the same result but requires one more step.

Handling nested frames

Some websites might use iframes embedded within other iframes, creating a hierarchy of frames. Each frame has its own DOM and context. In such cases, chain your frame selectors carefully:

1. **Locate the parent iframe**: Use `page.frameLocator` to select the top-level iframe.
2. **Locate the nested iframe**: Use `frameLocator` on the parent frame to select the nested iframe.
3. **Interact with elements**: Use `locator` to find and interact with elements in the nested iframe.

Let's look at an example of how you might work with nested iframes:

```
import { test, expect } from '@playwright/test';

test('should correctly find text in all nested frames', async ({ page })
=> {
  await page.goto('https://the-internet.herokuapp.com/nested_frames');

  // Locate the top frame (which contains the nested frames)
  const topFrame = page.frameLocator('frame[name="frame-top"]');

  // Locate the frames nested inside the 'topFrame'
  const leftFrame = topFrame.frameLocator('frame[name="frame-left"]');
  const middleFrame = topFrame.frameLocator('frame[name="frame-middle"]');
  const rightFrame = topFrame.frameLocator('frame[name="frame-right"]');

  // Locate the bottom frame (which is at the same level as 'topFrame')
  const bottomFrame = page.frameLocator('frame[name="frame-bottom"]');

  // Assert the text content of each frame
  await expect(leftFrame.locator('body')).toHaveText('LEFT');
  await expect(middleFrame.locator('body')).toHaveText('MIDDLE');
  await expect(rightFrame.locator('body')).toHaveText('RIGHT');
  await expect(bottomFrame.locator('body')).toHaveText('BOTTOM');
});
```

This test helps us verify that a web page with several nested frames displays the right text in each section. First, we locate the frame-top frame. Inside it, we find the three nested frames: frame-left, frame-middle, and frame-right. We also locate the frame-bottom, which sits below the top frame at the same level. We then use the `expect` function to confirm that each frame contains the correct text.

> If your iframes are sourced from a different origin, browser security policies (such as the same-origin policy) might limit what you can do. Playwright does a great job handling many cross-origin situations, but it's always good to keep potential restrictions in mind.

When you're working with modern web apps (especially ones that use Web Components), you might run into some challenges when trying to interact with elements inside the Shadow DOM. Fortunately, Playwright has tools to help with that. That leads us to the next important topic.

Handling Shadow DOM components

In web development, the **Shadow DOM** lets you encapsulate parts of the DOM (such as custom components) so their styles and elements don't accidentally interfere with the rest of the page. This makes it a bit tricky to access or interact with those nested elements using traditional DOM selectors. Let's take a look at ways to pierce through this boundary and interact with these encapsulated elements.

Locating the host element

This is often the most direct way to access elements within a Shadow DOM. You first locate the host element that has the Shadow DOM. From this root locator, you can then query for elements within it using standard Playwright locators.

Let's imagine you have a custom web component like this:

```
<my-widget>
  #shadow-root
    <div class="internal-button">Click me!</div>
    <style>
      .internal-button { color: blue; }
    </style>
</my-widget>
```

Here's how you'd interact with the button in Playwright:

```
import { test, expect } from '@playwright/test';
test('interacting with shadow dom component', async ({ page }) => {
  await page.goto('webpage.html');

  // Locate the host element
  const widget = page.locator('my-widget');

  // Now you can locate elements within the shadow root
  const internalButton = widget.locator('.internal-button');
```

```
  // Perform actions on the internal element
  await internalButton.click();
  const buttonText = await internalButton.innerText();
  console.log(buttonText);

  // You can add assertions here to verify the behavior
  // For example, if clicking the button changes something
  // on the page:
  // await expect(page.locator('#some-indicator')).toHaveText('Button
Clicked!');
});
```

In this example, `page.locator('my-widget')` gives us a new locator that is scoped to the shadow root of the `<my-widget>` element. We can then use familiar locator strategies such as `.locator(".internal-button")` on `shadow_root` to find the button.

Using the >>> combinator

Playwright also provides a piercing selector syntax that makes it straightforward to target elements within an open shadow DOM. The key operator here is the >>> symbol, which tells Playwright to traverse the shadow boundaries.

Let's say we use the same HTML structure as before:

```
import { test } from '@playwright/test';

test('interacting with shadow dom using deprecated combinators', async ({
page }) => {
  await page.goto('webpage.html');

  const internalButton = page.locator('my-widget >>> .internal-button');

  await internalButton.click();
  const buttonText = await internalButton.innerText();
  console.log(buttonText);
});
```

`>>>` acts as an instruction to pierce into any open shadow root. This syntax is also effective for nested shadow DOM components. If you have multiple layers, you can chain the selectors:

```
// Chaining through multiple shadow boundaries:
await page.click('parent-component >>> child-component >>> button');
```

Here, Playwright automatically handles crossing into each shadow boundary defined by the custom elements.

Keep in mind that this code would also work without the >>> symbol. Modern versions of Playwright automatically traverse open shadow roots, so you can use regular CSS, text, or role-based locators without any special syntax (though XPath selectors do not pierce by default).

> Closed Shadow DOMs aren't accessible from outside the component. That means Playwright locators won't work in those cases. This isn't a limitation of Playwright specifically. It's part of the web standard for encapsulation.
>
> For a deeper dive into the Shadow DOM, see Faraz's article, *Understanding Shadow DOM*:
>
> `https://blog.logrocket.com/understanding-shadow-dom-v1-fa9b81ebe3ac/`
>
> It explains the core ideas behind the Shadow DOM specification and explores practical use cases.

Summary

In this chapter, you've explored some of Playwright's most useful tools for navigating the ever-changing landscape of modern web interfaces. You've gotten hands-on with the reliable `getBy*` locators and learned when it's best to fall back on traditional selectors.

You also discovered how Playwright's smart waiting features can help you handle dynamic content smoothly, which makes your tests less prone to flakiness.

On top of that, you learned how to deal with system dialogs, work with iframes, and interact with shadow DOMs, which are key skills for testing today's complex, component-driven UIs.

As you proceed with building your tests, always remember that the goal is to mimic genuine user interactions while ensuring your code remains resilient in the face of change.

In our next chapter, we will shift focus to browser-agnostic testing, which ensures tests work across Chromium, Firefox, and WebKit.

3

Browser-Agnostic Testing Across Chromium, Firefox, and WebKit

In modern web development, ensuring that your application behaves consistently across all major browsers is no longer optional: it's essential. In this chapter, we'll introduce you to Playwright's browser-agnostic testing capabilities, showing you how to run a single suite of end-to-end tests against all major browsers with zero code duplication. You'll learn how to define multiple *projects* in your Playwright configuration, each customized to a different browser or device profile, and how to launch them in parallel to catch compatibility issues early in your development cycle.

Next, we'll dive into all the ways you can tweak your browser contexts: adjusting viewport sizes and user agents, emulating various devices, and even setting permissions. This lets you mirror real-world user scenarios and catch potential problems before they reach your users. We'll also cover how to save and reuse storage state for fast test flows, and how to target branded channels such as Microsoft Edge or Google Chrome when accuracy really matters.

By the end of the chapter, you'll have a clear, step-by-step plan for creating reusable tests that run reliably everywhere.

The chapter is structured into these sections:

- Configuring Playwright for multi-browser testing
- Handling browser-specific behaviors
- Writing tests for cross-browser compatibility
- Debugging browser-specific test failures

Let's get started with configuring Playwright for your tests.

Technical requirements

The source code for this chapter is available at

`https://github.com/PacktPublishing/Hands-On-Automated-Testing-with-Playwright/tree/main/Chapter03`.

Configuring Playwright for multi-browser testing

If you want to run your Playwright tests on different browsers, such as **Chromium**, **Firefox**, and **WebKit**, without writing the same tests multiple times, Playwright makes it easy with a feature called **projects**. By setting up projects in your config file, you can define which browser to use, along with any custom settings such as viewport size, device emulation, or specific test options. Playwright then takes care of running your tests in parallel across all the configured browsers.

Running tests with Playwright projects

A project defines the following:

- Which browser engine to use (`browserName`: `'chromium'`, `'firefox'`, or `'webkit'`)
- Browser-specific options and arguments
- Device emulation (such as viewport size, user agent, and touch support)
- Other configuration options specific to that project (such as `baseURL`, `use` options such as `storageState`, etc.)

Playwright Test will then run tests in parallel using worker processes. These workers will pick up test files to execute based on the configured projects. Within the `playwright.config.ts` file, you'll find a `projects` array. This is where you define the different browser configurations you want to run your tests against.

The following is an example of a `playwright.config.ts` file showing a basic multi-browser configuration:

```
projects: [
    {
      name: 'chromium',
      use: { ...devices['Desktop Chrome'] },
    },

    {
      name: 'firefox',
      use: { ...devices['Desktop Firefox'] },
    },

    {
      name: 'webkit',
      use: { ...devices['Desktop Safari'] },
    },
  ],
```

Let's take a closer look at the `projects` array:

- `name`: This is a descriptive name for this project, which will be used in the test reports to identify which browser the tests ran on.
- `use`: This object contains configuration options specific to this project. Playwright provides preconfigured device emulations in the `devices` object. By using the spread syntax (`...`), you inherit all the default settings for a desktop version of each browser (such as viewport size, user agent, etc.).

You can further customize how each browser is launched by adding more options within the `use` object of each project.

Customizing browser launch options

Within the `use` object of each project in your `playwright.config.ts` file, you can add various options that Playwright will pass along when it launches the browser. You can specify a different viewport size, user agent, or even pass command-line arguments to the browser.

Here are some common and useful options.

userAgent

By default, Playwright uses the real user agent of the browser it launches, but you can simulate different devices or browsers by overriding the user agent string. This is useful for testing how your site behaves across platforms.

Here is an example:

```
{
  name: 'webkit-ipad',
  use: {
    ...devices['Desktop Safari'],
    userAgent: 'Mozilla/5.0 (Windows NT 10.0; Win64; x64; rv:138.0)
Gecko/20100101 Firefox/138.0',
  },
},
```

Note that user agent spoofing alone doesn't change browser engine behavior. If you spoof Firefox's user agent while running Safari, you're still using Safari's rendering engine. To simulate a device such as an iPhone or Galaxy, use predefined devices in Playwright (such as `devices['iPhone 16 Pro']`), which we'll discuss later in this chapter.

deviceScaleFactor

This option sets the device scale factor, which is important for testing on high-DPI screens. By default, it's set to 1.

Here is an example:

```
{
  name: 'chromium-high-dpi',
  use: {
    ...devices['Desktop Chrome'],
    viewport: { width: 1280, height: 720 },
    deviceScaleFactor: 2,
  },
},
```

Setting a value of 2 means that one device-independent pixel equals two physical pixels in both width and height. In other words, the browser will display content at double the pixel density of a standard screen (where `deviceScaleFactor` would be `1`).

This helps websites and web apps look crisp and clear on high-resolution displays, since they can adjust images and styles based on the screen's pixel density. By using `deviceScaleFactor: 2`, you're telling Playwright to mimic a high-DPI environment.

viewport

This option allows you to set the initial viewport size of the browser window. This is essential for responsive design testing.

Here is an example:

```
{
  name: 'chromium-large',
  use: {
    ...devices['Desktop Chrome'],
    viewport: { width: 1920, height: 1080 },
  },
},
{
  name: 'firefox-mobile',
  use: {
    ...devices['Desktop Firefox'],
    viewport: { width: 375, height: 667 },
  },
},
```

isMobile

This accepts a Boolean value indicating whether to emulate a mobile device. This often goes hand-in-hand with setting `viewport` and `userAgent`.

Here is an example:

```
{
  name: 'chromium-mobile-only',
  use: {
    ...devices['Desktop Chrome'],
    viewport: { width: 390, height: 844 },
```

```
    isMobile: true,
  },
},
```

javaScriptEnabled

You can explicitly control whether JavaScript is enabled in the browser. This is useful for testing how your application behaves with JavaScript disabled.

Here is an example:

```
{
  name: 'chromium-no-js',
  use: {
    ...devices['Desktop Chrome'],
    javaScriptEnabled: false,
  },
},
```

ignoreHTTPSErrors

By default, tests will fail if they encounter HTTPS errors, such as those caused by self-signed certificates or other SSL/TLS issues. To bypass these errors, you can configure Playwright to ignore HTTPS errors by setting the `ignoreHTTPSErrors` option to `true` in the browser context configuration.

Here is an example:

```
{
  name: 'chromium-ignore-https',
  use: {
    ...devices['Desktop Chrome'],
    ignoreHTTPSErrors: true,
  },
},
```

Just keep in mind that it's best to be cautious when using this in production environments, as ignoring HTTPS errors might hide real security problems or misconfigurations.

proxy

Setting up a proxy server for your browser lets you route its network traffic through an intermediary server. This can be useful if your app is meant to be accessed through a proxy.

Proxies can also help you simulate different network scenarios. For example, you can mimic users from various geographic locations or test how your app performs under certain network restrictions.

To set up a proxy in Playwright, you'll use a configuration object with the following options:

- `server` (string): This is the key setting. It tells Playwright which proxy server to use, and should include the full address: protocol (`http://`, `https://`, or `socks5://`), hostname or IP, and port number.
- `username` (string, optional): If the proxy requires a login, you can provide the username here.
- `password` (string, optional): Add the password here if your proxy needs it for authentication.
- `bypass` (string or array of strings, optional): You can list domains or hosts that should skip the proxy. This is handy for accessing local resources or specific websites directly.

Here is an example:

```
{
  name: 'chromium-with-proxy',
  use: {
    ...devices['Desktop Chrome'],
    proxy: {
      server: 'http://username:password@yourproxy.com:8080',
    },
  },
},
```

With this configuration, any tests run using the `chromium-with-proxy` project will launch a Chromium browser configured to route its traffic through the specified proxy server.

In a real setup, avoid hardcoding credentials in your configuration files. Instead, store them securely using environment variables or a secrets manager. See *Chapter 14, Security and Authentication.*

permissions

Playwright allows you to manage browser permissions (such as access to geolocation, camera, or microphone) before your tests even start. This is helpful when you're testing features that depend on these permissions, so you don't have to manually click through permission prompts during test runs.

You can set permissions globally for all your tests, for individual projects, or even for specific test cases. Just use the `use` option in your Playwright configuration file or inside a `test.use()` block. Within `use`, the `permissions` field takes an array of strings, each one representing a browser permission you'd like to allow.

Here's an example:

```
{
  name: 'chromium-with-location',
  use: {
    ...devices['Desktop Chrome'],
    permissions: ['geolocation'], // Grants geolocation permission
  },
}
```

In this setup, the `chromium-with-location` project uses the `Desktop Chrome` device profile and explicitly grants access to `geolocation`.

If you want to block all permissions instead, you can pass an empty array:

```
{
  name: 'chromium-no-camera',
  use: {
    ...devices['Desktop Chrome'],
    permissions: [], // Blocks all permissions
  },
}
```

With this setup, the browser won't ask for any permissions, and features that rely on them will be blocked.

Playwright supports a variety of permissions, though the exact list can vary a bit depending on the browser and version. Some commonly supported ones include the following:

- `geolocation`
- `camera`
- `microphone`
- `notifications`
- `clipboard-read`
- `clipboard-write`
- `midi`
- `accelerometer`
- `gyroscope`
- `magnetometer`
- `ambient-light-sensor`
- `background-sync`
- `payment-handler`
- `storage-access`

By setting permissions up front, your tests become easier to maintain.

storageState

Playwright makes it easy to save the current browser storage (such as cookies, local storage, and IndexedDB) at any point during your test and store it in a file (usually a JSON file). Later, you can load that saved state at the start of another test.

One of the biggest perks of using `storageState` is that it helps speed up your tests by skipping the repetitive login steps. Many web apps require users to log in before they can do much, and without `storageState`, you'd have to go through the login process in every single test: visiting the login page, typing in credentials, and submitting the form. That adds up quickly.

Instead, you can log in once, save the cookies, and then reuse that logged-in snapshot in future tests. This way, your tests can jump straight into the action with an authenticated session.

First, write a `login` script that logs in and writes out `storageState`:

```
// Open a page and perform login.
// Then save storage state to a file:
await context.storageState({ path: 'logged_in_state.json' });
```

Now, you can reference that file in your `playwright.config.ts` project configuration:

```
{
  name: 'chromium-logged-in',
  use: {
    ...devices['Desktop Chrome'],
    storageState: 'logged_in_state.json', // Path to a saved file
  },
},
```

If you'd like to see how this setup scales across multiple projects, check out *Chapter 14, Security and Authentication*. It shows how you can create a setup project to generate and share `storageState` data across tests.

Browser-specific channels for branded browsers

Playwright normally comes bundled with its own open source builds of Chromium, Firefox, and WebKit. But if you want to test against the official, branded versions such as Microsoft's Edge or Google Chrome that might include extra codecs or match your company's policies, you can do that too. Simply use the `channel` option in your Playwright setup.

The `channel` setting tells Playwright exactly which release channel to launch, whether it's `stable`, `beta`, `dev`, or `canary`. It's a great way to make sure your tests behave the same way on the exact browser builds your users have installed. Here is an example:

```
{
  name: 'edge-stable',
  use: {
    ...devices['Desktop Edge'],
    channel: 'msedge', // Stable channel
  },
},
{
  name: 'chrome-beta',
  use: {
    ...devices['Desktop Chrome'],
    channel: 'chrome-beta', // Beta channel
  },
}
```

When you pick a channel, Playwright will try to use that specific branded browser already installed on your system. If it can't find the one you asked for, it'll let you know with an error message.

You can find the full list of configurable browser launch options in the Playwright documentation here: `https://playwright.dev/docs/api/class-browser`.

Running tests on a specific browser

Playwright provides a very convenient way to target particular browser configurations. The primary way to do this is by using the `--project` command-line flag when you execute your Playwright tests, which allows you to specify one or more project names that you've defined within the `projects` array of your `playwright.config` file. Playwright will then only run the tests using the browser configurations associated with those project names.

Let's assume you have the following `projects` configuration in your `playwright.config.ts` file:

```
projects: [
  {
    name: 'chromium',
    use: { ...devices['Desktop Chrome'] },
  },
  {
    name: 'firefox',
    use: { ...devices['Desktop Firefox'] },
  },
  {
    name: 'webkit',
    use: { ...devices['Desktop Safari'] },
  },
  {
    name: 'mobile-chrome',
    use: { ...devices['Pixel 5'] },
  },
],
```

To execute your tests solely using the Chromium browser configuration, you would open your terminal in your project's root directory and run the following:

```
npx playwright test --project chromium
```

Playwright will then launch Chromium and run all your tests (within your specified test files) using that browser.

You can target multiple browsers by using the `--project` flag multiple times, each followed by the name of the project you want to include:

```
npx playwright test --project chromium --project firefox
```

In this case, Playwright will run your tests twice: once in Chromium and once in Firefox. If you have defined custom project configurations, such as the preceding `mobile-chrome` example, you can target them in the same way:

```
npx playwright test --project mobile-chrome
```

Note that project names are case-sensitive: make sure you use the exact same casing for the project names as you defined them in your `playwright.config` file; `'chromium'` is different from `'Chromium'`.

If you run `npx playwright test` without any `--project` flags, Playwright will, by default, run your tests against all the projects defined in your configuration file.

You can combine the `--project` flag with other Playwright CLI options, such as `--grep` to filter tests by name, to run a specific set of tests on a specific browser.

Here is an example:

```
npx playwright test --project chromium --grep "user login"
```

This would run only the tests that have `"user login"` in their title, but only within the Chromium browser.

When writing end-to-end tests, subtle differences in how each engine implements standards can lead to unexpected failures or flaky behavior. Let's look at how Playwright makes it easy to detect which browser you're running so that you can branch your test logic only when necessary.

Handling browser-specific behaviors

Playwright provides a straightforward way to determine which browser engine your test is currently running against. This is important for implementing conditional logic.

You can access the browser name through the `browser` fixture or from the page object. Using the `page.context().browser().browserType().name()` chain of methods will return a string indicating the browser type, such as `'chromium'`, `'firefox'`, or `'webkit'`:

```
import { test, expect } from '@playwright/test';

test('should log browser name', async ({ page }) => {
  const browserName = page.context().browser().browserType().name();
  console.log(`Currently running on: ${browserName}`);

  if (browserName === 'firefox') {
    console.log('This is a Firefox-specific step.');
    // Add Firefox-specific actions or assertions
  } else if (browserName === 'chromium') {
    console.log('This is a Chromium-specific step.');
    // Add Chromium-specific actions or assertions
  }
});
```

Once you can identify which browser is being used, you can use conditional statements such as `if`, `else if`, `else`, or `switch` to run different code depending on the situation.

Another option is to use the `browserName` fixture directly from `@playwright/test`. The test runner conveniently provides `browserName` as a built-in fixture, so you can access it easily in your tests. This lets you customize your tests depending on the browser and device type. For instance, on a mobile device, the **Sign in** link might be tucked away behind a hamburger menu, so your test would need an extra click to open it first:

```
import { test, expect } from '@playwright/test';

test('demonstrating device-specific logic', async ({ page, browserName,
isMobile }) => {
  await page.goto('https://github.com/');

  console.log(`Currently running on: ${browserName}, Is mobile:
${isMobile}`);

  if (isMobile) {
```

```
    // Mobile-specific behavior: Click hamburger menu to reveal SignIn
link
    await page.getByRole('button', { name: 'Toggle navigation' }).click();
    await expect(page.getByRole('link', { name: 'Sign in' })).
toBeVisible();
  } else if (browserName === 'firefox') {
    // Firefox might render a specific element differently
    await expect(page.getByRole('link', { name: 'Sign in' })).
toBeVisible();
  } else {
    // Default behavior for other browsers
    await expect(page.getByRole('link', { name: 'Sign in' })).
toBeVisible();
  }
});
```

This Playwright test shows how you can use the `browserName` and `isMobile` fixtures to add logic that adapts to different browsers and devices when testing GitHub's web page.

If it's on mobile, the test clicks the hamburger menu (`getByRole('button', { name: 'Toggle navigation' })`) to open the navigation and checks that the **Sign in** link is visible (`getByRole('link', { name: 'Sign in' })`). On desktop, it uses `browserName` to account for differences between browsers such as WebKit (Safari), Firefox, or Chromium, and verifies that the **Sign in** link is already visible without any extra steps.

This setup can be really handy for applying different assertions when a feature behaves differently, skipping specific test steps that don't apply or cause issues in certain browsers, or adjusting how you wait for elements if rendering times or behaviors differ.

Customizing tests for different browsers is a great start, but what about making sure your site looks good and works well on different devices? That's where device emulation steps in. It lets you easily see how your site behaves across all kinds of devices, without needing a drawer full of devices.

Using device emulation

Device emulation in Playwright lets you mimic how your website behaves on smartphones, tablets, and even various desktop setups.

Device emulation does more than just resizing your browser window. It can simulate a full range of properties. Emulation also comes in handy for checking how touch interactions work (things such as swipes, taps, and even virtual keyboards).

Using predefined devices in Playwright

Playwright comes with a predefined list of common device descriptors, which makes emulation very convenient. The full list of predefined devices is maintained in the source code available on GitHub: `https://github.com/microsoft/playwright/blob/main/packages/playwright-core/src/server/deviceDescriptorsSource.json`.

You can also see what predefined devices Playwright offers inside your code, without having to go to external docs or GitHub:

```
import { devices } from '@playwright/test';

console.log(devices);
```

This will log all the available device descriptors you can use.

Manually configuring emulation parameters

Playwright comes with a useful collection of ready-made device profiles you can pick from, but sometimes you'll want to tweak settings just a bit more or emulate a gadget that isn't on that list. That's when you should set up your own emulation parameters as you spin up a new browser context.

A browser context is an isolated session that's equivalent to an incognito profile: it keeps its own cookies, local storage, and session data all to itself. By creating a fresh context with custom options, you're essentially telling Playwright exactly what "environment" you want for every page that lives inside it.

When you create a new browser context using `browser.newContext()`, you can pass an `options` object to customize its behavior. This `options` object allows you to set various properties that influence how the browser behaves.

Some of the key parameters you can manually configure include the following:

- `hasTouch`: This Boolean indicates whether the emulated device supports touch events.
- `geolocation`: You can provide an object with latitude, longitude, and optional accuracy to emulate a specific geographic location. This is useful for testing location-aware features, such as `{"latitude": 40.7128, "longitude": -74.0060}`.
- `locale`: This string allows you to emulate the user's locale, which affects language and regional settings, such as `"en-US"`.

- `timezoneId`: You can set the time zone of the browser context, which is important for testing applications that handle dates and times, such as `"America/New_York"`.
- `permissions`: This array of strings allows you to grant specific permissions to the browser context, such as `'geolocation'`, `'notifications'`, or `'camera'`.
- `colorScheme`: You can emulate the user's preferred color scheme, such as `'light'` or `'dark'`.
- `viewport`: This object allows you to set the dimensions of the viewport in pixels. You can specify width and height, such as `{"width": 1280, "height": 720}`.
- `userAgent`: You can set a custom user agent string to emulate a specific browser or device. This string is sent in the HTTP headers and can be used by websites to serve different content or layouts, such as `"Mozilla/5.0 (Windows NT 10.0; Win64; x64) AppleWebKit/537.36 (KHTML, like Gecko) Chrome/135.0.0.0 Safari/537.36 Edg/135.0.0.0"`.
- `deviceScaleFactor`: This number specifies the device scale factor, which is the ratio between physical pixels and logical pixels. It's useful for emulating high-DPI displays.
- `isMobile`: Setting this Boolean to `true` enables mobile emulation, which affects things such as touch events and the presence of a mobile user agent (if not explicitly set).

By combining these parameters, you can create a customized emulation environment that precisely matches the characteristics of a specific device or browser scenario that is not available in Playwright's default device list.

Here's a basic example:

```
import { test } from '@playwright/test';

test('Emulate Android device and open github.com', async ({ browser }) =>
{
  const context = await browser.newContext({
    viewport: { width: 360, height: 640 },
    userAgent: 'Mozilla/5.0 (Linux; Android 10; SM-G975F)
AppleWebKit/537.36 (KHTML, like Gecko) Chrome/83.0.4103.106 Mobile
Safari/537.36',
    deviceScaleFactor: 2,
    isMobile: true,
    hasTouch: true,
    geolocation: { latitude: 48.856613, longitude: 2.352222 },
    locale: 'fr-FR',
```

```
    timezoneId: 'Europe/Paris',
    permissions: ['geolocation'],
  });

  const page = await context.newPage();
  await page.goto('https://github.com');

  // Add assertions or interactions here

  await context.close();
});
```

This manual configuration provides precision when the built-in device presets are not sufficient for your testing needs.

> While you can define these parameters directly in your test, it's best practice to move them into the `use` object inside your `playwright.config.ts` file. This keeps your test code clean and makes it easier to manage environment-specific settings in one place.

Overriding specific properties of a device descriptor

While predefined device descriptors are very useful, you sometimes need to modify one or two properties for a specific test scenario without creating an entirely new descriptor from scratch. To do this, you'll use what's called **spreading a predefined descriptor**. This basically means you're starting with all the settings from a device such as a Pixel 8 or iPhone 16 and building on top of it.

You do this using the spread syntax (`...devices['Device Name']`), which copies over all the device's properties into a new object. Once you've spread the base settings, you can customize whatever you need by adding or changing properties right in the same object. If the same property is listed more than once, the last one wins, meaning your custom values will override the defaults.

Here's a quick example:

```
{
  name: 'Pixel 8 Dark Mode',
  use: {
    ...devices['Pixel 8'], //Bring in all the default settings for Pixel 8
    colorScheme: 'dark',   // Customize to dark mode
```

```
      locale: 'fr-FR',        // Set the Locale to French
    },
  }
```

In this setup, you're creating a new project that starts with everything the regular Pixel 8 offers (such as viewport size and user agent) but then tweaks the color scheme to `'dark'` and changes the locale to French (`'fr-FR'`). This way, you can test how your app looks in specific scenarios.

You can also do this programmatically. Here's how:

```
import { test, expect, devices } from '@playwright/test';

test.use({
  ...devices['iPhone 16'],                    // Start with iPhone 16 settings
  viewport: { width: 390, height: 600 }, // Override the screen size
  locale: 'es-ES',                           // Switch to Spanish
});

test('iPhone16 viewport & locale test', async ({ page }) => {
  // Verify page elements
});
```

This creates a new browser context that's based on an iPhone 16, but with a custom screen size and a Spanish locale.

Always make sure your overrides come *after* the spread (`...devices['Device Name']`). JavaScript processes properties from left to right, so anything defined later will overwrite earlier values. If you put your overrides *before* the spread, they'll get overwritten.

Whenever you can, try to use configuration instead of adding conditional logic directly in your test files. If you're seeing differences because of setup, environment, or browser capabilities, it's usually best to handle those in your `playwright.config.ts` file. This keeps your test code cleaner and easier to maintain.

So, achieving browser-agnostic testing requires that your automated tests run reliably across Chromium, Firefox, and WebKit. Playwright does a great job of simplifying this with its unified API, but creating tests that handle the subtle (and sometimes not-so-subtle) differences between browsers still takes some thoughtful planning. This leads us to the next section.

Writing tests for cross-browser compatibility

When you write tests, aim for one unified suite that runs smoothly on every browser without constantly troubleshooting browser-specific issues, and when you're writing your assertions, put yourself in the user's shoes and focus on what they actually see and do.

It's better to validate outcomes that are visible or meaningful to the end user rather than internal details that might behave differently between browsers. For example, checking that a button is visible is more robust than checking its exact CSS color value (unless that color is a specific requirement).

Playwright's `expect` API is a great tool for this. It comes with built-in auto-retrying, which helps with minor timing differences between browsers. If you're asserting something like `await expect(locator).toBeVisible()`, Playwright will automatically keep checking until the condition is met or the timeout is reached.

Also, keep in mind that visual rendering can differ slightly from browser to browser. Expecting pixel-perfect precision across engines is rarely realistic. If you need strict visual checks, it's worth integrating visual regression tools (see *Chapter 10, Setting Up Visual Regression Testing*). For most functional tests, though, it's best to focus on whether elements are present, in the right state, and contain the correct content.

Some features, such as `backdrop-filter`, the `:has()` CSS selector, or certain animations in the Web Animations API, might not be fully supported everywhere. When you're using newer or less common features, it's a good idea to check `caniuse.com` for browser compatibility first.

If a browser behaves a little differently, you can use conditional logic in your test code to handle those cases. For instance, if a WebKit-specific timing issue affects an animation, you can write a conditional check to adjust behavior only when the test runs in WebKit. Just be sure to document why that condition exists, and avoid overusing this approach. It should be the exception, not the rule.

Ideally, one test should run across all browsers without issue. But sometimes, browser-specific bugs or intentional behavior differences make that impossible. In those cases, Playwright allows you to skip specific tests (or parts of tests) based on the browser being used. This is handy when a known issue in one browser causes a test to fail unnecessarily.

Here is an example:

```
test('feature X works', async ({ page, browserName }) => {
  if (browserName === 'webkit' && someKnownWebKitIssue) {
    test.skip(true, 'Skipping due to known WebKit issue XYZ');
  }
  // ... rest of the test logic ...
});
```

If skipping isn't enough, and a certain workflow is truly different in a particular browser, you can write a separate test for it. This should be a last resort, though. Maintaining separate tests adds overhead and can violate the **Don't Repeat Yourself** (**DRY**) principle, so it's best used only when absolutely necessary and always with clear documentation explaining why the test diverges.

Remember, don't wait until the end of development to run cross-browser tests. It's much easier to catch and fix issues if you integrate testing into your workflow early on. Run your tests against all browsers frequently, even as you're developing new features or writing new tests. This helps you spot compatibility problems before they grow into larger issues.

By testing across browsers from the beginning, you'll naturally write more portable and resilient tests. Plus, you'll save yourself from frustrating surprises during late-stage QA.

Debugging browser-specific test failures

Even with a solid cross-browser testing strategy in place, you'll occasionally hit situations where a test passes in one browser but fails in another. These browser-specific failures can be very frustrating.

The first thing you should do is confirm that the failure is actually limited to a specific browser. Start by running the test individually in the browser where the issue occurs. If your test suite normally runs across all browsers, narrowing it down helps you isolate the problem and speeds up the debugging process.

For example, as we discussed earlier in this chapter, you can run a specific test in Firefox with the following:

```
npx playwright test --project="Firefox"
```

Once you've isolated the browser, run the test in `headed` mode. This means the browser window will be visible during the test, allowing you to watch what's happening in real time. Often, you'll spot visual inconsistencies or timing issues just by watching the test run.

Here's how you can do that in WebKit:

```
npx playwright test --project="WebKit" --headed
```

If visual inspection doesn't reveal the issue right away, try slowing things down. Playwright offers a `slowMo` option, which slows the browser's actions so you can better observe what's going on. You can enable this in your `playwright.config.ts` file like so:

```
projects: [
  {
    name: 'chromium',
    use: {
      ...devices['Desktop Chrome'],
      launchOptions: {
        slowMo: 1000, // pauses for 1000 milliseconds between actions
      }
    }
  }
]
```

Another useful tool is `page.pause()`. You can insert this directly into your test code at the point where things start to go wrong. When Playwright hits this command, it pauses the test and opens the Playwright Inspector. From there, you can step through the commands and closely examine the page state.

Here is an example:

```
import { test, expect } from '@playwright/test';

test('Change article language to Deutschtest  ', async ({ page }) => {
  await page.goto('https://en.wikipedia.org/wiki/Playwright_(software)');
```

```
  await page.getByRole('button', { name: 'Go to an article in another'
}).click();
  await page.getByRole('link', { name: 'Deutsch' }).click();
  await page.waitForURL('https://de.wikipedia.org/wiki/Playwright_
(Software)', { timeout: 5000 });

  // Pauses execution for manual inspection
  await page.pause();

  console.log('Successfully navigated to German Wikipedia.');
});
```

This test script pauses for manual inspection before logging a success message.

> `page.pause()` is great for debugging, but remember to take it out before you commit your code or run tests in your automation pipeline.

Before introducing any browser-specific workarounds, take a moment to understand why the behavior varies. Is it a bug in your application when viewed in a specific browser? A known incompatibility? Or an intentional difference in how that browser functions? Understanding the root cause will help you choose the right solution.

Developer tools can help you inspect computed styles to check for differences in display, visibility, opacity, transform, or element dimensions. Pay attention to console logs in the failing browser to catch subtle JavaScript errors. If you're relying on modern features, consider implementing feature detection both in your application and your tests. That way, you can handle any differences more smoothly.

If your app adapts for different screens, be sure to try it out at each breakpoint. A layout that looks correct in Chrome might behave differently in Firefox, such as a menu being pushed off-screen.

Browser-specific bugs can be tricky and time-consuming to debug, but with Playwright's tools and a step-by-step approach, you can create tests that run smoothly across all major browsers. Take your time, stay organized, and you'll save yourself a lot of frustration later on.

We'll take a deeper look at debugging techniques in *Chapter 8, Headless Testing and Debugging*.

Summary

When writing tests for your application, aim to achieve consistent behavior across all the browsers you support. Cross-browser compatibility should be your top priority. While it's sometimes necessary to include browser-specific code due to genuine differences in how browsers behave or support features, these cases should be the exception, not the norm. Keep any such logic isolated to avoid cluttering your tests.

By now, you've seen just how approachable it is to run the same test suite across Chromium, Firefox, and WebKit without reinventing the wheel for each engine. Playwright gives you the tools to spot and fix issues before they ever reach your users. You've learned how to set up multi-browser configurations, write resilient and reusable tests, and handle the little surprises each browser engine might throw your way.

In our next chapter, we will explore how AI tools can improve Playwright test creation by generating scripts from natural language and refining tests for reliability.

4

AI-Powered Test Generation

Writing and maintaining automated tests can be time-consuming, especially when web apps are constantly changing. Luckily, there's a smarter way to handle it. With the help of AI, we can now generate tests faster, improve reliability, and cut down on the repetitive work that usually comes with test automation.

In this chapter, we'll start by exploring Playwright Codegen, a tool that turns your clicks and keystrokes into real test scripts, and then show how you can supercharge that experience using GitHub Copilot and **Playwright Model Context Protocol** (**MCP**).

You'll see how you can generate tests just by interacting with a website or even by typing out what you want in plain English. We'll also explore how to handle flaky tests, deal with dynamic content, and make your tests resilient when something changes.

The chapter is structured into these parts:

- Generating Playwright scripts with Codegen
- Setting up Playwright MCP for test automation
- Generating Playwright tests using MCP + Copilot
- Refining AI-generated scripts for reliability
- Implementing a resilient locator strategy

Let's jump in and see how AI can make test generation not only easier but actually kind of fun.

Technical requirements

The source code for this chapter is available at

`https://github.com/PacktPublishing/Hands-On-Automated-Testing-with-Playwright/tree/main/Chapter04.`

Generating Playwright scripts with Codegen

Playwright Codegen is a handy feature in the Playwright framework that automatically generates test scripts as you interact with a website. While it's not an AI tool in itself, it fits nicely into an AI-powered testing workflow, especially when paired with AI-assisted tools or copilots. It's perfect for speeding up test automation and learning how Playwright works without writing everything from scratch.

Recording tests

When you use Codegen, it records your actions (such as clicking buttons, filling out forms, or navigating through pages) and turns them into Playwright code in real time.

To launch Codegen, just run the following command in your terminal:

```
npx playwright codegen https://www.google.com/
```

You'll see two windows pop up:

- **Browser**: This is where you perform actions on your site
- **Playwright Inspector**: This shows the code being generated in real time based on your interactions

> You can leave the URL out in your terminal command and just navigate to your target site manually once the browser opens.

As you explore the website, Codegen records each interaction and translates it into readable Playwright code. It even chooses smart, reliable selectors (such as roles, text, or test IDs) and refines them when needed to make sure each element is uniquely targeted.

Once you're done recording, copy the generated code from the Inspector and paste it into your test file. From there, you can customize it: refactor, add logic, or include test data. We'll dive into how to do that a bit later in this chapter.

Adding assertions

If you want to check whether something is visible or contains the right text, you can use the **assertion tools** in the Inspector:

1. Click the assertion icon in the toolbar.
2. Select the element you want to check.
3. Choose the type of assertion (such as visibility, text, or value).

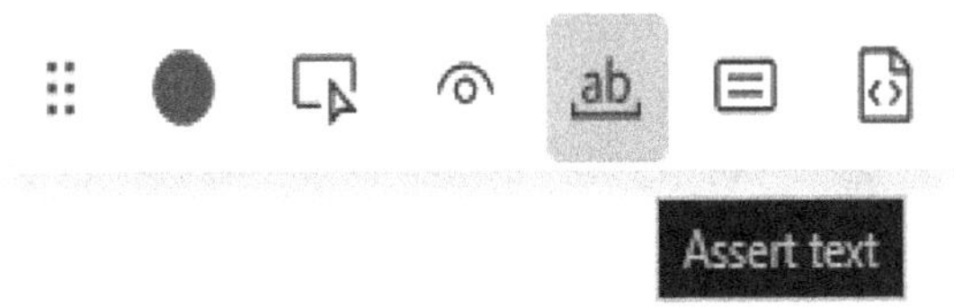

Figure 4.1: Selecting the type of assertion in the toolbar

Codegen will add that assertion right into your script.

Be sure to add assertions in your tests so you can verify that everything on the page works as expected. Without assertions, your test might just click around your app without really checking whether things are functioning properly. Assertions help confirm that your app behaves the way it should and let you catch any unexpected changes early on.

Choosing your language

If you prefer working in a specific programming language, Codegen supports the following:

- TypeScript
- JavaScript
- Python
- C#
- Java

Just pick your preferred language from the Inspector.

You can also specify the output language in your terminal by using the `--lang` flag, as in this example:

```
npx playwright codegen --lang=python
```

Using the Pick Locator tool

Even if you're not recording, you can still use the **Pick Locator** tool in Codegen. Hover over elements in the browser to instantly see the generated selectors. It's a great way to find solid locators for your tests without writing a line of code.

Figure 4.2: Hovering over an element to see the generated selector

Limitations of Codegen

While Codegen is a great starting point, it does have some limitations to be aware of. The scripts it generates are often fairly basic. They're great for capturing straightforward user flows, but for more complex scenarios (such as handling dynamic content), you'll likely need to refine the code manually.

Another limitation is that Codegen doesn't handle logic on its own. It won't include conditional statements, loops, or error handling in the generated code. If your test requires decision-making or needs to adapt to different conditions, you'll need to add that logic yourself.

Lastly, while Codegen does a good job at picking reliable selectors, it's not foolproof. You may find that some locators need adjustment to ensure your tests remain stable and don't break due to small changes in the UI.

To make handling these kinds of issues easier, it helps to use tools that give you more insight and control during testing. That's where Playwright MCP comes in.

Setting up Playwright MCP for test automation

Playwright Model Context Protocol (**MCP**) is a tool built on top of the Playwright automation framework. What makes it special is that it gives AI models (such as ChatGPT or Claude) the ability to actually *see* and *interact* with websites using structured snapshots of web pages. In simpler terms, Playwright MCP gives AI models *eyes* to see web content and *hands* to interact with it by clicking, typing, uploading files, and more.

The easiest way to get started is by installing the Playwright MCP server using the VS Code CLI. In VS Code, go to the top menu and choose **Terminal** | **New Terminal**, or press *Ctrl* + ` (backtick) on Windows/Linux or *Cmd* + ` on macOS.

Then, just run this command:

```
code --add-mcp '{"name":"playwright","command":"npx","args": ["@
playwright/mcp@latest"]}'
```

If you get an error such as `code: command not found`, that means the code CLI isn't available in your system path. To fix that, open the Command Palette in VS Code by pressing *Ctrl* + *Shift* + *P* on Windows/Linux or *Cmd* + *Shift* + *P* on macOS and run `Shell Command: Install 'code' command in PATH`. Restart your terminal and try again.

Alternatively, head over to the Playwright MCP GitHub repo (`https://github.com/microsoft/playwright-mcp`) and click the **Install in VS Code** button. Once it's installed, the MCP server will be available to use with your GitHub Copilot agent in VS Code.

GitHub Copilot can suggest code snippets, complete functions, and generate tests based on context, comments, or natural language prompts. When paired with MCP, Copilot can interact with Playwright to automate browser actions and generate test scripts.

> If you don't have the GitHub Copilot extension installed, just open the **Extensions** sidebar (or press *Ctrl* + *Shift* + *X* on Windows/Linux or *Cmd* + *Shift* + *X* on macOS), search for `GitHub Copilot` and `GitHub Copilot Chat`, and click **Install** on both official extensions by GitHub.

To use Copilot with MCP, follow these steps:

1. Open the secondary sidebar (*Ctrl* + *Alt* + *B* on Windows/Linux, or *Cmd* + *Alt* + *B* on macOS).
2. At the bottom of the Copilot chat window, switch from **Ask** mode to **Agent** mode. This allows Copilot to use Playwright commands to interact with web pages.
3. Choose **Claude** as the Copilot model.

Figure 4.3: Switching to Agent mode

Now that we have set up Playwright MCP and Copilot, we can ask them to generate tests for us.

Generating Playwright tests using MCP + Copilot

This useful duo helps you speed up test creation with less hassle. Let's try something. Tell Copilot to do the following: `Open the Playwright MCP repo. Then click the Watch button and select all activities to monitor.`

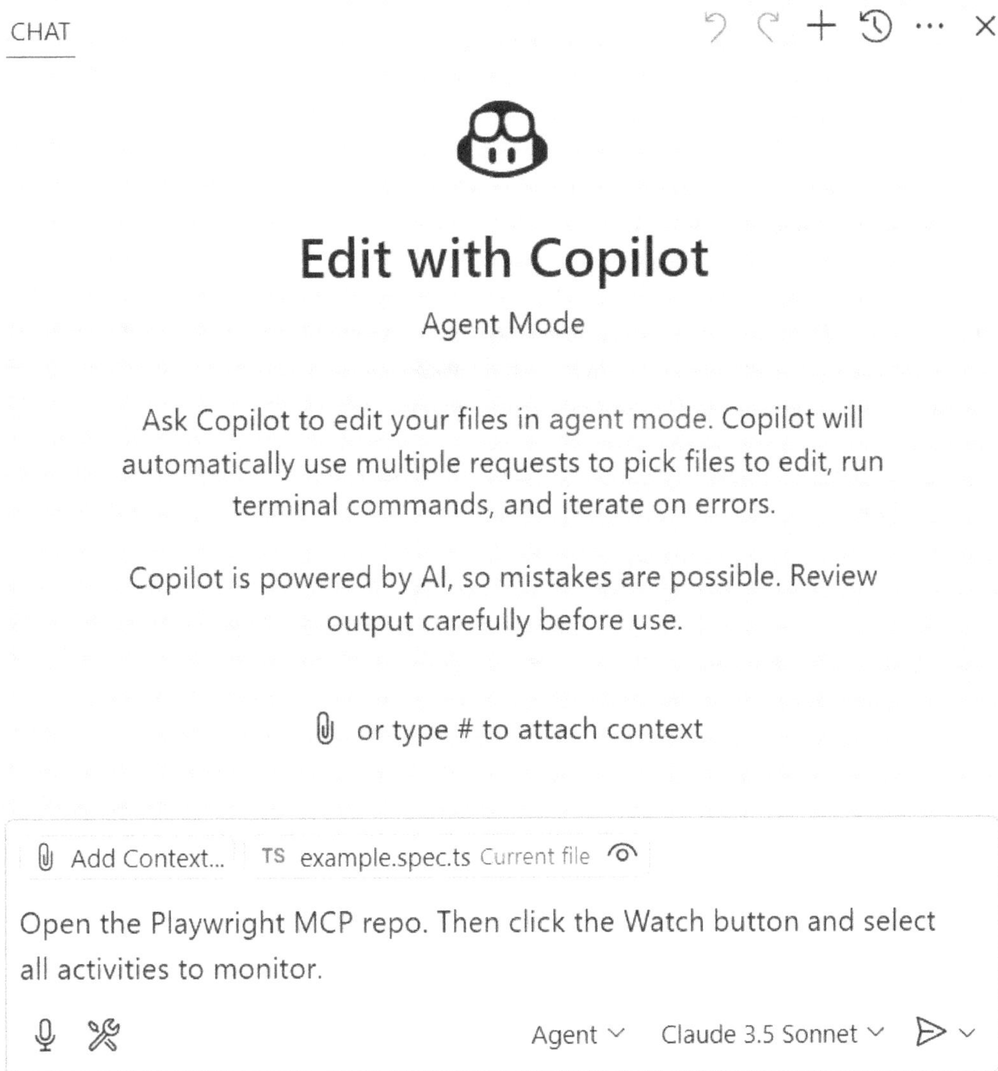

Figure 4.4: Writing a command in the secondary sidebar

Copilot will ask for your confirmation (just for safety), so go ahead and click **Continue**. You'll see it launch a browser, navigate to the right page, and even notice that you need to be signed into GitHub. It uses Playwright's snapshot tool to figure this out, and then clicks the **Sign In** button. It can identify the login form and fields for username/email and password.

> Heads-up: Copilot will warn you not to share passwords with AI. No problem: you can just manually click into the form, paste in your credentials, and handle two-factor authentication as usual.

Once you're signed in, you can tell Copilot to watch the repo. And that's it. Watching the code get generated as you interact with the site is a great way to learn about Playwright's API and how it interacts with elements on the page.

This is a big step forward in letting AI agents safely and intelligently interact with real websites. Copilot, through the MCP server, interacts with the web page, analyzes its accessibility tree, and generates a Playwright test script tailored to the prompt.

Let's say you want to test that a blog page loads correctly, the search bar works, and clicking on a tag filters the posts.

You simply tell Copilot the following:

```
Using Playwright, generate a test to verify the blog at mashable.com loads, the search input works, and clicking a tag filters posts correctly.
```

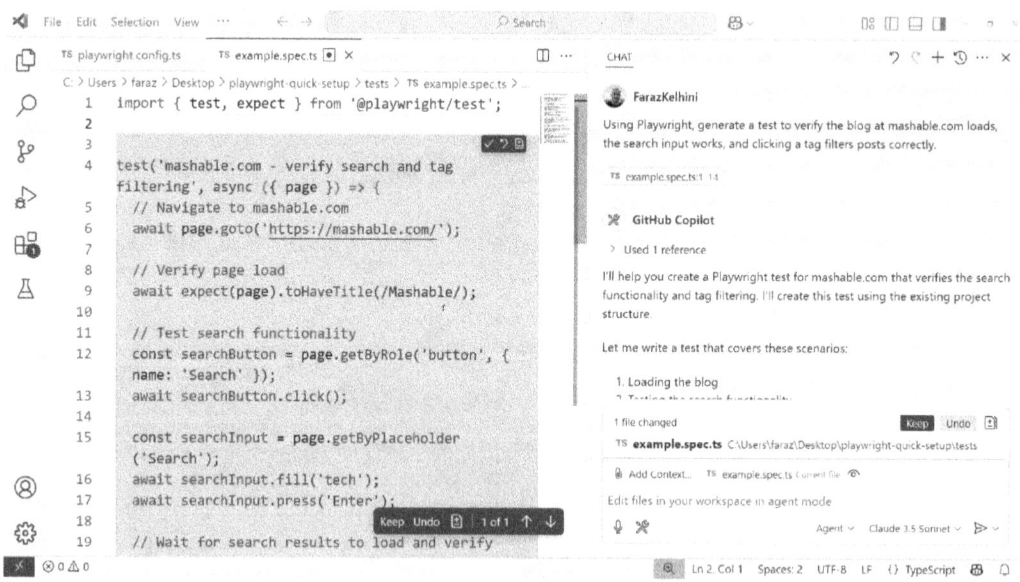

Figure 4.5: Interacting with a web page using Copilot

Copilot responds with a full Playwright test script and will ask you whether you want to run it:

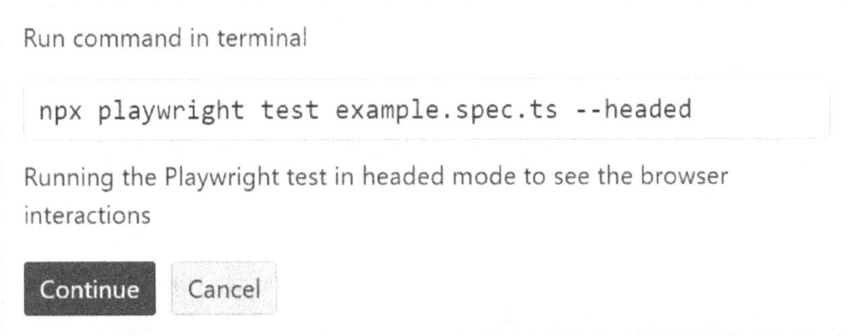

Figure 4.6: You can run your script with Copilot

You can also run the script right away using the Playwright CLI:

```
npx playwright test
```

Don't forget to review the output. Copilot does a great job, but it might miss some edge cases. As we'll see shortly, you can refine it by adding assertions for specific content or handling scenarios such as empty search results. If the test fails, you can even ask Copilot to analyze the failure and suggest a fix.

So, when you bring together Copilot, MCP, and Playwright, you get a supercharged way to create tests quickly with the help of AI. You can automate tasks without needing access to the source code, and instead of writing scripts by hand, you can just use natural language prompts.

> You can also add a `.github/copilot-instructions.md` file to your repository to give GitHub Copilot extra context about your project. This file can include details such as how your app is built, tested, and deployed, or specific coding conventions that your team follows. Copilot will automatically reference these instructions when suggesting code within that repository, which helps it generate responses that better fit your project's setup.
>
> For even more precision, consider looking at the `github/awesome-copilot` (`https://github.com/github/awesome-copilot`) repository, which is a fantastic resource for large code bases or multi-language projects where code style varies between components. These pre-written instruction files give you a running start on framework-specific guidance.
>
> For your Playwright tests, you can take advantage of the following instructions:
>
> `https://github.com/github/awesome-copilot/blob/main/instructions/playwright-typescript.instructions.md`

Always remember that reviewing the generated code is key. The AI gets you 80–90% of the way there, but your insights ensure full coverage. And that brings us to the next section.

Refining AI-generated scripts for reliability

AI-generated scripts can be a great starting point, but they often need a bit of polishing to meet best practices and suit your project's specific needs. They usually include the basics such as navigation, clicking buttons, or simple assertions, but may fall short on things such as context-aware logic, error handling, or element selection.

Take a few moments to check for the following:

- **Fragile selectors** such as `div:nth-child(3)`. These can easily break if the page structure changes.
- **Missing waits**, which can cause flaky tests when dealing with dynamic content.

For example, a basic AI-generated script might test a button like this:

```
await page.click('button');
```

This works, but the selector isn't very specific. Instead, aim for role- or text-based selectors (such as `getByRole` or `getByText`) and custom data attributes, such as (`data-testid`), if available:

```
await page.getByRole('button', { name: 'Submit' }).click();
```

Critical actions can be wrapped in `try-catch` blocks to gracefully handle failures. And don't forget to assert expected outcomes using `expect`.

Here is an example:

```
// AI-generated:
import { test, expect } from '@playwright/test';

test('netlify.app - click on button', async ({ page }) => {
  await page.goto('https://sweetshop.netlify.app/');
  await page.click('.btn');
});
```

We can improve this AI-generated script like this:

```
// Improved:
import { test, expect } from '@playwright/test';
```

```
test('netlify.app - click on button', async ({ page }) => {
  try {
    await page.goto('https://sweetshop.netlify.app', {timeout:30000});
    await expect(page.getByText('Welcome')).toBeVisible();
    await page.getByRole('link', { name: 'Browse Sweets' }).click();
  } catch (error) {
    console.error('Something went wrong:', error);
    throw error;
  }
});
```

Here, we use a `try-catch` block to catch any errors: if something goes wrong, we log the issue and throw an error. As you will learn in *Chapter 7, Integrating Workflows with CI/CD Pipelines*, the `catch` block also comes in handy for capturing screenshots for failed tests.

Remember, validate outcomes, not just actions. It's not enough to click buttons: you also want to check that the expected result actually happened.

For example, the following code simulates a user clicking the **Submit** button and validates the outcome by checking that a **Success** message appears after the click:

```
await page.getByRole('button', { name: 'Submit' }).click();
await expect(page.getByText('Success')).toBeVisible();
```

If you stop after the click, your test might pass, even if nothing actually happened. But the page might display an error or stay stuck on the same screen. Without checking the result, you wouldn't know.

Some AI agents might write the tests as standalone scripts, and you will want to convert them into structured tests.

For example, here is an AI-generated test written as a standalone script:

```
// AI-generated (standalone):
const { chromium } = require('playwright');
(async () => {
  const browser = await chromium.launch();
  const page = await browser.newPage();
  await page.goto('url');
```

```
  await page.click('button');
  await browser.close();
})();
```

Ask the AI to convert the code into a test runner script, or rewrite it manually yourself:

```
// Improved (test runner):
import { test, expect } from '@playwright/test';

test.describe('Login Tests', () => {
  test('should log in successfully', async ({ page }) => {
    await page.goto('url');
    await page.getByRole('button', { name: 'Log In' }).click();
    await expect(page.getByText('Welcome')).toBeVisible();
  });
});
```

With a few thoughtful tweaks, you can turn an AI-generated script into a much more reliable test.

Next, let's explore the **Copy prompt** feature.

Using the Copy prompt feature

When a Playwright test fails, a **Copy prompt** button appears in the error details within the following tools:

- **HTML report**
- **Trace Viewer**
- **UI Mode**

We'll explore **Trace Viewer** in *Chapter 6, Test Parallelization and Performance Optimization*, and **UI Mode** in *Chapter 8, Headless Testing and Debugging*. What you need to know now is that clicking the **Copy prompt** button copies a pre-filled, structured prompt to your clipboard.

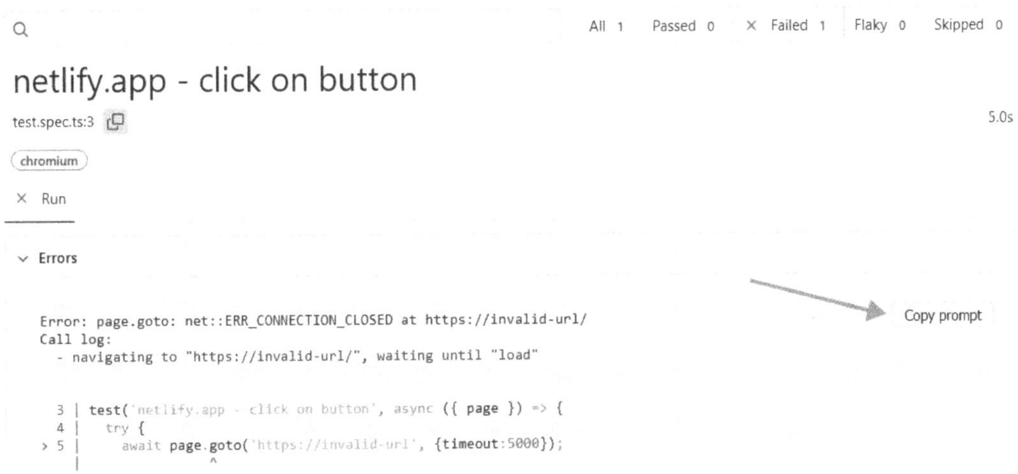

Figure 4.7: The Copy prompt button in the HTML report

You then paste this into your preferred LLM (such as ChatGPT, Grok, or GitHub Copilot) to get explanations, root cause analysis, and suggested fixes. This reduces the manual effort of describing issues to an AI, which makes debugging faster and more accurate.

In the following section, we'll walk through how to implement fallback locators so that your test automation adapts dynamically to changes and maintains reliability over time.

Implementing a resilient locator strategy

Modern web apps change fast: elements shift around, IDs get updated, and new classes appear all the time. If your automated tests rely on static locators, these changes can break them easily. That's where fallback locators come in handy.

Fallback locators allow you to recover from common issues such as missing elements, stale references, or small UI changes. Instead of failing right away, they try alternative ways to find elements or retry actions. This helps cut down the need for constant manual updates.

Using fallback locators

Without fallback logic, you're stuck constantly fixing tests because of minor changes. Here's a simple example of how to make your test resilient by trying multiple locators:

```
import { test, expect } from '@playwright/test';

test('Google search button', async ({ page }) => {
```

```
  await page.goto('https://google.com');

  const locators = [
    page.getByTestId('submit-button'),
    page.getByRole("button", { name: "Google Search" }),

    page.getByText('Google Search'),
  ];

  for (const locator of locators) {
    try {
      await locator.click({ timeout: 5000 });
      console.log('Success!');
      return;
    } catch {
      console.warn(`Locator failed: ${locator}, trying next...`);
    }
  }
  throw new Error("All locators failed for Submit button");

});
```

This code checks for the button in a few different ways: by its role and name, a `data-testid` attribute, and by looking for the word `Submit` inside a button. This makes the function flexible in case the button is coded differently in various versions of the page.

It goes through each option one by one and tries to click it. If one doesn't work within 5 seconds, it moves on to the next and logs a warning to let you know what happened. If none of them work, it throws an error to let you know the button couldn't be found or clicked. It's a simple way to make sure your script keeps running even if the page changes a bit.

Adding fallback locators makes your tests more reliable, especially in CI/CD environments where stability is key.

Handling temporary failures with retry logic

Playwright's built-in retry features are extremely useful. Actions such as click, fill, and others will automatically retry until the element is ready, meaning it's visible, enabled, and so on. You can also adjust timeouts in your `playwright.config.ts` file (check out *Chapter 1, Quick Setup Refresher*, for details).

But if you need more control, you can take advantage of Playwright's `expect().toPass()` assertion:

```
// Waits until the loader disappears (retries until it passes)
await expect(async () => {
  // Assert that the loader is no longer visible
  await expect(page.locator('.loader')).not.toBeVisible();
}).toPass({
  timeout: 3000,     // Try for 3 seconds
  interval: 1000,    // Check every half second
});
```

`expect().toPass()` will repeatedly run the function until it passes (or times out).

If you want even more control, you can implement your own custom retry logic like this:

```
async function retryAction(action, maxAttempts = 3) {
  for (let attempt = 1; attempt <= maxAttempts; attempt++) {
    try {
      await action();
      return;
    } catch (error) {
      console.warn(`Attempt ${attempt} failed: ${error}`);
      if (attempt === maxAttempts) throw error;
      await new Promise(res => setTimeout(res, 1000));
    }
  }
}

// Usage
await retryAction(() => page.getByText("Login").click());
```

This code sets up a function designed to repeatedly attempt an action up to a specified number of times. The function takes two arguments: `action`, which is a function returning a promise, and `maxAttempts`, an optional number specifying how many times the action should be retried upon failure.

If the action works on the first try, great! If not, it catches the error, logs a warning, waits a second, and tries again. If it keeps failing after all the allowed attempts, it throws the error so you can handle it however you like.

In this case, we have used the function to try clicking a **Login** button on the page. So, if the button takes a second to load or isn't ready right away, this function will patiently try again instead of crashing the test. It's a simple way to make your automated tests less sensitive to little hiccups on the page.

> It's important to cap retries. Limiting attempts helps prevent infinite loops that waste resources and time.

Dealing with dynamic content

When working with web pages that load parts of their content *after* the initial page load (such as a **Load More** button or a list that populates a bit later), it's important to wait for elements to be ready before interacting with them. If you try to click or check something too early, your test might fail just because the content wasn't there yet, not because something was actually wrong.

To handle this, Playwright offers tools such as **explicit waits**, as in this example:

```
await page.waitForSelector('img', {
  state: 'visible',
  timeout: 10000,
});
```

Here, you're telling Playwright, *Wait up to 10 seconds for this specific element to become visible before doing anything else.*

But what if there's no clear selector change to wait for? In that case, you can use `waitForFunction`:

```
await page.waitForFunction(() => document.querySelector('.loaded') !==
null, {
  timeout: 15000,
});
```

This code keeps checking your custom condition (in this case, whether an element with the `.loaded` class exists) until it becomes `true`, or until the timeout is hit. It's perfect when you need more control or when the usual selector-based waits aren't enough.

Trying an alternative path

Sometimes, you might try clicking on a button or link, but for some reason (maybe it's hidden, slow to load, or covered by another element) the click doesn't actually work.

Instead of letting your test fail, you can add a **fallback plan**:

```
import { test, expect } from '@playwright/test';

test('should navigate to sweets page', async ({ page }) => {
  await page.goto('https://sweetshop.netlify.app/',
                 { waitUntil: 'domcontentloaded' });

  try {
    // Attempt to click Dashboard link
    await page.getByRole('link', { name: 'Browse Sweets' })
             .click({ timeout: 5000 });
    // Verify successful navigation
    await expect(page).toHaveURL(/sweets$/, { timeout: 5000 });
  } catch (error) {
    console.warn('Link click failed, navigating directly...');
    await page.goto('https://sweetshop.netlify.app/sweets',
                   { waitUntil: 'domcontentloaded' });
    // Verify fallback navigation
    await expect(page).toHaveURL(/sweets$/, { timeout: 10000 });
  }
});
```

This script attempts to find and click a link labeled `Browse Sweets`. If, for some reason, the link doesn't show up in time or can't be clicked, the script catches the error and logs a warning. As a fallback, it directly navigates to the `/sweets` page URL. In both cases, whether the link is clicked successfully or fallback navigation is used, it checks that the final URL ends with `/sweets` to confirm successful navigation.

The `waitUntil` option in the `page.goto()` method tells Playwright when it should consider the page "ready" before moving on. In this case, we're using `waitUntil: 'domcontentloaded'`, which happens when the browser finishes loading the main HTML, but before things such as images, stylesheets, or iframes are fully loaded. That's usually enough for most testing needs, especially if you're just checking or interacting with text, buttons, or other elements that are part of the main page structure. It also makes your test run faster because it doesn't wait for everything else to load.

But if you do need to wait for everything to be fully loaded (say, for checking whether an image is visible), you might want to use a different option, such as `'load'`.

Using AI-powered self-healing

Sometimes, a simple change to a website, such as moving a button or changing its color, completely breaks your automated tests. It's a common and frustrating problem that costs a lot of time.

AI-powered self-healing allows your automated tests to intelligently adapt to changes in your application's **user interface** (**UI**) and automatically fix themselves when something breaks. Instead of failing right away, the tests can "heal" on the fly and continue running.

Although Playwright doesn't have built-in AI for self-healing, you can integrate commercial tools such as Testim or Mabl. Imagine you write a test to click a **Submit** button. A traditional test would look for that button using a very specific address, such as its unique ID. If a developer later changes that ID, the test gets lost and fails.

An AI-powered self-healing framework does things differently. When you first create the test, the AI engine collects information about that **Submit** button:

- What text it has (**Submit**)
- What it looks like (its size and color)
- Where it's located on the page (next to the **Cancel** button, inside a specific form)
- Its unique ID

If the test runs later and can't find the button using its original ID, the AI doesn't give up. It quickly scans the web page, using all those other clues to find the button. It might find a button with the exact same text (**Submit**) in the same general area, and realize, "Aha! This must be the one."

The test then updates its script with the new address and keeps going. The best part is that the system logs this change, so you can see exactly what was fixed, and the AI learns from it to be even smarter next time.

Test maintenance is one of those tasks that can quietly eat up hours of your day. With self-healing, you drastically cut down on the time you'd normally spend fixing broken tests, freeing you up to focus on more important things. It also makes your tests a lot more reliable. Instead of failing because someone changed a button's color or moved a label, your tests only fail when there's a real bug. That means you can actually trust the results and spend less time second-guessing your test failures.

In short, AI-powered self-healing takes away the most tedious part of test automation, letting you focus on what really matters: building and shipping amazing software.

Despite their benefits, self-healing tests come with trade-offs. One drawback is slower test execution. Also, while self-healing can handle minor UI adjustments, it won't protect you from major redesigns or structural changes. Such overhauls will still cause tests to fail.

There's also a risk of false positives. If your recovery logic becomes too aggressive, it may mask genuine issues that should cause test failures. Finally, implementing AI-powered or advanced self-healing tools adds complexity to your testing stack, which requires extra setup. For most smaller projects, the effort and overhead might not be worth the benefits.

Summary

AI is changing the game when it comes to test automation, and tools such as Playwright Codegen, Playwright MCP, and GitHub Copilot make it easier to get started. Instead of writing every test by hand, you can now generate solid test scripts just by interacting with a website or using natural language prompts. It's fast and can boost your productivity.

Of course, AI doesn't get everything perfect. The scripts it creates are a great starting point, but they usually need a bit of polishing. Things such as fragile selectors, missing waits, or skipped edge cases can still trip you up. That's where your skills come in: refining what the AI gives you, adding better locators, wrapping actions in error handling, and making sure tests actually check for expected results.

Adding a resilient locator strategy takes things a step further. With a few smart techniques, your tests can handle changes in the UI without falling apart, which is perfect for keeping things stable in fast-moving projects.

In the end, the real magic happens when you combine the speed of AI with your own experience. You let the AI do the heavy lifting, and you fine-tune the results to make them ready for the real world. It's an exciting time to be working in test automation.

In the next chapter, we focus on scaling tests efficiently by running them in parallel and optimizing performance.

5

Crafting Scalable Tests with the Fixture System

Testing modern web applications can get complex if every test has to manage its own setup and cleanup. Imagine repeatedly launching a browser, logging in, and setting up the environment for each test. It's not only time-consuming but can also lead to inconsistent and unreliable results.

This is where Playwright's **fixtures** come in. Inspired by Python's `pytest` framework, fixtures act as reusable building blocks that handle essential resources. They manage all the behind-the-scenes work, which allows you to focus on what you're actually testing. You can even create custom fixtures to perfectly fit your project's needs.

In this chapter, you'll discover how to use Playwright's fixture system to its full potential. We'll start with the built-in fixtures, then move on to creating your own and understanding how fixture scope and life cycle affect your tests. We'll also cover more advanced topics such as nesting fixtures, integrating them with the page object model, and designing a scalable architecture that keeps your test suite easy to manage.

As such, we will cover the following topics in the chapter:

- Examining built-in fixtures
- Creating custom fixtures
- Understanding fixture scope and life cycle
- Practical fixture examples

Technical requirements

The source code for this chapter is available at `https://github.com/PacktPublishing/Hands-On-Automated-Testing-with-Playwright/tree/main/Chapter05`.

Examining built-in fixtures

Built-in fixtures are handy tools that come ready-to-use with the Playwright Test framework. They are prepackaged helpers that take care of common tasks such as setting up and tearing down browsers, pages, and contexts. They make your tests easier to write.

You don't have to do anything special to use fixtures. They're available by default. Just declare them as parameters in your test functions, and Playwright will handle the rest.

The core mechanism is **dependency injection**. When you define a test, you list the fixtures you need as parameters in the `test` function. The Playwright test runner sees these parameters, initializes the corresponding objects behind the scenes before your test runs, and then passes them to your test. After the test finishes, it automatically cleans them up.

For example, let's say you write a test like this:

```
import { test, expect } from '@playwright/test';

test('my first test', async ({ page }) => {
  await page.goto('https://playwright.dev/');
  await expect(page).toHaveTitle(/Playwright/);
});
```

Here, you never wrote any code to launch a browser or create a new page. The `{ page }` argument tells the test runner, "Hey, I need a fresh browser page for this test." The runner then performs these steps for you:

1. **Sets up**: Launches a browser, creates a new browser context, and creates a new page
2. **Injects**: Passes the page object into your test function
3. **Executes**: Runs your test code
4. **Tears down**: Closes the page, the context, and the browser automatically

The following is an overview of the main built-in fixtures, what they do, and how you can use them in your tests. Once you're familiar with these Playwright fixtures, we'll look at how you can create your own to handle reusable setup and teardown logic that's tailored to your testing needs.

The browser fixture

The browser fixture provides a new browser instance (Chromium, Firefox, or WebKit) for the test. The browser instance is launched when the test starts and closed when the test ends. You can use it when you need to control the browser directly, such as launching a new context or managing browser-level settings.

Here is an example:

```
import { test, expect } from '@playwright/test';

test('manage browser-level settings', async ({ browser }) => {
  // Create a new context with custom settings
  const context = await browser.newContext({
    userAgent: 'My Custom User Agent',
    locale: 'fr-FR',
    // other options like timezoneId, colorScheme, etc.
  });

  // Create a page inside this context
  const page = await context.newPage();
  await page.goto('url');

  // Your test actions and assertions here

  await context.close();
});
```

Another browser fixture is browserName, which is just a string indicating the name of the browser being used ("chromium", "firefox", or "webkit"). This is useful for conditional logic based on the browser type.

Here is an example:

```
import { test } from '@playwright/test';

test('check browser', async ({ browserName }) => {
  if (browserName === "chromium") {
    console.log(`Running on ${browserName}`);
  }
});
```

The page fixture

The page fixture provides a single, isolated browser page (tab) for a test, which is automatically created within a new browser context. It's ideal for testing individual web pages or user flows, as it comes preconfigured with a context and is closed after the test. This is the most commonly used fixture because most tests interact with a single page.

Here is an example:

```
import { test, expect } from '@playwright/test';

test('visit page', async ({ page }) => {
  await page.goto('https://www.google.com/');
  await expect(page).toHaveTitle(/Google/);
});
```

In contrast, the `browser` fixture we discussed previously provides a full `browser` instance (Chromium, Firefox, or WebKit), which gives you control over the entire browser, including the ability to create multiple contexts, manage browser-level settings, or launch multiple pages. But it requires manual context and page creation. Essentially, the page fixture is a higher-level abstraction for simpler, single-page tests, while the `browser` fixture offers lower-level control for more complex scenarios. The page fixture is also automatically configured using the settings defined in your `playwright.config.ts` file, such as default browser type and viewport size (as we discussed in *Chapter 1, Quick Setup Refresher*), which makes it convenient for most tests.

The context fixture

The `context` fixture provides a `BrowserContext` object. A context is like an incognito browser profile, with its own cookies and local storage. All pages created within the same context will share these. This is useful for tests where you need to manage login states across multiple tabs.

Here is an example:

```
import { test, expect } from '@playwright/test';

test('should share cookies between pages in the same context', async ({
context }) => {
  // Create two pages within the same context
  const page1 = await context.newPage();
  const page2 = await context.newPage();
```

```
    // Set a cookie on page1
    await page1.goto('https://playwright.dev/');
    await page1.context().addCookies([{
      name: 'test_cookie',
      value: 'test_value',
      domain: '.example.com',
      path: '/',
    }]);

    // Navigate to the same domain on page2
    await page2.goto('https://playwright.dev/');

    // Verify that page2 has access to the same cookie
    const cookies = await page2.context().cookies();
    const testCookie = cookies.find(cookie => cookie.name === 'test_
  cookie');
    expect(testCookie).toBeDefined();
    expect(testCookie.value).toBe('test_value');

    // Clean up
    await page1.close();
    await page2.close();
  });
```

Here, the script uses the `context` fixture to create two pages (`page1` and `page2`) within the same `context` fixture. It navigates `page1` to `'https://playwright.dev/'`, sets a cookie, and then navigates `page2` to the same domain. The test verifies that `page2` can access the same cookie by retrieving the context's cookies and checking that `'test_cookie'` exists with the expected value. This shows how pages in the same context share cookies. Once that's verified, both pages are closed to clean up resources.

The request fixture

The `request` fixture gives you an `APIRequestContext` instance for making HTTP requests (such as `GET` or `POST`) to APIs or other endpoints. This fixture is useful for testing APIs or setting up test data via HTTP requests.

Here is an example:

```
import { test, expect } from '@playwright/test';

test('API request', async ({ request }) => {
  const response = await request.get('https://jsonplaceholder.typicode.
com/todos/1');
  expect(response.ok()).toBeTruthy();
});
```

Built-in fixtures come out of the box, but you can also create custom ones to tailor things perfectly for your application.

Creating custom fixtures

Without a centralized approach, you might end up writing the same setup steps (such as launching a browser, going to a URL, or logging in) and teardown steps (such as closing the browser) in multiple places, sometimes in every test file or even every single test.

This leads to duplicated code that's harder to maintain and can create inconsistencies, which, in turn, can cause flaky tests. On top of that, making changes to the setup or teardown later means you'll need to update it in many different spots. That's where project-level fixtures really shine. They let you share things such as a browser instance across all tests in a given project.

To set up your own custom fixtures in Playwright, you'll start by extending the base test object. First, import the base test from `@playwright/test`. Then, use the `test.extend()` method to add your fixtures. Each fixture is just an `async` function that takes in any dependencies along with a `use` callback. This gives you a nice flow: do any setup work first, hand control back to the test with `use`, and then wrap things up with teardown once the test is finished.

For example, say you have many tests that require a logged-in user. You can define a custom fixture like this:

```
// fixtures/auth.ts
import { test as base } from '@playwright/test';

export const test = base.extend<{ loggedInPage: Page }>({
  loggedInPage: async ({ page }, use) => {
    // --- Setup: Log the user in ---
    await page.goto('https://www.saucedemo.com/');
    await page.getByPlaceholder('Username').fill('standard_user');
```

```
    await page.getByPlaceholder('Password').fill('secret_sauce');
    await page.getByRole('button', { name: 'Login' }).click();
    await page.waitForURL('https://www.saucedemo.com/inventory.html');

    console.log('User logged in!');

    // Provide the logged-in page to the test
    await use(page);

    // --- Teardown ---
    // Example: Log out if needed
    // await page.click('#logout-button');
    console.log('Test finished, loggedInPage fixture torn down.');
  },
});
```

Notice how we pass the fixture's value to the use callback using `await use(value)`, which hands over the resource to the test for execution. At the end of the script, you can implement the teardown logic after the use call to clean up resources. This ensures test isolation and prevents side effects such as lingering data or open connections.

Now, you can use the fixture in your code:

```
import { test } from '../fixtures/auth';
import { expect } from '@playwright/test';

test('should display shopping cart after login', async ({ loggedInPage })
=> {
  const cartLink = loggedInPage.locator('.shopping_cart_link');
  await expect(cartLink).toBeVisible();
});
```

Using fixtures this way comes with lots of benefits:

- The login logic is defined once, so each test can focus on what it's actually testing
- You can use the same fixture across many tests without repeating code
- Each test gets its own fresh `loggedInPage` fixture (default is test scope), which helps prevent one test from accidentally affecting another
- Setup and teardown behave the same way everywhere, which helps keep your tests reliable (we'll go over this in the *Fixture life cycle* section)

You can also group tests by project type (such as *Desktop Chrome* vs. *Mobile Safari*) and run each group in its own isolated environment with the right emulation settings. Inside your tests, you simply use the built-in page fixture and let Playwright handle the page life cycle for you.

> If you need to reuse the same logged-in page across tests within a worker, consider defining your fixture with the `scope: 'worker'` option. This ensures the page is created once per worker and shared across its tests. For more details, see the Playwright docs on worker-scoped fixtures (`https://playwright.dev/docs/test-fixtures#worker-scoped-fixtures`).

So far, we've looked at what fixtures are, how to use the built-in ones, and how to create your own for custom setups. But knowing what a fixture does is only half the story. To really use them effectively, you also need to understand how long they live, when they're created, and when they're torn down.

Understanding fixture scope and life cycle

Fixture scope and life cycle concepts define the boundaries of a fixture's existence: whether it's spun up fresh for every test, or reused across multiple tests in the same worker. Getting this right can mean the difference between a slow, flaky suite and one that runs smoothly at scale.

Fixture scope

A fixture's scope defines how long its resource stays active and how it's shared across tests during a run. Playwright offers two fixture scopes, **test** and **worker**, each designed for different scenarios:

- **Test**: The **test scope** is the default and provides the strongest isolation. A fixture with test scope is created and cleaned up for each individual test, so every test gets a brand-new instance of the resource. For example, the built-in page fixture is test-scoped, which means every test runs with a fresh browser page. This prevents any state from leaking between tests and ensures full independence. The trade-off is performance: creating and tearing down resources for every test can slow things down, especially in larger test suites.

- **Worker**: The **worker scope** offers a middle ground between isolation and performance. A fixture with worker scope is created once per worker process and then shared across all tests running in that worker. A worker in Playwright is a single Node.js process that runs multiple tests in sequence, and you can run multiple workers in parallel (using the `--workers` option) to speed things up. The built-in `browser` fixture is worker-scoped, since launching a new browser for every test would be very resource-heavy. Worker scope is a great fit for expensive resources that can be reused safely within a worker, but you need to be mindful of the state to avoid tests interfering with one another.

Fixture life cycle

The fixture life cycle describes the journey a fixture goes through during test execution: its setup, use, and cleanup. Playwright takes care of these steps automatically, so resources such as browsers, pages, or custom objects are managed efficiently:

- **Setup**: This is the starting point of a fixture's life cycle, where Playwright creates the resource that the fixture needs. Setup happens lazily only when a test or another fixture actually requires it. For instance, if a test uses the built-in `page` fixture, Playwright will launch a browser (if it's not already running), spin up a new context, and then create a page inside that context. For custom fixtures, setup might mean steps such as navigating to a login page or connecting to a database. The goal is to have everything ready before the test begins.
- **Usage**: Once the setup is done, the fixture's resource is handed off to the test or another fixture. This is where the actual test logic runs, whether it's navigating to URLs, clicking buttons, or making API calls. The scope of the fixture determines how it behaves: a test-scoped fixture, such as `page`, provides a clean instance for each test. A worker-scoped fixture, such as `browser`, is shared across tests running in the same worker process.
- **Teardown**: After the test (or group of tests, depending on the scope) finishes, Playwright automatically cleans up the fixture in the teardown stage. For test-scoped fixtures, such as `page`, resources are closed right after each test. Worker-scoped fixtures, such as `browser`, are cleaned up when the worker process ends.

To make things easier, let's look at a diagram that maps out the fixture scopes and their life cycles:

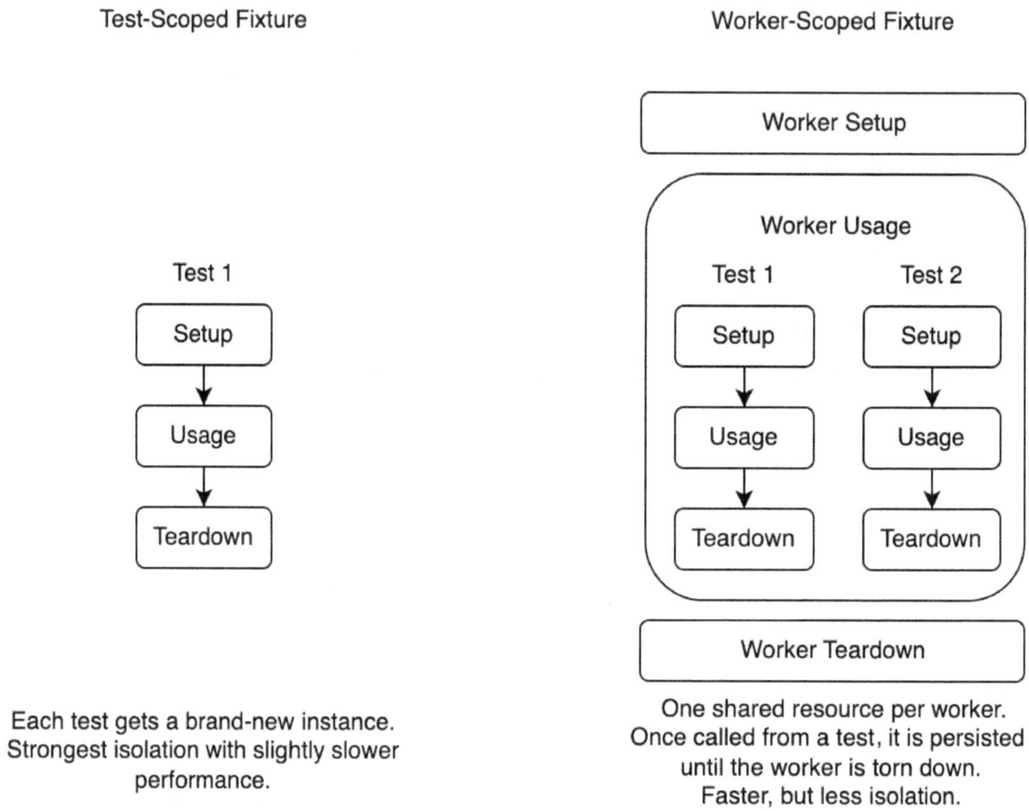

Figure 5.1: Overview of fixture scope and life cycle

Now that you have a solid grasp of how fixtures work in Playwright, it's time to look at some practical examples.

Practical fixture examples

The real value of fixtures comes alive when you put them into practice. In this section, we'll walk through practical examples that demonstrate how to apply fixtures in real-world testing scenarios. We'll explore how to chain fixtures together for a logged-in workflow, detect broken images automatically, and capture console logs right at page load.

Creating a page object fixture that depends on a logged-in user fixture

The **page object model** (**POM**) is a popular design pattern that helps organize test code by separating *what* a test does from *how* it interacts with the application. Instead of scattering locators and interaction logic directly inside your test files, POM bundles them neatly into page classes.

It knows where the important elements are (locators such as buttons, forms, or links) and it knows how to interact with them. This way, your tests don't need to know the nitty-gritty details of selectors or DOM structure: they simply call methods such as `login()` or `search()`, which makes tests much more readable.

> Learning a framework or programming language is rarely a straight path. We'll return to POMs in *Chapter 15, Best Practices for Test Maintainability*, but for now, our focus is on how to use them together with fixtures. If you find this topic a bit challenging, it may help to review *Chapter 15* first.

As we have learned, fixtures act like helpers that automatically provide reusable objects (including page objects) to your tests. Without fixtures, you'd have to manually create and initialize your page objects inside every single test. That works for small projects, but quickly becomes repetitive and hard to maintain. Fixtures solve this problem by letting you define page objects once and then *injecting* them into any test that needs them. This combination (POM for structure and fixtures for automation) gives you easy-to-maintain test suites.

For example, you can define a `LoginPage` class like this:

```
// pages/LoginPage.ts
import { Page, Locator } from '@playwright/test';

export class LoginPage {
  private readonly page: Page;
  private readonly usernameInput: Locator;
  private readonly passwordInput: Locator;
  private readonly submitButton: Locator;

  constructor(page: Page) {
    this.page = page;
    this.usernameInput = page.getByPlaceholder('Username');
```

```
    this.passwordInput = page.getByPlaceholder('Password');
    this.submitButton = page.getByRole('button', { name: 'Login' });
  }

  async navigate() {
    await this.page.goto('https://www.saucedemo.com/');
  }

  async login(username: string, password: string) {
    await this.usernameInput.fill(username);
    await this.passwordInput.fill(password);
    await this.submitButton.click();
  }
}
```

Here, the class encapsulates all the details of how the login page works. Tests don't care about locators or which button submits the form: they just call `loginPage.login('user', 'pass')`.

Then, they create a fixture for it:

```
// fixtures/login.fixture.ts
import { test as base } from '@playwright/test';
import { LoginPage } from '../pages/LoginPage';

export const test = base.extend({
  loginPage: async ({ page }, use) => {
    const loginPage = new LoginPage(page);
    await loginPage.navigate();
    await use(loginPage);
  },
});

export { expect } from '@playwright/test';
```

This fixture ensures that any test that declares `loginPage` as a dependency will automatically get an initialized `LoginPage` instance. You don't need to repeat setup logic across multiple tests:

```
// tests/dashboard.spec.ts
import { test, expect } from '../fixtures/login.fixture';
```

```
test('login test', async ({ loginPage }) => {
  await loginPage.login('standard_user', 'secret_sauce');
  await expect(loginPage.page).toHaveURL('https://www.saucedemo.com/
inventory.html');
});
```

Notice how the test now reads almost like a sentence:

1. Log in with these credentials.
2. Check that we landed on the inventory page.

There's no mention of selectors or button clicks: the details are safely hidden inside the page object.

The combination of the POM and fixtures brings several important advantages to test design. Tests become more maintainable, since any change to a page's structure only requires updating the locator in one place, the page object, instead of across dozens of tests.

The fixture adds another layer of efficiency by making page objects easily reusable throughout the suite. It automatically handles setup and teardown, so you don't repeat boilerplate code. This approach is highly scalable, as fixture dependencies can model complex flows without cluttering test logic.

Building a fixture to test for broken images

To help lock in your understanding of fixtures, let's build one that checks a page for any images that might be causing issues. This test is designed to fail because the target website (`https://with-bugs.practicesoftwaretesting.com/#/`) intentionally contains broken images. The test output will clearly report the URL of the broken image and its HTTP status, which confirms that our new fixture is working perfectly.

This fixture-based approach is very useful here because you can now add it to any test to quickly check for broken images without duplicating code:

```
// fixtures/image-validator.fixture.ts
import { test as base, expect } from '@playwright/test';

/**
* Provides a function to check for broken images by examining src
* attributes, HTTP status codes, and image content validity.
*/
export const test = base.extend({
```

```
  imageValidator: async ({ page }, use) => {
    const validateImages = async () => {
      const allImages = await page.locator('img').all();
      const brokenImages = [];

      for (const img of allImages) {
        const src = await img.getAttribute('src');

        if (!src) {
          brokenImages.push({
            src: 'Missing src attribute',
            status: 'N/A'
          });
          continue;
        }

        const absoluteSrc = new URL(src, page.url()).href;

        try {
          const response = await page.request.get(absoluteSrc);

          if (!response.ok()) {
            brokenImages.push({
              src: absoluteSrc,
              status: response.status()
            });
          } else {
            const isCorrupted = await img.evaluate(image => image.
naturalWidth === 0);
            if (isCorrupted) {
              brokenImages.push({
                src: absoluteSrc,
                status: 'OK but corrupted (naturalWidth is 0)'
              });
            }
          }
        } catch (error) {
```

```
          brokenImages.push({
            src: absoluteSrc,
            status: `Error: ${error.message}`
          });
        }
      }

      const errorMessage = `Found ${brokenImages.length} broken images:\
n${JSON.stringify(brokenImages, null, 2)}`;
      expect(brokenImages, errorMessage).toEqual([]);
    };

    await use(validateImages);
  },
});
```

This fixture contains a `validateImages()` function that handles the main logic for checking images on a page. It starts by locating all `<img>` elements with a locator, then goes through each one to verify its validity.

For every image, it first checks whether the `src` attribute is missing. If it is, the image is logged as broken. If a `src` attribute is present, the function builds an absolute URL and sends a network request to confirm the response status. Any unsuccessful responses (such as `404`) mark the image as broken.

> Keep in mind that this code checks each image sequentially (one after another). This means that if a page has many images (say, hundreds), the test will take longer to finish, since each image validation must complete before the next one starts. For pages with many images, you could improve performance by running image checks in parallel using the `Promise.all()` method. Feel free to check out this resource if you wish to delve deeper: `http://mdn.io/Promise/all`.

Even when the network request succeeds, the fixture performs an additional check in the browser: it inspects the image's `naturalWidth` property. A value of `0` means the image content is invalid and therefore treated as broken.

All detected issues are collected in an array. If the array isn't empty, the test fails and provides a clear error message listing each broken image.

Now, in our test file, we can use the following:

```
// tests/broken-images.spec.ts
import { expect } from '@playwright/test';
import { test } from "../fixtures/image-validator.fixture.ts;

test.describe('Broken Images Validation', () => {
  test('should not find any broken images on the page', async ({ page,
imageValidator }) => {
    await page.goto('https://with-bugs.practicesoftwaretesting.com/#/');

    await expect(page.locator('[data-test="product-1"]')).toBeVisible();

    await imageValidator();
  });
});
```

First, we import the fixture from `image-validator.fixture.ts`. In this example, we are not exporting `expect` from the fixture, so we have to get `expect` from Playwright itself.

The test navigates to the website, waits for the main content to become visible to ensure images have started loading, and then calls the `validateImages` function we imported from the `imageValidator` fixture.

The code should find two broken images on the website and log them to the console:

```
Error: Found 2 broken images:
[
  {
    "src": "https://with-bugs.practicesoftwaretesting.com/broken.png",
    "status": 404
  },
  {
    "src": "https://with-bugs.practicesoftwaretesting.com/broken.png",
    "status": 404
  }
]
```

This separation of concerns allows the fixture to be reused across multiple test cases or projects.

Creating a fixture to check for console logs on page load

Many apps silently log errors or warnings in the console without breaking the UI. You can define a fixture that fails the test if unexpected `console.error()` or `console.warn()` entries appear:

```
// fixtures/console.fixture.ts
import { test as base, expect } from '@playwright/test';

/**
* Checks for console logs on page load
*/
export const test = base.extend({
  noConsoleErrors: async ({ page }, use) => {
    const consoleErrors = [];

    // Set up a listener for the 'console' event.
    page.on('console', msg => {
      // Check if the message type is 'error'.
      if (msg.type() === 'error') {
        consoleErrors.push('\n' + msg.text());
      }
    });

    // Use the fixture in the test. The test code will run here.
    await use();

    // After the test, assert that no console errors were logged.
    // This part is the "teardown" of the fixture.
    expect(consoleErrors, `Unexpected console errors: ${consoleErrors.
join()}`).toHaveLength(0);
  },
});
```

By wrapping the base test with `base.extend()`, we are introducing a new fixture (`noConsoleErrors`) that integrates automatically into the test life cycle. This means that any test using `test` from this file will automatically benefit from console error monitoring without needing to write extra code in every test file.

Inside the fixture, Playwright attaches an event listener to the page object that listens for `console` events emitted by the browser. Each time a `console` message is logged, the fixture checks whether the message type is `error`. If it is, the message text is pushed into an array called `consoleErrors()`. This effectively collects all JavaScript errors that appear in the page's console while the test is running.

We can use this fixture like this:

```
import { test } from '../fixtures/console.fixture.ts';

test.describe('Page Load Console Logs', () => {
  test('should load the page without any console errors', async ({
noConsoleErrors, page }) => {
    // Navigate to the URL.
    // The `noConsoleErrors` fixture is active during this navigation.
    await page.goto('https://with-bugs.practicesoftwaretesting.com/#/');
  });
});
```

In this test, we aren't importing `expect` directly into the test like we typically have. Instead, it's being run as part of the fixture. While there's always a bit of risk when moving assertions out of the test file, in this case, it makes sense and keeps things cleaner.

When you test the website, you should get the following output:

```
Error: Unexpected console errors:
Failed to load resource: the server responded with a status of 404 (),
Failed to load resource: the server responded with a status of 401
(Unauthorized),
ERROR {message: Unauthorized}
```

This fixture can be used to stop developers from shipping code that spams the console with debug logs, warnings, or deprecations.

If you want the fixture to run automatically for every test without manually importing or calling it, you can mark it as an **automatic fixture** using `{ auto: true }`. This ensures that no console errors slip through anywhere in your test suite. Check out this documentation for more details on automatic fixtures: `https://playwright.dev/docs/test-fixtures#automatic-fixtures`.

Summary

In this chapter, we saw how Playwright's fixtures make testing more scalable. Instead of writing the same setup and cleanup code over and over, fixtures handle that work for you, so your tests can stay focused on what really matters.

We explored the built-in fixtures such as `browser`, `page`, `context`, and `request`, and then moved on to creating custom ones for tasks such as logging in or validating application states. Along the way, we learned about fixture scope and life cycle, which decide how long resources stick around and when they get cleaned up. Finally, we put it all into practice with examples. Combined with patterns such as the POM, fixtures let you focus on intent rather than plumbing, which keeps your test code clean.

The next chapter focuses on scaling tests efficiently by running them in parallel and optimizing performance.

6

Test Parallelization and Performance Optimization

As your test suite grows, waiting a long time for it to run can really slow you down, especially when you're trying to ship quickly and frequently. That's where test parallelization and performance optimization come in. The good news is that Playwright makes it surprisingly easy to boost performance without losing reliability.

In this chapter, we'll explore how Playwright's parallelism model works under the hood and how you can take full advantage of it. You'll learn how to run tests in parallel across multiple workers, split test suites across **continuous integration** (**CI**) machines, and even run individual tests in parallel when it makes sense. We'll also look at practical ways to optimize performance, such as controlling resource usage, blocking unnecessary network requests, and keeping your system from getting bogged down.

On top of that, we'll show you how to monitor things such as CPU and memory usage, and how to use Playwright's built-in tracing tools to catch performance issues early.

By the end of this chapter, you'll have a solid playbook for keeping your tests lean and reliable so you can spend less time watching progress bars and more time delivering great software.

The chapter is structured into these parts:

- Optimizing parallel testing in Playwright
- Managing resources to avoid bottlenecks
- Measuring and monitoring resource usage

Let's get started!

Technical requirements

The source code for this chapter is available at `https://github.com/PacktPublishing/Hands-On-Automated-Testing-with-Playwright/tree/main/Chapter06`.

Optimizing parallel testing in Playwright

Playwright is able to speed up your tests by running them in parallel. But to really get the most out of it, it helps to understand how it all works. Let's look at how Playwright handles parallelism.

Understanding Playwright's parallelism model

Playwright's test runner (Playwright Test)is built from the ground up to make running tests in parallel easy. When you run `npx playwright test`, the runner automatically starts up a pool of workers, each one running in its own Node.js process. Playwright figures out how many workers to use by looking at your machine's CPU count. By default, it uses one less than the total number of logical cores, but it always uses at least one.

Each worker picks up one complete test file at a time and runs it in isolation. It launches its own browser contexts to make sure nothing gets shared so that things such as cookies or local storage stay completely separate.

At runtime, Playwright distributes entire test files across all available workers. So, if you've got 20 test files and 4 workers, each worker will process about 5 files. Inside any given test file, the test cases run one after another (serially), unless you tell Playwright to run them in parallel (which we'll cover later).

Because each worker creates its own fresh browser context, you don't have to worry about tests accidentally sharing state. Every browser instance starts off clean, and your tests stay isolated.

Controlling the number of workers

You have two primary ways to customize how many workers Playwright uses. From the command line, you can use the `--workers` flag. For instance, to launch exactly four workers, you can write the following:

```
npx playwright test --workers=4
```

To disable parallelism entirely, you can write this:

```
npx playwright test --workers=1
```

You can also use a percentage string, such as `--workers=50%`, and Playwright will allocate that percentage of your machine's logical cores, rounding down to the nearest whole number. This approach is often convenient in scripts or on CI machines where you want to tie concurrency to available resources without hardcoding a number.

If you prefer to bake the setting into your repository, you can set the `workers` field in your `playwright.config.ts` file. For example, setting `workers: 6` in the configuration file means Playwright will never run with more than six workers, regardless of how many cores are detected. If you omit the `workers` field or set it to `undefined`, Playwright reverts to its auto-detection logic.

It's common to guard against running too many workers in CI by conditionally reducing concurrency based on environment variables. For instance, you might check whether `process.env.CI` is truthy and then set `workers` to a lower number, which lets Playwright auto-detect only when running locally:

```
import { PlaywrightTestConfig } from '@playwright/test';

const config: PlaywrightTestConfig = {
  workers: process.env.CI ? 2 : undefined,

  use: {
    // Other browser options
  },
};

export default config;
```

Parallelizing tests within a file

By default, once a worker picks up a test file, Playwright executes the tests inside that file one after another, in series. If you have multiple small test cases that could safely run at the same time, you can opt in to intra-file parallelism.

Playwright offers `test.describe.parallel()`, which lets you do group tests and have the runner treat each test in that group like its own worker task, all while still running within the same OS process:

```
import { test, expect } from '@playwright/test';

test.describe.parallel('Parallel test suite', () => {
```

```
  test('Test 1 - Google.com has correct title', async ({ page }) => {
    await page.goto('https://google.com');
    await expect(page).toHaveTitle('Google');
  });

  test('Test 2 - Playwright.dev has correct title', async ({ page }) => {
    await page.goto('https://playwright.dev');
    await expect(page).toHaveTitle(/Playwright/);
  });

  test('Test 3 - GitHub has correct title', async ({ page }) => {
    await page.goto('https://github.com');
    await expect(page).toHaveTitle(/GitHub/);
  });

});
```

In practice, when a worker hits a `test.describe.parallel` block, it spins up a separate browser context for each test and runs them at the same time (within the global worker limit).

So, this feature helps you speed up test suites with lots of small, independent tests by launching multiple browser contexts at once.

Another option to achieve the same result is to use the `test.describe.configure()` method, as in this example:

```
import { test, expect } from '@playwright/test';

test.describe.configure({mode: 'parallel'});

test('Test 1 - Google.com has correct title', async ({ page }) => {
  await page.goto('https://google.com');
  await expect(page).toHaveTitle('Google');
});

test('Test 2 - Playwright.dev has correct title', async ({ page }) => {
  await page.goto('https://playwright.dev');
  await expect(page).toHaveTitle(/Playwright/);
```

```
});

test('Test 3 - GitHub has correct title', async ({ page }) => {
  await page.goto('https://github.com');
  await expect(page).toHaveTitle(/GitHub/);
});
```

`test.describe.configure()` lets you configure how tests inside `test.describe()` blocks are run. Even though our tests aren't wrapped in a `test.describe()` block in this example, this configuration still affects the overall test file. It ensures that each test can run concurrently.

Just keep in mind that running too many parallel contexts can use up your system's RAM or file descriptors, so it's a good idea to balance your level of parallelism with the resources you have.

Running all your Playwright tests in full parallel mode

By default, Playwright runs test files in parallel, but the tests within each file run one after another in the same worker process. If you'd like to make all tests across all files run at the same time, you can turn on full parallel execution by setting `fullyParallel: true` in your Playwright config:

```
// playwright.config.ts
export default defineConfig({
  fullyParallel: true,
});
```

Once that's set, Playwright will try to run every test (no matter which file it's in) in parallel, as long as your system has enough resources.

If you have multiple projects defined in your config (for example, different browsers, environments, or configurations), you don't have to make all of them fully parallel. You can enable it just for certain ones:

```
projects: [
  {
    name: 'chromium',
    use: { browserName: 'chromium' },
    fullyParallel: true, // only this project runs all tests in parallel
  },
```

```
    {
      name: 'firefox',
      use: { browserName: 'firefox' },
    },
  ],
```

So basically, `fullyParallel: true` in the root affects all projects, while `fullyParallel: true` inside a project affects only that project.

Sharding (splitting up your tests)

If your team runs tests across multiple CI machines, you can speed things up by splitting your test suite into smaller chunks. This is called **sharding**. Playwright makes this easy with the `--shard=X/Y` flag.

Let's say you have two CI runners (Runner A and Runner B). You can divide the test suite like this:

- Runner A:

  ```
  npx playwright test --shard=1/2
  ```

- Runner B:

  ```
  npx playwright test --shard=2/2
  ```

Playwright will automatically split the total test files into two equal parts and assign each runner its portion. Inside each shard, it will still use the configured number of workers to run tests in parallel, as in this example:

- You have 40 test files
- Runner A (`--shard=1/2`) runs files 1–20
- Runner B (`--shard=2/2`) runs files 21–40
- Each runner can still use, say, four workers to process its assigned files even faster

You can also add a `shard` field under the `projects` array or directly in the config. The `shard` setting has two fields: `total` and `current`. The `total` field specifies how many shards you want to split the test suite into (in other words, how many parallel parts you will run):

```
// playwright.config.ts

import { defineConfig } from '@playwright/test';
```

```
export default defineConfig({
  shard: {
    total: 3,      // Total number of shards (splits)
    current: 1,    // This shard instance
  },
});
```

The current field specifies which shard this particular Playwright process should run. The value of current starts from 1, so a value of `current: 1` represents the first shard, `current: 2` the second shard, and so on. Each shard will receive a distinct subset of the test files, and together, all shards will cover the entire test suite.

Suppose you have 300 tests, and you want to run them split across 3 machines:

- Machine 1 config:

  ```
  shard: { total: 3, current: 1 }
  ```

- Machine 2 config:

  ```
  shard: { total: 3, current: 2 }
  ```

- Machine 3 config:

  ```
  shard: { total: 3, current: 3 }
  ```

So, each machine runs about 100 tests.

When you have a large number of test files, sharding helps you run the entire suite much faster. It's a great way to cut your test time in half (or even more) and keep your pipelines moving quickly.

Fine-tuning parallelism

When deciding how many workers to run or how many tests to execute in parallel, it's important to balance both CPU and memory usage. Spawning too many workers on a machine with limited RAM can cause thrashing or even **out of memory (OOM)** errors. A good starting point is to retrieve the number of CPU cores programmatically:

```
// playwright.config.js
const { defineConfig } = require('@playwright/test');
const os = require('os');
```

```
const cpuCount = os.cpus().length;

module.exports = defineConfig({
  workers: Math.max(1, cpuCount - 1),
  // other config options...
});
```

This code starts by importing Node.js's built-in `os` module, which gives you handy info about the operating system. It then uses `os.cpus()` to find out how many logical CPU cores your machine has. For example, if you have a quad-core CPU with hyperthreading, it might show eight cores because each physical core appears as two logical ones.

Next, it calculates the number of test workers with `Math.max(1, cpuCount - 1)`. In other words, Playwright will run tests in parallel using one fewer worker than the total number of CPU cores, always leaving at least one worker running. This is similar to just leaving the number of workers `undefined` and letting Playwright decide for you.

The reason for subtracting one is to avoid maxing out your machine's CPU completely. Running too many processes can slow things down or make your system unstable, especially during heavy testing. You get the benefit of faster tests thanks to parallel processing, but without overloading your computer.

From there, keep an eye on CPU and memory usage during your test runs. If you notice your CPU maxing out or your memory getting tight, it's a good idea to lower the number of workers to keep things running smoothly.

Running tests in parallel also brings up some new challenges with test isolation. Since multiple workers will be executing tests at the same time, you need to make sure they aren't writing to the same files, database rows, or any other shared resources. Otherwise, you risk race conditions and flaky test results.

As discussed, Playwright spreads test files across workers, but tests within a single file still run serially. If you choose to run tests in parallel inside a file (using `test.describe.parallel`), be aware of system limits: launching too many browser contexts at once can quickly use up file descriptors or memory.

If you have some especially slow **end-to-end** (E2E) tests, consider placing them in a separate folder or marking them with custom annotations (such as `@slow` or `@e2e`) so you can run them with fewer workers:

```
# Fast unit tests (50 files, short)
npx playwright test tests/unit --workers=8

# Slow E2E tests (5-10 files, longer)
npx playwright test tests/e2e --workers=2
```

If your tests are very CPU-heavy, adding more workers may not help much: you'll just end up fighting over CPU time. On the other hand, if your tests are mostly waiting on network or server responses (I/O-bound), you can often run more workers without overwhelming your CPU.

If you have a test that needs a bit more time to run (maybe it's dealing with network requests, database operations, or animations), you can use the `test.slow()` method to help it out.

Calling `test.slow()` tells the test runner to give that test extra time by tripling the usual timeout, so it won't fail just because it's taking longer than normal.

You can use `test.slow()` in two ways: either for a single test or for an entire test suite. For an individual test, just call `test.slow()` inside the test function, like this:

```
import { test, expect } from '@playwright/test';

// Fast test
test('quick test', async ({ page }) => {
  await page.goto('https://google.com');
  await expect(page).toHaveTitle('Google');
});

// Slow test
test('very slow test', async ({ page }) => {
  test.slow(); // Marking this test as slow

  // Simulate long-running test (1 minute)
  await page.waitForTimeout(60000);
});
```

Another option is to mark an entire test suite as slow by calling `test.slow()` inside a `describe` block. This way, all the tests in that suite will automatically be treated as slow.

You can also add a custom reason for marking a test as slow, such as `test.slow(true, 'Waiting for long API response')`. This can be helpful for debugging or keeping your logs informative.

> Remember, in large test suites, if some tests take a long time to run, they might "block" or delay other tests from starting, especially if the test runner runs tests in parallel but has a limit on concurrency (number of workers).

Before we dive into specific strategies for managing browsers, contexts, and network requests, it's useful to understand why these optimizations matter. In the next section, we'll explore practical tips to avoid resource contention and keep your Playwright tests running fast.

Managing resources to avoid bottlenecks

When using Playwright, it's easy to run into *invisible* resource bottlenecks if you're not careful, such as launching dozens of browser instances at once, leaking pages/contexts, or loading heavy assets when you don't need to. Let's look at the most common pain points and practical strategies for managing CPU, memory, and I/O.

Identifying common sources of bottlenecks

The first step to avoiding performance issues is knowing where they usually start. In Playwright, a common pitfall is launching too many browser instances. Every time you call `browser.launch()`, it spins up a brand-new process (Chromium, Firefox, or WebKit), which uses CPU power and memory.

The same goes for opening lots of contexts or pages. Each new context creates its own browser profile on disk and takes up memory to handle rendering and JavaScript execution. If your scripts or tests are constantly creating and closing browsers or contexts without limits, those small costs can quickly add up.

Another source of resource contention is unbounded parallelism. Ironically, this can slow down your whole test suite instead of speeding it up. If you're running dozens of tests at once (especially heavy E2E tests), your machine can get overwhelmed. Running too many tests in parallel can max out CPU cores, run out of file descriptors, or clog up the network adapter with too many simultaneous resource requests.

Another thing to watch out for is that Playwright will load everything on the page by default unless you tell it otherwise. That means every image, CSS file, font, JavaScript bundle, ad, and analytics beacon will get downloaded. But if you don't actually need the full page to render (say you're just checking for a heading or testing an API call), waiting on all those extra assets is a waste of CPU, memory, and network bandwidth.

Lastly, it's a good idea to close pages or contexts when you're done with them. Leaving them open can quietly use up system resources. If you forget to call `page.close()` or `context.close()`, or rely on Node.js's garbage collector to handle it, you might end up with orphaned headless rendering processes.

Even though the garbage collector will eventually clean things up, your machine could run low on memory or even start swapping (that's when it borrows disk space as *fake* RAM, which is much slower) before it gets the chance. This can lead to flaky tests, unexpected crashes, or trouble starting new browser instances, all things we'd like to avoid.

Reusing browser instances and contexts

One of the easiest ways to speed things up and save resources is to avoid launching a brand-new browser every time you visit a page. Instead, you can launch a single browser once and then create new contexts and pages within it as needed.

For example, rather than writing a loop that calls `chromium.launch()` for every URL, you can launch the browser once at the start of your script, then open new contexts for each page visit. This cuts out the delay and heavy memory usage that comes with starting a new browser process each time.

Here's what *not* to do:

```
// anti-pattern:
for (const url of urls) {
  const browser = await chromium.launch();
  const context = await browser.newContext();
  const page = await context.newPage();
  await page.goto(url);
  // ...
  await browser.close();
}
```

Instead, try this approach:

```
// recommended:
const browser = await chromium.launch();

for (const url of urls) {
  const context = await browser.newContext();
  const page = await context.newPage();
  await page.goto(url);
  // do your checks...
  await context.close();
}

await browser.close();
```

While each `browser.newContext()` method still uses some memory (since it creates a new profile and browser state), it's much lighter than launching a full browser process every time. Plus, closing each context when you're done helps free up memory and disk space quickly.

Blocking or stubbing unnecessary network requests

By default, each Playwright page will load all resources referenced by the web page, but you don't always need everything for your tests. Playwright allows you to intercept and control network traffic through its **page routing** feature. This lets you block, modify, or simulate network requests as needed.

For example, if your test is only checking text content or validating a specific API call, you can skip loading image formats such as `.png`, `.jpeg`, `.svg`, and so on:

```
await page.route('**/*.{png,jpg,jpeg,svg,gif}', (route) => route.abort());
```

Or, if you want to be more targeted, you can block requests to specific domains, such as `ads` or `analytics`:

```
await page.route('**/ads.googleads.com/**', (route) => route.abort());
await page.route('**/analytics.googleads.net/**', (route) => route.
abort());
```

Blocking unnecessary requests like this reduces CPU load because the browser does not need to decode large image files, saves memory by not allocating textures for images, and speeds up navigation by eliminating potentially slow third-party requests.

You can also take it a step further by simulating network responses. With Playwright's route interception, you can "fake" responses for API calls, which is handy when you don't want to rely on a live backend. For example, here's how you can stub the `/api/user/profile` call:

```
await page.route('**/api/user/profile', (route) => {
  route.fulfill({
    status: 200,
    contentType: 'application/json',
    body: JSON.stringify({ name: 'Test User', id: 123 }),
  });
});
```

This trick is especially useful for tests involving multiple API calls: it helps ensure consistent test results, avoids putting extra load on your test servers, and can greatly speed up your test runs.

For a comprehensive overview of page routing in Playwright, check out the official docs here: `https://playwright.dev/docs/api/class-route`.

Limiting heavy artifacts: screenshots, videos, and traces

Screenshots, videos, and performance traces are extremely useful for debugging test failures, but saving them for every single test can quickly eat up disk space and slow down your tests. You can configure Playwright to capture these artifacts only when you need them, such as when a test fails or is retried.

A great starting point is to set your configuration like this:

```
test.use({
  trace: 'on-first-retry',
  screenshot: 'only-on-failure',
  video: 'retain-on-failure',
});
```

With this setup, you'll still get all the rich debugging data when something goes wrong, but your storage won't fill up with large files from passing tests.

If you want to capture an artifact in a specific test (say, a one-off screenshot), you can still do so easily:

```
await page.screenshot({ path: `screenshots/test-A-${Date.now()}.png`,
fullPage: false });
```

Of course, if you truly need video for every test (perhaps for compliance reasons or client demos), you can absolutely do that. Just be mindful of performance: lower the video resolution, run in a container with fast disk I/O, or adjust recording intervals to keep things running smoothly, even if lots of `.webm` files are generated.

Now, let's see how monitoring your web pages' resource usage can help catch performance issues early.

Measuring and monitoring resource usage

While Playwright doesn't generate resource usage reports out of the box, it gives you everything you need to gather valuable metrics, just like you would in a real browser. You can tap into browser performance APIs, use the **Chrome DevTools Protocol** (**CDP**) for Chromium-based browsers, and leverage Playwright's built-in tools such as `page.evaluate`, CDP sessions, network event listeners, and tracing.

Here's how resource tracking can help you:

- If a new code change accidentally adds a memory leak or makes your scripts too CPU-heavy, tests that monitor performance will catch it before it impacts users.
- Playwright allows you to simulate various scenarios, like a low-end mobile device or a slow network. By benchmarking your app in these environments, you can make sure it works well for everyone.
- You can set thresholds such as keeping Largest Contentful Paint under 2 seconds (we'll explain what that means soon) and write tests that fail if those limits are exceeded. This helps you maintain consistent performance as your app evolves.

Next, we'll walk through some common techniques, complete with code examples to help you get started.

Using built-in browser performance APIs

Modern browsers give us a set of useful performance APIs (such as **Navigation Timing**, **Resource Timing**, **Paint Timing**, **Memory**, and **Web Vitals**) that we can access right from JavaScript. With Playwright's `page.evaluate` method, you can run these calls directly in the browser context and get back raw performance data to analyze.

Navigation and resource timing

The **Navigation Timing API** gives you detailed timestamps for each stage of the page load process: everything from **Domain Name System** (**DNS**) lookup to **Transmission Control Protocol** (**TCP**) handshake to **Document Object Model** (**DOM**) processing.

You can pull this data like so:

```
import { test } from '@playwright/test';

test('Measure navigation timings', async ({ page }) => {
  await page.goto('https://playwright.dev/');

  // Wait until the page is fully loaded
  await page.waitForLoadState('load');

  // Extract navigation timing metrics
  const timing = await page.evaluate(() => {
    const navEntry = performance.getEntriesByType('navigation')[0];
    return {
      startTime: navEntry.startTime,
      connectEnd: navEntry.connectEnd,
      domContentLoaded: navEntry.domContentLoadedEventEnd,
      loadTime: navEntry.loadEventEnd - navEntry.startTime,
    };
  });

  // Log the timings (you can also add assertions here if you want)
  console.log('Navigation timings:', timing);

  // Example assertion: ensure loadTime is less than 5 seconds
  // expect(timing.loadTime).toBeLessThan(5000);
});
```

These numbers give you a clear picture of how long each part of the page load takes, which is helpful for identifying bottlenecks:

- `startTime`: When navigation started
- `connectEnd`: When the connection to the server finished (including DNS and TCP handshake)
- `domContentLoaded`: When the `DOMContentLoaded` event finished firing (meaning the initial HTML has been completely loaded and parsed)
- `loadTime`: The total page load time

Likewise, the **Resource Timing API** lets you see when each individual resource (images, scripts, stylesheets, etc.) starts and finishes downloading, and how big it is:

```
const resources = await page.evaluate(() => {
  return performance.getEntriesByType('resource').map(r => ({
    name: r.name,
    startTime: r.startTime,
    duration: r.duration,
    decodedBodySize: r.decodedBodySize,
    transferSize: r.transferSize,
  }));
});
console.log('Resource timings:', resources);
```

This code builds and returns an object containing five key metrics:

- `name`: The resource URL
- `startTime`: When the resource started loading
- `duration`: How long it took to load
- `decodedBodySize`: The uncompressed size of the resource
- `transferSize`: The actual size transferred over the network

This helps you quickly spot large or slow-loading assets that may be dragging down your load times.

Paint timing and web vitals

Paint timing gives you great insight into how fast and smoothly your web page is loading for users. Two key metrics to start with are **First Paint** and **First Contentful Paint** (**FCP**). These tell you when the browser first starts drawing anything on the screen and when it displays the first actual content. You can capture them using the **Paint Timing API**:

```
import { test } from '@playwright/test';

test('Measure paint timings', async ({ page }) => {
  await page.goto('https://playwright.dev/');

  const paintMetrics = await page.evaluate(() => {
    const paintEntries = performance.getEntriesByType('paint');
    return paintEntries.map(e => ({
      name: e.name,
      startTime: e.startTime,
    }));
  });

  console.log('Paint timings:', paintMetrics);

});
```

This helps you understand how quickly your page starts showing something useful to the user.

For deeper insights, metrics such as **Largest Contentful Paint** (**LCP**) and **Cumulative Layout Shift** (**CLS**) are helpful. These go beyond the initial paint and tell you when the largest piece of content finishes loading, and whether any annoying layout shifts happen during the load.

Tracking LCP requires a bit more work: you can use the `PerformanceObserver` API inside the page to watch for `largest-contentful-paint` events. The observer keeps track of the latest LCP value and stores it in a simple global function (`window.__lcp`) that you can call later to retrieve the result after navigation is done.

Here's an example of tracking LCP:

```
import { test, expect } from '@playwright/test';

test('measure LCP on google.com', async ({ page }) => {
  // Inject the LCP observer *before* navigation
  await page.addInitScript(() => {
    let lcp;
    new PerformanceObserver((entries) => {
      entries.getEntries().forEach((e) => {
        lcp = e.startTime;
      });
    }).observe({ type: 'largest-contentful-paint', buffered: true });
    window.__lcp = () => lcp;
  });

  await page.goto('https://www.google.com', { waitUntil: 'load' });

  // Wait a bit to let paints complete
  await page.waitForTimeout(3000);

  // Read the LCP value
  const lcpValue = await page.evaluate(() => window.__lcp());
  console.log('Largest Contentful Paint:', lcpValue, 'ms');

  // Good LCP is <= 2s
  expect(lcpValue).toBeLessThanOrEqual(2000);
});
```

The core of this script is the use of `page.addInitScript`. This command injects a JavaScript snippet into the page's environment before the page itself starts to load. This injected script sets up `PerformanceObserver`, a standard browser API designed to listen for performance events. By setting it up early, the script guarantees it can capture the `largest-contentful-paint` event whenever it occurs during the page load process. The observer stores the LCP time in a global window variable, `window.__lcp`, making it accessible later.

After navigating to Google and waiting a few seconds for the page to fully render, the test retrieves the captured LCP value. Keeping an eye on these paint and layout metrics is valuable because they highlight parts of the user experience that really matter: how fast the page feels and how stable it looks. No one enjoys a site that loads slowly or jumps around while you're trying to read it.

If the page you're testing performs redirects (for example, `amazon.com` redirecting to a regional domain), specify the final destination URL or disable redirects to ensure accurate LCP measurements.

Memory usage

In Chrome or a Chromium-based browser, you can check out JavaScript heap memory statistics with the `window.performance.memory` object. This handy object gives you detailed info about how much memory the JavaScript engine is using. For example, `usedJSHeapSize` tells you how much of the JavaScript heap is currently being used, while `totalJSHeapSize` shows the total size that's been allocated.

If you'd like to grab this info programmatically, here's a simple script you can use:

```
const memoryUsage = await page.evaluate(() => {
  return performance.memory
    ? {
        usedJSHeap: performance.memory.usedJSHeapSize,
        totalJSHeap: performance.memory.totalJSHeapSize,
      }
    : null;
});
console.log('Memory usage:', memoryUsage);
```

This code checks whether `performance.memory` is available. If it is, the code returns an object with the current and total JavaScript heap sizes; if not, it simply returns `null`.

It's good to keep in mind that `performance.memory` is a non-standard API. This means it isn't part of any official web specification and generally only works in Chromium-based browsers (such as Chrome and Edge). Because of this, it's not a reliable option for memory profiling across different browsers.

Capturing metrics via Chrome DevTools Protocol (CDP)

Capturing performance metrics through the **Chrome DevTools Protocol** (**CDP**) gives you a great way to peek under the hood of your browser and see what's really going on beyond what typical in-page APIs can show. In browsers based on Chromium (such as Chrome or Edge), Playwright's `newCDPSession` object makes it easy to open a direct line of communication with the browser's inner workings.

This lets you tap into detailed performance and network data, such as the effects of CPU throttling, the number of bytes transferred, DOM complexity, and key timing details.

Getting started is straightforward: first, launch a Chromium instance and create a browser context and a page. Then, use `newCDPSession` to create a session tied specifically to that page. Once you're connected, you can enable the `Performance` and `Network` domains with `Performance.enable` and `Network.enable`:

```
import { test } from '@playwright/test';

test('Collect performance metrics with throttling', async ({ browser }) =>
{
  const context = await browser.newContext();
  const page = await context.newPage();

  // Create a CDP session for this page:
  const session = await context.newCDPSession(page);
  await session.send('Performance.enable');
  await session.send('Network.enable');

  // Optionally throttle network & CPU:
  await session.send('Network.emulateNetworkConditions', {
    offline: false,
    latency: 100,              // ms
    downloadThroughput: 75000,  // bytes/sec
    uploadThroughput: 25000,
  });
  await session.send('Emulation.setCPUThrottlingRate', { rate: 4 }); //
Simulate 4x slower CPU

  // Navigate and wait for load:
```

```
    await page.goto('https://playwright.dev');

    // Retrieve performance metrics:
    const metricsResponse = await session.send('Performance.getMetrics');
    console.log('CDP Performance metrics:', metricsResponse.metrics);

    await context.close();
  });
```

This kicks off the collection of rich metrics, such as when `DomContentLoaded` fires, when `FirstMeaningfulPaint` occurs, CPU usage patterns, and much more. You can even tweak network conditions to see how your site behaves for users on slower connections.

One of the coolest features of a CDP session is the ability to emulate different performance scenarios. With `Network.emulateNetworkConditions`, you can simulate network latency or throttle bandwidth, perfect for testing on mobile or under low-bandwidth conditions. Likewise, `Emulation.setCPUThrottlingRate` lets you artificially slow down CPU performance to mimic less powerful devices (for example, applying a 4× slowdown to simulate older smartphones). After setting up these conditions, you simply navigate to your target URL and wait for the page to load.

Once the page is ready, you can grab the collected performance data with `Performance.getMetrics`. The browser returns an array of metrics, each with a name and value. These typically include `Timestamp` (current time), `Documents` and `Frames` (number of open documents and frames), `JSEventListeners` (active event listeners), `Nodes` (DOM node count), `LayoutCount` and `RecalcStyleCount` (layout and style recalculation counts), `ScriptDuration` (JavaScript execution time), `TaskDuration` (main-thread task time), and memory usage details such as `JSHeapUsedSize` and `JSHeapTotalSize`.

By diving into these numbers, you can gain valuable insights into your site's performance, such as the following:

- Divide `JSHeapUsedSize` by `JSHeapTotalSize` to estimate current memory usage
- Look at `TaskDuration` to understand how busy the main thread has been
- Check `ScriptDuration` to see how much time is spent running JavaScript
- Examine `Nodes` and `RecalcStyleCount` to assess DOM complexity and how often style recalculations are triggered

So, CDP sessions give you a flexible way to automate performance testing and analysis. You can simulate a wide variety of real-world scenarios and gather detailed metrics that will help guide your optimization efforts and deliver a better user experience.

Listening to network events for resource-level data

Listening to network events while automating a browser is a great way to capture detailed data about every network request a page makes. If you want to know exactly how long each request takes and how large the responses are, you can use the `requestfinished` event provided by the page object. This event fires whenever a network request has fully completed (meaning the entire response has been received).

To set this up, you can start with a simple array called `networkRequests` to store information about each request. Then, add an event listener to `page.on('requestfinished')`. Inside the event handler, you can retrieve the `response` object for the completed request by calling `await request.response()`. This object provides useful details such as timing information and response headers:

```
import { test, expect } from '@playwright/test';

test('Capture network request details', async ({ page }) => {
  // Store network request data
  const networkRequests = [];

  // Listen for requestfinished event
  page.on('requestfinished', async (request) => {
    const response = await request.response();
    const timing = request.timing();

    networkRequests.push({
      url: request.url(),
      method: request.method(),
      resourceType: request.resourceType(),
      status: response?.status(),
      responseSize: (await response?.body())?.length || 0,
      duration: timing.responseEnd - timing.requestStart,
      startTime: timing.startTime
    });
  });
```

```
  // Navigate to the test page
  await page.goto('https://playwright.dev/');

  // Wait for page to load completely
  await page.waitForLoadState('networkidle');

  // Log collected network requests
  console.log('Network Requests:', networkRequests);

  // Basic assertion to verify page loaded
  await expect(page).toHaveTitle(/Playwright/);

  // Example assertions for network requests
  expect(networkRequests.length).toBeGreaterThan(0);
  expect(networkRequests.some(req => req.status === 200)).toBe(true);
});
```

Once the page has fully loaded (usually after you call `page.goto()`), you can check the `requests` array to see all the data you've collected `networkRequests.push({...})` helps you create a detailed log of everything happening on the network while your test runs. Every time a network request completes, its key details are captured and added as a neatly structured object to the `networkRequests` array.

Let's look at the properties being added to each object:

- `url: request.url()`: Retrieves the full URL of the network request.
- `method: request.method()`: Gets the HTTP method used for the request (such as `GET`, `POST`, or `PUT`).
- `resourceType: request.resourceType()`: Identifies the type of resource being requested (such as `document`, `stylesheet`, `image`, `script`, or `fetch`).
- `status: response?.status()`: Gets the HTTP status code of the response (such as `200` for `OK`, and `404` for `Not Found`). The `?` character (optional chaining) is used because the response might be `null` in some edge cases (though less common for `requestfinished`).
- `responseSize: (await response?.body())?.length || 0`:
    - `await response?.body()`: Asynchronously retrieves the raw body of the response
    - `.length`: Gets the size of the response body in bytes
    - `|| 0`: Provides a default value of `0` if the response body is `null` or `undefined`

- `duration: timing.responseEnd - timing.requestStart`: Calculates the duration of the request from its start to the end of the response. `timing` is an object obtained from `request.timing()` that provides various timestamps related to the request life cycle.
- `startTime: timing.startTime`: Records the precise timestamp when the request started.

Later in the script, we use this `networkRequests` array to ensure that some requests occurred and that at least one request returned a `200` status code:

```
expect(networkRequests.length).toBeGreaterThan(0);
expect(networkRequests.some(req => req.status === 200)).toBe(true);
```

This approach is helpful for performance tuning and debugging because it gives you a clear view of how each resource affects your page's load time and bandwidth usage.

> Ensure that all resources have loaded before grabbing metrics. Relying solely on `page.goto` might miss late-loading assets (web fonts and analytics scripts).

Leveraging Playwright tracing for deeper profiling

Tracing in Playwright is more than just capturing test logs or screenshots: it gives you an interactive trace file that helps you really understand what's happening in your application during automated tests. Tracing records a series of snapshots, tracks network activity, captures console logs, monitors DOM changes, and can even include video recordings while your test runs.

You usually start tracing at the beginning of a test or around a section you want to inspect, and then stop it once the key interactions are done. This generates a `.zip` trace file that you can open in Playwright's **Trace Viewer**. The viewer gives you an easy-to-navigate timeline and a visual playback of each step, so you can *rewind* and explore exactly how the browser state changed over time.

It's simple to configure tracing in your `playwright.config.ts` file:

```
import { defineConfig } from '@playwright/test';

export default defineConfig({
  use: {
    trace: 'on-first-retry', // Options: 'on', 'off', 'retain-on-failure', 
'on-first-retry'
  },
});
```

Trace options include the following:

- 'on': Records a trace for every test. Useful when you are actively debugging or developing tests, but can create large trace files.
- 'off': Disables tracing (default). No trace files are generated.
- 'retain-on-failure': Records traces for all tests but only saves them for failed tests. A good balance between debugging information and storage usage.
- 'on-first-retry': Records a trace only on the first retry of a failed test. Recommended for CI environments to minimize storage while still capturing useful debug information for flaky tests.

You can also turn on tracing on the fly when running tests from the command line:

```
npx playwright test --trace on
```

This is great when you want to enable tracing temporarily, without having to edit your config file.

Alternatively, enable trace recording in your test file like this:

```
import { test } from '@playwright/test';

test.use({ trace: 'on' }); // or 'retain-on-failure' etc.

test('test', async ({ page }) => {
  // your test steps here
});
```

After running tests, Playwright will generate trace files, usually stored in the following:

```
./test-results/<test-name>/trace.zip
```

You can open Trace Viewer by running this command:

```
npx playwright show-trace test-results/test-name/trace.zip
```

This will launch an interactive Trace Viewer in your browser.

If you're using Playwright Test and HTML reports, the report itself will have **Show Trace** links for each test (if a trace was recorded). So, you can also open Trace Viewer by running the following:

```
npx playwright show-report
```

Then, click on **Show Trace** on the desired test.

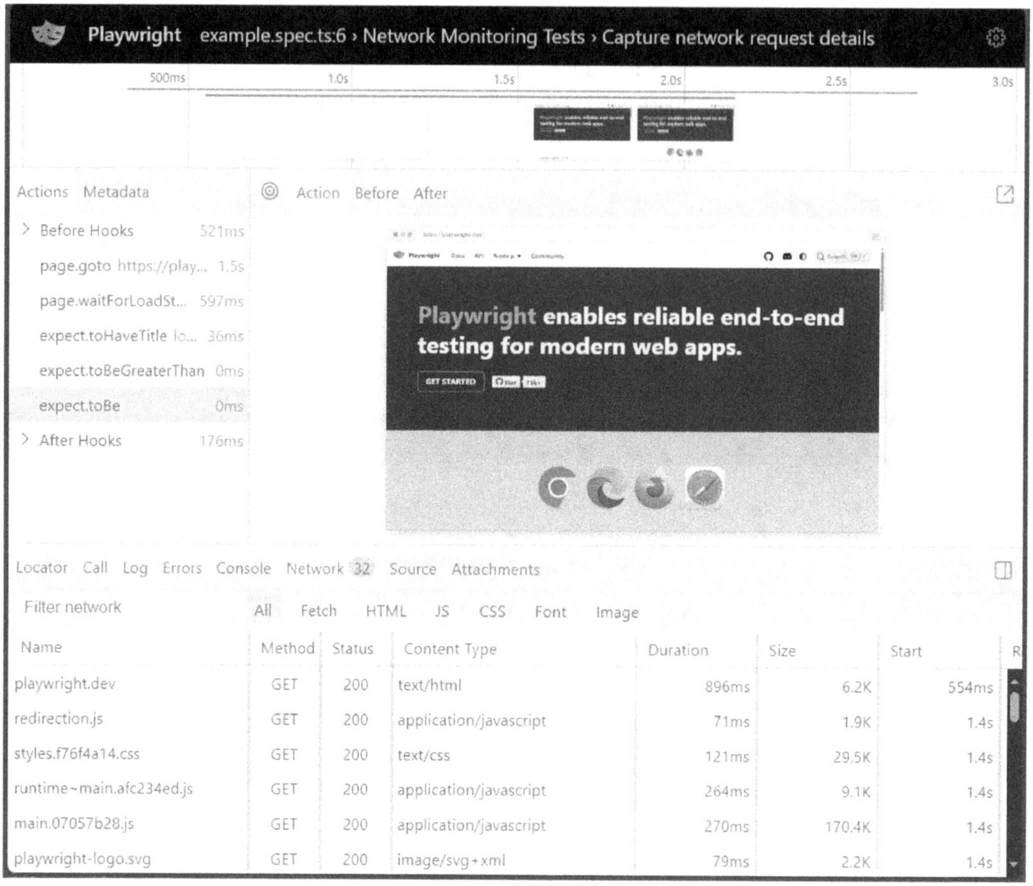

Figure 6.1: Playwright Trace Viewer

Tracing is particularly helpful in CI environments. Debugging failed tests in CI can be tricky, but saving a trace artifact lets you reproduce the issue locally with all the context they need. The trace viewer makes it easy to answer questions such as *Which API request failed? Was the button actually clickable? Did something weird happen during rendering?*

Use tracing strategically. It adds a bit of overhead and produces large trace files, so it's best to enable it selectively for flaky tests, important user flows, or focused profiling sessions. Many teams choose to enable tracing only on test failures, so they can capture valuable debugging info without slowing down every test run.

If you prefer a higher-level abstraction, `playwright-performance-metrics` (`https://github.com/Valiantsin2021/playwright-performance-metrics`) automates much of the work of capturing web vitals, resource timings, and **core web vitals** in your Playwright tests. Core web vitals are a set of key metrics that Google uses to measure how good the user experience is on a website. They focus on how fast your page loads, how quickly it responds to user actions, and how stable the layout looks while loading.

The plugin internally uses CDP's *Performance* and *Resource Timing* domains to gather information such as the following:

- FCP
- LCP
- **Total Blocking Time** (**TBT**)
- CLS
- Total bytes downloaded
- Detailed per-resource timing

From a performance standpoint, tracing helps you spot slow areas in your app. You can inspect the recorded timeline to see exactly where time is being spent, whether it's waiting for a server response, executing JavaScript, or rendering on the client side. This insight can guide optimizations such as lazy loading assets or improving script performance.

Overall, tracing is an invaluable tool that not only simplifies debugging but also provides deep insights into your app's behavior and performance.

Summary

In this chapter, we explored how Playwright's built-in parallelization features and smart performance optimizations can help you run your tests faster and more efficiently. We looked at how to manage workers, parallelize tests inside and across files, and shard your test suite to take full advantage of CI machines.

We also talked about practical ways to avoid common performance pitfalls, such as reusing browsers and contexts, blocking unnecessary network requests, and controlling how many artifacts (screenshots, videos, and traces) you generate. And finally, we saw how to track and measure resource usage so you can catch performance issues early and keep your app running smoothly.

With these techniques, you'll speed up your test runs and make them easier to maintain. Playwright gives you all the tools you need to keep your tests fast and your feedback loop tight. In the next chapter, we'll discuss incorporating Playwright tests into CI/CD workflows using GitHub Actions.

7

Integrating Workflows with CI/CD Pipelines

Shipping software can be stressful. Bugs sneak in, things break at the last minute, and getting code from your laptop to production can feel like a juggling act. That's where CI/CD comes in. Short for **Continuous Integration/Continuous Deployment**, **CI/CD** helps take the stress out of software delivery by automating testing and deployment.

In this chapter, we'll explore how CI/CD pipelines can supercharge your workflow, especially when paired with automated testing tools such as Playwright. You'll learn how to set up GitHub Actions to run your tests every time you push code, generate reports you can actually use, and even publish them online with just a few clicks. We'll also look at using Docker to create consistent test environments that work the same everywhere, whether you're on your laptop or in the cloud.

By the end, you'll have everything you need to build an automated pipeline that helps you catch bugs early, ship updates faster, and sleep a little better at night.

As such, we will cover the following main topics in the chapter:

- Embracing CI/CD for faster, safer software delivery
- Using GitHub Actions
- Handling test reports and artifacts
- Running tests on multiple browsers and operating systems with matrix builds
- Using Docker to create consistent, containerized test environments

Technical requirements

For this chapter, you'll need:

- A Playwright project already set up
- Basic knowledge of GitHub

The source code for this chapter is available at

`https://github.com/PacktPublishing/Hands-On-Automated-Testing-with-Playwright/tree/main/Chapter07`.

Embracing CI/CD for faster, safer software delivery

In this section, we'll explore why CI/CD matters, how automated testing keeps releases safe, and some of the popular platforms that make it all possible.

Importance of CI/CD in modern software development

With **Continuous Integration** (**CI**), every time code is committed, it's automatically built, tested, and validated. This means bugs and integration issues get caught early, before they turn into bigger problems. You also get instant feedback, which builds confidence and saves time that would otherwise be spent on manual testing or fixing messy code conflicts. So, teams can easily manage dozens or even hundreds of code changes a day while keeping the product stable and reliable.

Continuous Deployment (**CD**) takes this a step further by automatically pushing each successful build to staging or even straight to production. Instead of waiting weeks or months for a release, new features and fixes can go live in just hours or minutes. This agility allows teams to respond quickly to user feedback, address urgent bugs right away, and try out new ideas in real-world environments. The entire development process becomes more adaptable, which helps you focus on what really matters: delivering value to users.

Why automated tests in CI/CD pipelines matter

Automated tests are like a safety net that helps keep fast, frequent deployments from turning into chaos. In a manual testing world, every new change brings the risk of unexpected issues or bugs, and it's often up to an already busy QA team (or worse, your users) to catch them.

By building automated tests right into your CI/CD pipeline, every code change, no matter how small, kicks off a series of checks that confirm everything works as expected, prevents old bugs from sneaking back in, and ensures new features play nicely with the existing system.

This constant feedback helps catch problems as soon as they happen (when they're easiest and cheapest to fix) rather than later in the release cycle or, even worse, in production.

Automated tests also give teams real confidence in their deployment process. When each merge or pull request passes a full suite of unit, integration, and end-to-end tests automatically, developers can quickly spot which changes broke the build and respond accordingly, whether that means rolling back or applying a quick patch. This fast feedback loop not only speeds up development but also promotes a culture of accountability: everyone knows their code is being held to a consistent quality standard. So, teams can safely deploy multiple times a day, try out new ideas, and keep improving features without worrying about breaking the system.

Common CI/CD platforms

Let's take a look at some of the most popular CI/CD platforms that help automate building, testing, and deploying software.

GitHub Actions feels like an extension of your repository: write a workflow file, push your code, and voilà, tests and builds run automatically whenever you open a pull request or push a commit. The best part is that you get access to a huge marketplace of readymade *actions*, and if you ever need more power, you can spin up your own selfhosted runners.

If you're already on **GitLab**, **GitLab CI** is a natural fit. Drop a `.gitlab-ci.yml` file in your project, and you can spin up pipelines that build, test, and even deploy your app. You get built-in Docker registry support, parent–child pipelines for complex workflows, and seamless issue tracking all in one place. It's ideal for teams who want the entire DevOps lifecycle under one roof.

For those who want flexibility, **Jenkins** is the granddaddy of CI. With an enormous plugin ecosystem, you can customize almost anything, but you'll need to manage the server yourself. If you'd rather leave infrastructure to the pros, **CircleCI**'s cloudfirst approach spins up jobs in **Docker containers**, uses smart caching to speed things up, and offers reusable *orbs* to share config snippets. If you're in the Microsoft ecosystem, Azure DevOps brings together pipelines, repos, boards, and more, all with first-class support for Azure services.

Go with whatever fits best in your workflow. In this chapter, we'll be using GitHub Actions, which is a popular choice among developers.

Using GitHub Actions

GitHub Actions lets you **automate workflows** directly within your GitHub repositories. Think of it as a way to respond automatically to events in your repo such as pushes, pull requests, or releases.

With GitHub Actions, you can do the following:

- Run tests and check code quality
- Build and package your applications
- Deploy to servers or cloud providers
- Automate issue management
- Trigger notifications or integrations with other services

It's highly flexible and works for nearly any programming language or platform.

Understanding key concepts

Before diving in, let's cover some essential terms:

- **Workflow**: A configurable process triggered by events in your repo (such as a push or PR). Workflows are defined in YAML files stored in `.github/workflows/`.
- **Job**: A set of steps that run together on the same runner. Workflows can have multiple jobs running sequentially or in parallel.
- **Step**: An individual task in a job, such as checking out code or running a shell script.
- **Runner**: A machine (virtual or physical) that executes your jobs. GitHub provides free hosted runners, or you can use your own self-hosted machines.
- **Action**: Reusable pieces of code you can use in steps. Actions might be community-built or custom scripts you create.

Creating the GitHub Actions workflow file

First, let's create a GitHub Actions workflow file. This is a YAML file placed in the `.github/workflows/` directory of your repository. You can name it something such as `playwright.yml`:

```
.github/workflows/playwright.yml
```

Within this file, define when the workflow should run, typically on `push` and `pull_request` events.

> If `npm init playwright@latest` already created `playwright.yml` for you, you can just modify it.

Add the following content. We'll be using the example code from the Playwright documentation (`https://playwright.dev/docs/ci-intro`):

```
name: Playwright Tests

on:
  push:
    branches: [ main, master ]
  pull_request:
    branches: [ main, master ]

jobs:
  test:
    timeout-minutes: 60
    runs-on: ubuntu-latest

    steps:
    - uses: actions/checkout@v4

    - uses: actions/setup-node@v4
      with:
        node-version: lts/*

    - name: Install dependencies
      run: npm ci

    - name: Install Playwright Browsers
      run: npx playwright install --with-deps

    - name: Run Playwright tests
      run: npx playwright test

    - uses: actions/upload-artifact@v4
      if: ${{ !cancelled() }}
      with:
        name: playwright-report
        path: playwright-report/
        retention-days: 30
```

This file automates the process of running Playwright tests whenever changes are pushed to your main or master branches, or when a pull request is opened targeting these branches.

Let's break down each section:

- `name: Playwright Tests`: This defines the name of your workflow. This name will appear in the **Actions** tab of your GitHub repository, making it easy to identify what the workflow does.
- `on`: This section specifies the events that trigger this workflow.
    - `push: branches: [ main, master ]`: The workflow will run whenever code is pushed to either the main or master branches.
    - `pull_request: branches: [ main, master ]`: The workflow will also run whenever a pull request is opened targeting either the main or master branches. This is crucial for ensuring that new code is tested before it's merged.
- `jobs`: Workflows are composed of one or more jobs. This workflow has a single job named `test`:
    - `timeout-minutes: 60`: This sets a maximum time for the test job to run. If the job exceeds 60 minutes, GitHub Actions will automatically cancel it. This prevents jobs from running indefinitely due to issues.
    - `runs-on: ubuntu-latest`: This specifies the type of runner (the virtual machine) that the job will execute on. `ubuntu-latest` is a common choice for its speed and compatibility with many tools. You could also choose `windows-latest` or `macos-latest` if your tests require a specific operating system environment.
    - `steps`: Jobs are made up of a sequence of steps. Each step can execute commands or use pre-built actions:
        - `- uses: actions/checkout@v4`: This step uses the checkout action (version 4) to download your repository's code onto the runner. This is essential for accessing your project files, including your Playwright tests. @v4 indicates that you are using version 4 of this action. It's good practice to pin to a specific version to ensure your workflows are stable and don't break due to backward-incompatible changes in newer versions of an action.
        - `uses: actions/setup-node@v4`: This step uses the setup-node action (version 4) to install Node.js on the runner, which is required to run Playwright and its dependencies.

    - `with: node-version: lts/*`: This specifies that the latest **Long Term Support (LTS)** version of Node.js should be installed.
    - `- name: Install dependencies`

      `run: npm ci`: This step runs the `npm ci` command. `npm ci` is preferred over `npm install` in CI/CD environments. `npm ci` deletes the existing `node_modules` folder and installs everything from scratch using the exact versions listed in `package-lock.json`. It ensures that the installed packages are exactly the same on every machine or server, which is crucial for CI/CD pipelines where reproducibility and reliability matter.

- `- name: Install Playwright Browsers`

  `run: npx playwright install --with-deps`: This step uses `npx` to execute the Playwright CLI command `install --with-deps`. This command downloads and installs all the necessary browser binaries (Chromium, Firefox, WebKit) that Playwright uses for testing, along with their system-level dependencies.

- `- name: Run Playwright tests`

  `run: npx playwright test`: This is the core step where your Playwright tests are executed. `npx playwright test` runs all tests found in your Playwright project.

- `- uses: actions/upload-artifact@v4`: This is an official action provided by GitHub that allows you to upload artifacts (files or directories) generated during your workflow run.
- `if: ${{ !cancelled() }}`: This `if` condition ensures that this step runs as long as the workflow has not been manually cancelled, even if previous steps (such as the Playwright tests) fail. This is useful when you still want to generate or upload the test report regardless of test failures, but want to skip the step if the entire workflow was intentionally stopped.
- `with:`
    - `name: playwright-report`: This gives a name to the uploaded artifact. In the **Actions** tab on GitHub, you'll see an artifact named **playwright-report**, which you can download.
    - `path: playwright-report/`: This specifies the directory containing the files to be uploaded.
    - `retention-days: 30`: This sets how long the artifact will be retained on GitHub's servers. After this period, it will be automatically deleted.

This is a standard setup for integrating Playwright tests into a GitHub-based CI/CD pipeline. Save your `playwright.yml` file, log in to your GitHub account, and commit it to your repository. Then, push your changes to GitHub:

```
git add .github/workflows/playwright.yml
git commit -m "Add Playwright tests GitHub Actions workflow"
git push
```

Once you push your code, GitHub Actions automatically detects the workflow and starts running it.

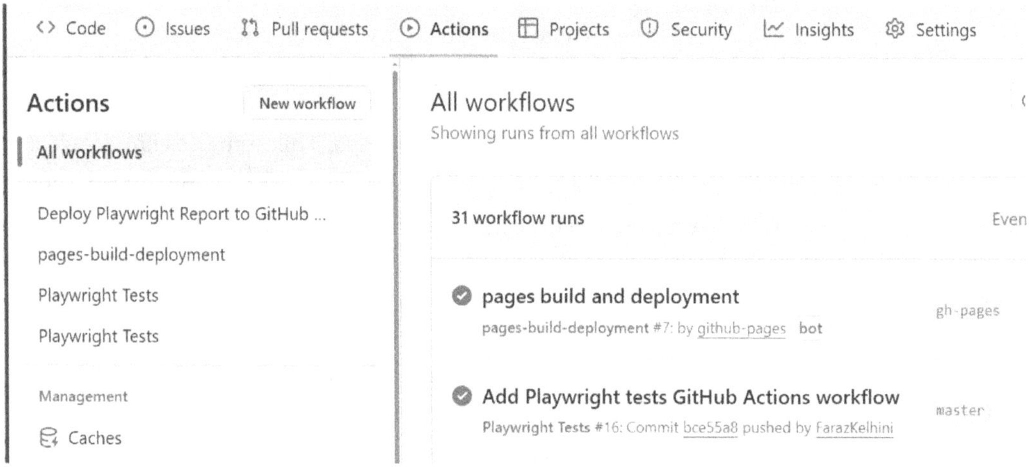

Figure 7.1: GitHub Actions runs

You can track its progress in the **Actions** tab of your repository:

1. Go to your GitHub repository.
2. Click on the **Actions** tab.
3. You will see your workflow runs. Click on the latest run.

4. You can then drill down into the `test` job and see the output of each step.
5. If tests fail, you'll see the error messages in the `Run Playwright tests` step.
6. In the **Summary** section of the workflow run, under **Artifacts**, you can download the `playwright-report.zip` file. Unzip it and open `index.html` in your browser to view a detailed interactive report of your test results.

Figure 7.2: GitHub Artifacts allow access to your report

When you open `index.html` from `playwright-report.zip`, you'll see the Playwright Test Report UI.

Inside it, each test shows details such as the following:

- Status (passed, failed, skipped)
- Error message & stack trace (if failed)
- Attachments (screenshots, videos, traces, logs)

- Test Steps: a step-by-step breakdown of what Playwright did, such as click button, fill input, and navigate to page

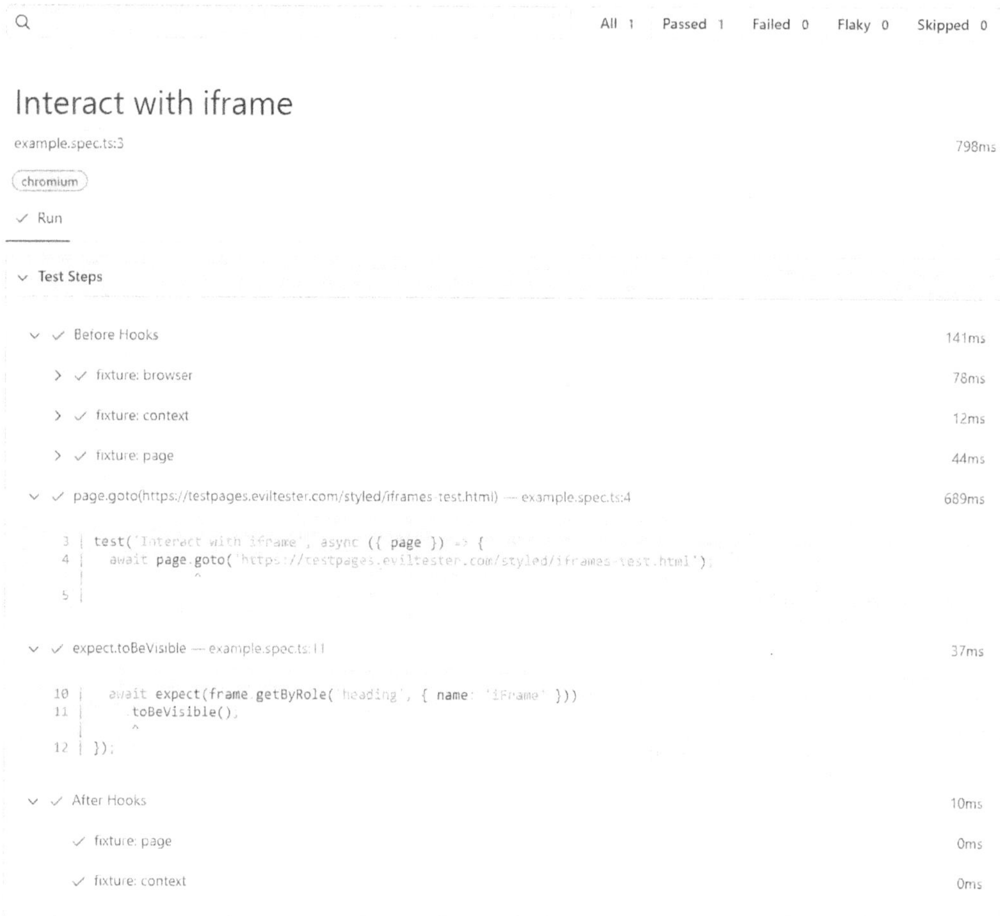

Figure 7.3: The Test Steps section shows a detailed, step-by-step breakdown of actions performed during a test

For large test suites, you can speed up execution by sharding your tests across multiple jobs or runners using Playwright's `--shard` flag. See *Chapter 6, Test Parallelization and Performance Optimization*, for reference.

Once your HTML report is ready, it's a good idea to store it as an artifact so you can easily access it after your workflow finishes running.

Handling test reports and artifacts

You can store your HTML report as an artifact with the `actions/upload-artifact@v4` action, where you'll define a name for your artifact (for example, `coverage-report`) and point to the folder that holds your generated HTML files (such as `playwright-report/`). The YAML file we discussed in the previous section already includes this action.

Publishing your HTML report online with GitHub Pages

If you want to share your Playwright HTML report online, you can host it using **GitHub Pages**. GitHub Pages is a free service from GitHub that lets you turn your code repositories into shareable websites. Instead of just storing code, you can use it to host project documentation, personal portfolios, or even full websites directly from your GitHub repository. You just push your project to a special branch, and GitHub will handle the rest.

First, generate your HTML report by running your Playwright tests with the HTML reporter enabled. If you want to do it only once, just run this command in your terminal:

```
npx playwright test --reporter=html
```

This will create a folder called `playwright-report`, which includes an `index.html` file plus all the necessary styles and scripts for an interactive test report. Next, you'll need a GitHub repository to host your report. You can either create a new repo or use an existing one.

You have a couple of options for where to host your report:

- On the main branch: You can place the `playwright-report` folder either at the root of the repo or inside a subdirectory such as `docs/`.
- On a separate branch (such as gh-pages): If you prefer to keep things tidy, you can create a dedicated `gh-pages` branch:

```
git checkout --orphan gh-pages
```

This command tells Git to create and switch to a new branch called `gh-pages` without any previous commit history. This is known as an **orphan** branch because it doesn't share history with the existing branches in your repository. Even though you're now on a brand-new branch, your working directory (the actual files sitting in your project folder) still contains all the files from the branch you were on previously, but Git considers them all as untracked files in this new context.

After that, copy the `playwright-report` folder into this branch, commit the changes, and push the branch to GitHub.

```
git add .
git commit -m "Publish Playwright report"
git push origin gh-pages --force
```

You need to use the `--force` flag here because the `gh-pages` branch is usually created as an **orphan branch**, meaning it doesn't share any history with your main branch. Because of that, a regular `git push` would fail since Git can't connect the two histories.

Using `--force` basically tells Git, *Go ahead and replace the remote branch with my local version, even if they don't match.* Just keep in mind that `--force` can be risky. If you use it on a shared branch, it might overwrite someone else's work or remove commits.

Once your files are on GitHub, head over to your repository settings and look for the **Pages** section. There, choose the branch where your report lives and specify the folder path for your report, such as the root directory or `docs/`:

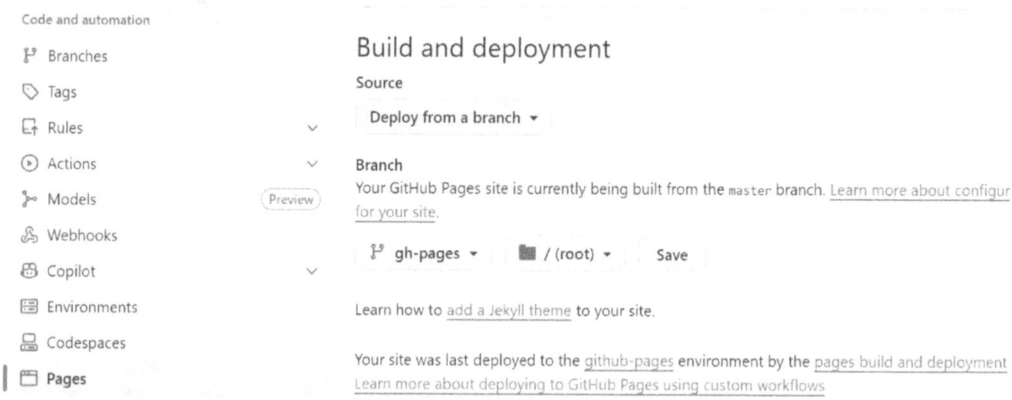

Figure 7.4: GitHub settings

After saving these settings, GitHub Pages will give you a URL, something like this:

```
https://<username>.github.io/<repository>/
```

If your report is inside a subdirectory, the URL will include that path. Here's an example:

```
https://<username>.github.io/<repository>/playwright-report/
```

When you open that link, GitHub Pages will serve the `index.html` file from your report, making it easy for anyone to view your interactive Playwright results in their browser.

Since playwright-report/ contains temporary test output rather than code you want to version, you should add it to .gitignore.

Automating the process with GitHub Actions

Manually pushing your Playwright HTML report every time can get tedious. Luckily, you can automate the whole process using GitHub Actions.

You can set up a job that automatically deploys it to the gh-pages branch whenever you push changes to your main branch. The workflow uses the peaceiris/actions-gh-pages action to publish the playwright-report folder:

```
- name: Deploy to GitHub Pages
        uses: peaceiris/actions-gh-pages@v4
        with:
          github_token: ${{ secrets.GITHUB_TOKEN }}
          publish_dir: ./playwright-report
          publish_branch: gh-pages
```

With this automation in place, your reports stay up to date without any manual steps. The line - name: Deploy to GitHub Pages simply gives this step a label, so when you look at your workflow logs on GitHub, you'll know that this part is handling the deployment.

The line uses: peaceiris/actions-gh-pages@v4 tells GitHub Actions to run a pre-built action called actions-gh-pages, created by a developer named peaceiris. This action is very popular because it makes it easy to push files to the GitHub Pages branch of your repository. By specifying @v4, you're choosing version 4 of this action.

Under the with section, there are inputs that customize how the action works. The first one, github_token: ${{ secrets.GITHUB_TOKEN }}, provides the action with permission to push changes back to your repository. GitHub automatically generates this token for each workflow run, so you don't need to manually create one. It's a secure way to allow the workflow to make changes, such as updating the gh-pages branch.

publish_dir: ./playwright-report tells the action which folder you want to publish to GitHub Pages. This action takes everything inside that folder and pushes it to the gh-pages branch used by GitHub Pages.

Now, you may get an error saying the GitHub Actions bot does not have permission to push to your repository. By default, `GITHUB_TOKEN` has read-only permissions on your repo unless you explicitly grant write permissions in your workflow YAML.

Add this top-level section to your workflow file:

```
permissions:
  contents: write
```

So, here's what our complete workflow snippet will look like:

```
name: Deploy Playwright Report to GitHub Pages

on:
  push:
    branches:
      - [ main, master ]

permissions:
  contents: write

jobs:
  deploy:
    runs-on: ubuntu-latest
    steps:
      - name: Checkout repository
        uses: actions/checkout@v4

      - name: Set up Node.js
        uses: actions/setup-node@v4
        with:
          node-version: lts/*

      - name: Install dependencies
        run: npm ci

      - name: Install Playwright Browsers
        run: npx playwright install --with-deps

      - name: Run Playwright tests
```

```
        run: npx playwright test

      - uses: actions/upload-artifact@v4
        if: ${{ !cancelled() }}
        with:
          name: playwright-report
          path: playwright-report/
          retention-days: 30

      - name: Deploy to GitHub Pages
        uses: peaceiris/actions-gh-pages@v4
        with:
          github_token: ${{ secrets.GITHUB_TOKEN }}
          publish_dir: ./playwright-report
          publish_branch: gh-pages
```

From now on, every time you push your code and your Playwright tests run successfully, your HTML report will automatically be published online with no manual steps required.

Once you've enabled GitHub Pages, check that your report is accessible by visiting the URL it provides. Make sure the `playwright-report` folder and its contents aren't listed in your `.gitignore` file, or they might not get uploaded.

If the report doesn't load as expected (for example, due to MIME type errors), double-check that GitHub Pages is set up to serve the right branch and folder. If you're working with a private repository, remember you can control who can see your GitHub Pages site through your repository settings.

You could also upload the report to external services such as AWS S3 or Firebase Hosting, depending on your needs.

Adding inline HTML into Job Summaries

GitHub's **Job Summaries** are a handy feature that lets you add nicely formatted content to the summary section of your GitHub Actions workflow runs. You can access this feature using the `GITHUB_STEP_SUMMARY` environment variable, and it's a great way to share extra information (such as links or important messages) using simple Markdown syntax.

For instance, you could add a link to a test report with a step like this:

```
- name: Add link to report in summary
  run: |
    echo "## Test Report" >> $GITHUB_STEP_SUMMARY
    echo "[View Test Report](https://${{ github.actor }}.github.io/test/
playwright-report/)" >> $GITHUB_STEP_SUMMARY
```

While Job Summaries do support Markdown, it's important to know that they don't handle large or complex raw HTML content. Markdown is meant to be lightweight and secure, so GitHub limits what you can include. You can definitely add text, links, headers, and lists, but if you try to add things such as full HTML documents, `<div>` blocks, or scripts, those will either be ignored or shown as plain text rather than rendered HTML.

For more complex content, you can use Markdown for the summary itself and link out to external resources where you can display richer details.

Ensuring your application works seamlessly across different environments is important for delivering a consistent user experience. One effective way to achieve this is by using matrix builds in your CI/CD pipeline.

Running tests on multiple browsers and operating systems with matrix builds

Matrix builds in GitHub Actions are a handy way to run the same job multiple times with different configurations (such as different browsers or operating systems), either in parallel or one after another.

With a matrix, you define a set of variables, and GitHub Actions automatically creates a separate job for each combination. This becomes especially powerful when you're testing across multiple environments.

Imagine you want to test on Linux, macOS, and Windows—and also across several browsers. A matrix build can generate all those combinations for you, so you don't have to write separate jobs for each pair. For instance, you'd easily get jobs such as Chromium on Linux, Firefox on macOS, and so on.

Here's a quick example:

```
runs-on: ${{ matrix.os }}
strategy:
  matrix:
    os: [ubuntu-latest, windows-latest, macos-latest]
    browser: [chromium, firefox]

steps:
  - uses: actions/checkout@v4
  - name: Install dependencies
    run: npm install
  - name: Run Playwright tests
    run: npx playwright test --project=${{ matrix.browser }}
```

This setup ensures that each job only runs tests for the browser specified by `matrix.browser`. For example, the Firefox job only runs Firefox tests, while the Chromium job only runs Chromium tests.

This would create six separate jobs (three operating systems × two browsers):

OS	Browser
ubuntu-latest	Chromium
ubuntu-latest	firefox
windows-latest	Chromium
windows-latest	firefox
macos-latest	Chromium
macos-latest	firefox

Table 7.1: Matrix expansion example (3 OS × 2 browsers)

Overall, matrix builds save you a lot of time and effort by handling the complexity of testing in multiple environments automatically.

If you're working on a Playwright report deployment workflow, for example, you could use a matrix build to run your Playwright tests across different browsers and then deploy either combined reports or browser-specific reports to GitHub Pages.

When building and testing software across multiple environments, consistency is key but often hard to achieve. Differences in operating systems, tools, or library versions can lead to unpredictable behavior and wasted debugging time. This is where containerization comes in.

Even with a well-integrated Playwright workflow, CI runs can sometimes behave unpredictably. To make your CI runs a bit more resilient, try adding "retries": 2 to your Playwright config. This tells Playwright to automatically rerun any failed tests up to two times. This is especially useful when dealing with flaky tests caused by timing or network instability. That said, retries shouldn't become a crutch. If you find yourself relying on them a lot, it might be a sign of something deeper, such as race conditions or misconfigured environments. So, it's worth digging in and fixing the root cause rather than just patching over it.

Another useful trick is turning on **Playwright traces** in your CI setup. Traces record screenshots, console logs, and network activity for each test, so you can actually replay what happened step by step. To enable traces, just add this to your `playwright.config.ts` file:

```
use: {
  trace: 'on-first-retry',
}
```

Using Docker to create consistent, containerized test environments

Docker is a tool that makes it easy to create consistent, repeatable test environments. It's especially helpful when working with CI/CD pipelines. With Docker, you can package your app and everything it needs (such as runtimes, dependencies, and tools) into a neat container that works the same way everywhere: on your laptop, in staging, or in production. That means no more "*It works on my machine*" headaches!

Instead of manually setting up your machine with specific versions of tools, you define everything once in a `Dockerfile`.

Another bonus is that containers are isolated. That means tests won't interfere with each other, which is great for running them in parallel and speeding up your workflow.

In CI/CD workflows, Docker shines when paired with tools such as GitHub Actions. By defining test environments in Docker images, every commit can be tested consistently. This is especially valuable for matrix builds, where tests span multiple configurations.

Setting things up

Before you begin, make sure Docker is installed and running on your machine:

- Download Docker Desktop for Windows or macOS:

  `https://www.docker.com/products/docker-desktop`

- Use Docker Engine if you're on Linux

Running your tests in Docker

In the root folder of your Playwright project, create a file named `Dockerfile` (no file extension). Paste in the following:

```
# Use an official Playwright base image (Node.js with browsers and
dependencies)
# It's recommended to pin to a specific version for reproducibility
FROM mcr.microsoft.com/playwright:v1.54.0-noble

# Set the working directory inside the container
WORKDIR /app

# Copy package.json and package-lock.json to install dependencies
# This leverages Docker's caching, so dependencies are only reinstalled if
these files change
COPY package*.json ./

# Install project dependencies
RUN npm install

# Copy the rest of your Playwright project files into the container
COPY . .

# Command to run Playwright tests when the container starts
# You can adjust this based on your specific needs
CMD ["npx", "playwright", "test"]
```

A `Dockerfile` is a script that contains instructions for building a Docker image. Here's what's happening here:

- `FROM mcr.microsoft.com/playwright:v1.54.0-noble`: We're starting from an official Playwright image that already has Node.js and all major browsers installed. Always *pin the version* to ensure consistent builds. You can find a list of available official Playwright images by visiting the Microsoft Artifact Registry at `https://mcr.microsoft.com/en-us/artifact/mar/playwright/tags`.
- `WORKDIR /app`: Sets where commands will run inside the container.
- `COPY package*.json ./`: Grabs your `package.json` files first to cache the install step (so it doesn't redo it every time unless dependencies change).
- `RUN npm install`: Installs all the Node.js dependencies defined in your `package.jason` file.
- `COPY . .`: Copies all the remaining files from your local project directory into the `/app` directory inside the container. This includes your Playwright tests, configuration, and any other project-specific files.
- `RUN npx playwright install --with-deps`: If you're using the official Playwright Docker image, the browsers are already included, and you don't need to install them manually. However, if you're using a more generic Node.js base image, running this command ensures that Playwright's browsers and their system dependencies are properly installed in the container.
- `CMD ["npx", "playwright", "test"]`: Defines the default command that will be executed when a container is launched from this image. In this case, it runs all your Playwright tests.

Building the Docker image

Now that you have your `Dockerfile`, let's build your Docker image. From your project's root directory, run the following:

```
docker build -t playwright-tests .
```

Let's break it down:

- `docker build`: The command to build a Docker image.
- `-t playwright-tests`: Tags the image with the name `playwright-tests`. You can choose any name you prefer.
- `.`: Specifies the build context, which is the current directory (where your `Dockerfile` is located).

The first build may take a little while as it downloads everything, but future builds will be much faster thanks to caching.

Running Playwright tests in a Docker container

After the image is built, you can run your Playwright tests in an isolated container using the `docker run` command:

```
docker run --rm -it --ipc=host playwright-tests
```

Let's break it down:

- `--rm`: Cleans up the container after it exits.
- `-it`: Lets you interact with the container (useful for reading test output).
- `--ipc=host`: It's recommended to use `--ipc=host` with Chromium to prevent memory issues. Without this flag, Chromium may run out of memory and crash.
- `playwright-tests`: That's the name of the image you just built.

When you run this command, Docker will create a container from your `playwright-tests` image, execute the command (`npx playwright test`), and display the test results in your terminal.

Viewing test reports and artifacts

By default, Playwright generates an HTML report in the `playwright-report` directory. To access this report (or any other artifacts such as screenshots or videos) generated inside the container, you need to *mount a volume*.

Modify your `docker run` command to include the `-v` flag:

```
docker run --rm -v "$(pwd)/playwright-report:/app/playwright-report"
playwright-tests
```

This mounts your local `playwright-report` directory (represented by `$(pwd)/playwright-report` on Linux/macOS or `%cd%/playwright-report` on Windows Command Prompt/PowerShell) to the `/app/playwright-report` directory inside the container. This means any reports generated by Playwright within the container will be saved directly to your local machine.

After the tests complete, you can open the `index.html` file in your local `playwright-report` directory in a web browser to view the detailed test report:

```
npx playwright show-report
```

With Docker in place, your test environments become fully portable, consistent, and isolated. It's a great way to simplify your CI/CD setup and avoid hard-to-track bugs.

Integration with GitHub Actions

Now that you've containerized your Playwright tests using Docker, the next step is to run them automatically as part of your CI pipeline. GitHub Actions makes this easy.

To integrate the Dockerized Playwright tests into your *Deploy Playwright Report to GitHub Pages* workflow, you'll primarily replace the steps that set up Node.js, install dependencies, and run Playwright directly on the runner with steps that build and run your Docker image.

First, you need to make sure to "check out" your code so that the Dockerfile and all your project files are available. Then, build your Docker image using the `Dockerfile`, and run your Playwright tests inside a container:

```
name: Deploy Playwright Report to GitHub Pages

on:
  push:
    branches:
      - master

permissions:
  contents: write

jobs:
  deploy:
    runs-on: ubuntu-latest
    steps:
      - name: Checkout repository
        uses: actions/checkout@v4

      - name: Build Docker image
        run: docker build -t playwright-tests .

      - name: Run Playwright tests in Docker
        run: docker run --rm -v "${{ github.workspace }}/playwright-
report:/app/playwright-report" playwright-tests
```

```
      - uses: actions/upload-artifact@v4
        if: ${{ !cancelled() }}
        with:
          name: playwright-report
          path: playwright-report/
          retention-days: 30

      - name: Deploy to GitHub Pages
        uses: peaceiris/actions-gh-pages@v4
        with:
          github_token: ${{ secrets.GITHUB_TOKEN }}
          publish_dir: ./playwright-report
          publish_branch: gh-pages
```

The original workflow had steps such as `Set up Node.js`, `Install dependencies`, and `Install Playwright Browsers`. These are no longer needed because your Docker image (`playwright-tests`) already encapsulates Node.js, Playwright, and all its dependencies within the container.

This step executes your Playwright tests inside the newly built Docker container:

```
    - name: Run Playwright tests in Docker
      run: docker run --rm -v "${{ github.workspace }}/playwright-report:/
  app/playwright-report" playwright-tests
```

The `-v "${{ github.workspace }}/playwright-report:/app/playwright-report"` part is crucial. It mounts a volume, effectively creating a shared directory. `${{ github.workspace }}` is a built-in variable pointing to the root of your cloned repository.

So, by mounting this volume, any reports, screenshots, or videos generated by Playwright inside the container will be directly written to the `playwright-report` directory in your GitHub Actions runner's workspace. This allows the subsequent `upload-artifact` and `peaceiris/actions-gh-pages` actions to access these files.

No changes to `upload-artifact` and `peaceiris/actions-gh-pages` are needed. These steps remain the same because, thanks to the volume mount, the `playwright-report` directory is available on the runner just as it would be if you ran the tests directly on the runner. They will correctly pick up the report generated by the Docker container.

This integrated workflow ensures that your Playwright tests are executed within a consistent, containerized environment, and their reports are still deployed to GitHub Pages.

> If your GitHub Actions workflow uses a matrix build to run Playwright tests across multiple configurations or shards, each job will generate its own report. To publish a single, unified report, you can use Playwright's blob reporting feature. Each shard uploads its results, and then a final job can merge them before deployment. For details and examples, see the Playwright docs:
>
> `https://playwright.dev/docs/test-sharding#github-actions-example`

That brings us to the end of this chapter.

Summary

Integrating automated tests into your CI/CD pipeline is one of the most impactful ways to increase development speed and gain confidence in frequent releases. In this chapter, you learned how to configure Playwright tests to run automatically on code changes, publish interactive HTML reports with GitHub Pages, and use Docker to ensure consistent test environments across machines. With features such as matrix builds and artifact uploads, your pipeline can now validate code across different systems and share results easily. Now you can spend less time worrying about infrastructure and more time building great features.

In the next chapter, we'll look at running tests in headless mode for efficiency and debugging failed tests with Playwright's tools.

8

Headless Testing and Debugging

When you're building and running automated tests, it's helpful to know what's going on behind the scenes and even more helpful when things don't go as planned. That's where this chapter comes in.

We're going to explore two important topics: **headless testing** and **debugging** in Playwright. Headless mode is great when you want your tests to run fast and quietly in the background. It's perfect for continuous integration or large test suites. But sometimes, you need to actually see what's happening on the screen. That's when headful mode (with the browser window open) comes in handy.

We'll also walk through some awesome debugging tools Playwright gives you, such as the Inspector, UI Mode, and ways to capture screenshots and videos of your tests in action. These tools make it way easier to figure out what went wrong and fix issues quickly.

By the end of this chapter, you'll know when to run tests silently and efficiently, when to watch them unfold step by step, and you'll have the tools to troubleshoot like a pro.

As such, we will cover the following main topics in the chapter:

- Configuring headless versus headful modes
- Debugging with Playwright's Inspector
- Exploring UI Mode for debugging
- Capturing screenshots for failed tests
- Recording videos of test runs

Technical requirements

To follow along with the chapter, make sure you're using a system that can run headless browsers (a GUI-enabled operating system).

The source code for this chapter is available at

`https://github.com/PacktPublishing/Hands-On-Automated-Testing-with-Playwright/tree/main/Chapter08.`

Configuring headless versus headful modes

Playwright offers two primary modes for running browser automation: **headless** and **headful** (sometimes called *headed*). The key difference lies in whether a visible browser window is displayed during execution.

We've already come across both modes back in *Chapter 1, Quick Setup Refresher*, but now let's take a closer look at each one.

Enabling headless mode

In headless mode, the browser operates without a **graphical user interface (GUI)**. This means you won't see a browser window pop up on your screen.

By default, Playwright runs in headless mode for speed and resource efficiency: without rendering any visuals, tests execute faster and consume fewer system resources. This makes headless mode especially well-suited for continuous integration environments or load testing scenarios where you don't need to see the browser's UI.

You can explicitly configure this setting in your `playwright.config.ts` file, under the use section:

```
// playwright.config.ts
import { defineConfig, devices } from '@playwright/test';

export default defineConfig({
  use: {
    headless: true,
    // ... other configurations
  },
});
```

Another way to run tests in headless mode is by using the `--headless` flag with the Playwright CLI:

```
npx playwright test --headless
```

If you're using multiple projects (such as Chromium, Firefox, and WebKit), you can also set it per project:

```
import { defineConfig, devices } from '@playwright/test';

export default defineConfig({
  projects: [
    {
      name: 'chromium',
      use: {
        ...devices['Desktop Chrome'],
        headless: false,
      },
    },
    {
      name: 'firefox',
      use: {
        ...devices['Desktop Firefox'],
        headless: true,
      },
    },
  ],
});
```

Running in headless mode saves both CPU and memory. Plus, it tends to be more consistent, since it avoids things such as screen size or display settings that can affect test results.

On the flip side, debugging in headless mode can be a bit tricky. Since you can't see the browser window, you'll often need to rely on things such as screenshots, recorded videos, or trace tools to figure out what went wrong. It also means you can't visually check how UI elements look or how animations and transitions play out, which can be important in some cases. While Playwright can help with this, some websites are more likely to flag headless browsers as bots, which might cause issues during testing.

That's where headful mode shines: by setting `headless: false`, you instruct Playwright to open the real browser window.

Enabling headful mode

Seeing the page render and actions play out in real time is invaluable when debugging flaky tests or developing new automation scripts. You can easily enable headful mode in your `playwright.config.ts` file:

```
// playwright.config.ts
import { defineConfig, devices } from '@playwright/test';

export default defineConfig({
  use: {
    headless: false,
    // ... other configurations
  },
});
```

You can also use the `--headed` flag with the Playwright CLI. If you're using multiple projects, you can also set it per project.

Running in headful mode does have a few trade-offs. The biggest one is performance: it tends to be slower than headless mode since it has to render the full graphical interface. This slowdown becomes more noticeable if you're running a lot of tests.

It's also a bit heavier on system resources. Headful mode uses more CPU and memory, which can limit how many tests you can run in parallel, something that's pretty important in fast-moving development workflows.

When you run Playwright tests in a CI environment (such as GitHub Actions), there's usually no graphical environment available, so browsers must run in headless mode. If you try to run them in headed mode, they'll fail because there's no display to render the UI.

A common pattern is toggling headless mode based on whether the tests are running in CI. Here's an example:

```
module.exports = defineConfig({
  use: {
    headless: !!process.env.CI,  // true in CI, false locally
  },
});
```

In GitHub Actions, the CI environment variable is automatically set to "true", so this logic works nicely.

Therefore, go with headless mode when doing the following:

- **Running CI/CD pipelines**: It's the default choice for automated testing in continuous integration setups
- **Handling large test suites**: It's faster and more efficient with system resources
- **Doing web scraping**: Perfect when you just need the data and don't need to see what's happening in the browser

Use headful mode when doing the following:

- **Developing or debugging locally**: Great for writing and troubleshooting tests
- **Testing interactive features**: Useful when you need to see how the app responds to user actions

Running your test directly in Node.js

If you prefer to run your test directly in Node.js, Playwright provides an option in the `launch()` method to toggle between headless and headful:

```
import { chromium } from 'playwright';

(async () => {
  // Headless mode
  const browser = await chromium.launch({ headless: true });
  const page = await browser.newPage();
  await page.goto(' https://playwright.dev/');
  // ... more actions
  await browser.close();
})();
```

To run a TypeScript test file with Node.js, first install the necessary packages:

```
npm install typescript ts-node @types/node
```

Then initialize a TypeScript config:

```
npx tsc --init
```

Now you can run your TypeScript file using `ts-node`:

```
npx ts-node example.spec.ts
```

That's it. You're up and running with TypeScript and Node.js.

In Node.js, you can even enable `devtools: true` to have the browser's developer tools pop open automatically, and you can add a `slowMo` delay to slow each action by a specified number of milliseconds, which gives you time to observe and interact with the page step by step:

```
import { chromium, Browser, BrowserContext, Page } from 'playwright';

(async () => {
  const browserHeadful: Browser = await chromium.launch({
    headless: false,
    devtools: true,
    slowMo: 50,
  });

  const context: BrowserContext = await browserHeadful.newContext();
  const page: Page = await context.newPage();
  await page.goto('https://playwright.dev/');
  await page.screenshot({ path: 'example.png' });

  await browserHeadful.close();
})();
```

Using this config gives you a clear visual of what's going on, which really helps when you're trying to spot and fix issues, especially UI-related bugs. It's also great for checking how things look, testing animations, and making sure interface behavior works as expected when a browser is actually visible.

Running Playwright directly in Node.js is useful for tasks such as web scraping or automating browser actions outside of a formal test automation suite. It's a handy way to interact with web pages programmatically (for example, extracting data or filling out forms) without integrating into a test runner such as Jest, Mocha, or Playwright Test.

If you're a QA engineer new to Node.js, think of it as more of a *scripted browser control* tool rather than a structured testing framework. Use it when your goal isn't to assert test results, but to automate or interact with the browser for utility purposes.

If you're looking to troubleshoot or just get a better understanding of what your Playwright tests are doing, the Playwright Inspector is a great tool to have in your toolkit.

Debugging with Playwright's Inspector

The **Playwright Inspector** gives you a visual interface where you can step through your test script, interact with the browser, and inspect elements and selectors in real time.

If a test fails inconsistently, the Inspector can help you zero in on the exact step where things go wrong and let you see what the page looked like at that moment. This makes debugging much easier.

It's also handy when you're working with locators. Before you commit a locator to your test script, you can use the Inspector's locator picker to make sure it accurately targets the element you want.

How to launch the Inspector

There are a few primary ways to launch the Playwright Inspector. Using the `--debug` flag is the most common way to debug. When you run your tests with this flag, Playwright will launch a browser in `headed` mode and open the Inspector alongside it:

```
npx playwright test --debug
```

To debug a specific test file or even a particular test within a file, you can use the following:

```
npx playwright test example.spec.ts --debug
npx playwright test example.spec.ts:10 --debug
```

The `:10` after `example.spec.ts` refers to line 10 in the `example.spec.ts` file. It tells Playwright to only run the test that is defined or starts on line 10 of the `example.spec.ts` file. This is a convenient way to run a specific test in a file that might contain multiple tests.

Another option is to launch your tests with debugging enabled by setting the `PWDEBUG=1` environment variable. For example, running `PWDEBUG=1 npx playwright test` will start your tests in debug mode and automatically open the Inspector window:

- Bash/Zsh (Linux/macOS):

  ```
  PWDEBUG=1 npx playwright test
  ```

- PowerShell (Windows):

  ```
  $env:PWDEBUG=1; npx playwright test
  ```

- Batch (Windows):

```
set PWDEBUG=1 && npx playwright test
```

When `PWDEBUG=1` is set, Playwright also applies some helpful defaults:

- Browsers launch in headed mode
- The default timeout is set to `0` (no timeout), preventing tests from failing prematurely during debugging

Using the Playwright Inspector

The Playwright Inspector consists of several parts. On the main side, it shows your test script with the current execution line highlighted. At the top, there are controls for pausing, resuming, and stepping through your test. Additionally, you can record user actions, which will be translated into code, and pick selectors by clicking on elements directly in the browser.

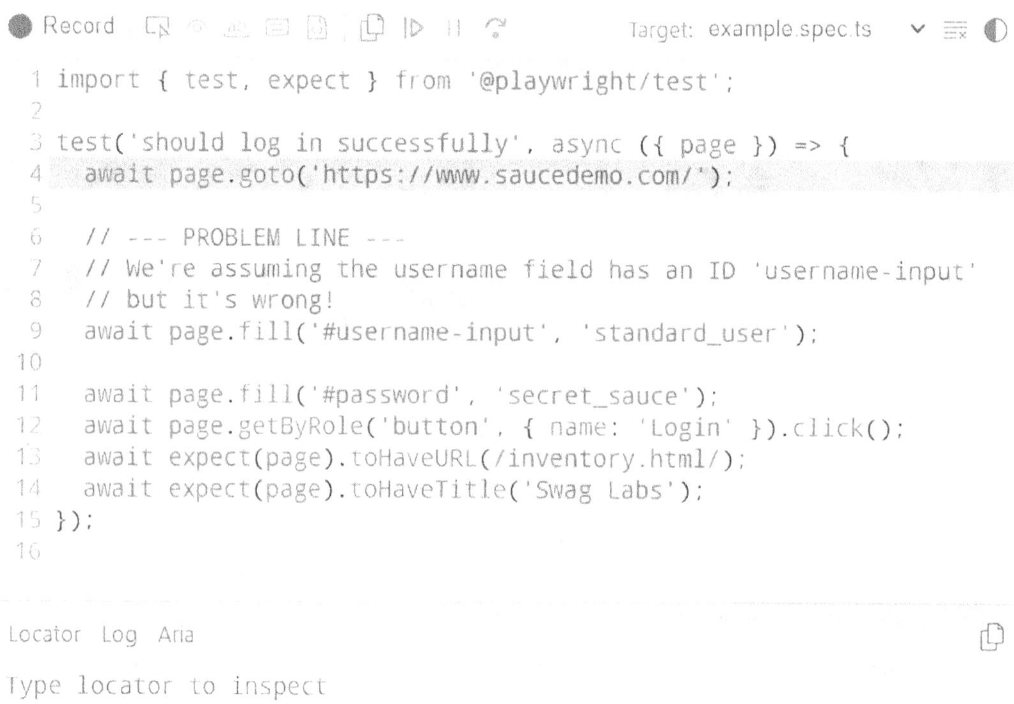

Figure 8.1: Playwright Inspector interface: controls are at the top left of the interface

When the Inspector opens, you'll see the following:

- **Actionability logs**: Provide detailed information about Playwright's actions, including why an element might not be interactive (not visible, not enabled, not stable). This is crucial for understanding why an action failed.
- **Toolbar for stepping**:
    - **Play/Resume**: Continues the test execution until the next `page.pause()` method or the end of the test.
    - **Step Over**: Executes the current Playwright action and pauses at the next one. This allows you to go through your test step by step.
- **Locator picker**:
    - This is a very useful feature. Click the **Pick Locator** button. Then, hover over elements in the browser window. Playwright will suggest locators for that element (prioritizing role, text, and test IDs).
    - Clicking an element will add its locator to the **Locator** tab in the Inspector. You can then live-edit this locator and see elements highlighted in the browser as you type, which helps you fine-tune your selectors.
    - You can copy the generated locator directly into your test code.

A practical example: fixing a failing login test

Suppose you're trying to automate a login process for a website. Your test code is failing because Playwright can't find the username input field:

```
import { test, expect } from '@playwright/test';

test('should log in successfully', async ({ page }) => {
  await page.goto('https://www.saucedemo.com/');

  // --- PROBLEM LINE ---
  // We're assuming the username field has an ID 'username-input'
  // but it's wrong!
  await page.fill('#username-input', 'standard_user');

  await page.fill('#password', 'secret_sauce');
  await page.getByRole('button', { name: 'Login' }).click();
```

```
    await expect(page).toHaveURL(/inventory.html/);
    await expect(page).toHaveTitle('Swag Labs');
});
```

Open your terminal in your Playwright project directory and run the test with the `--debug` flag:

```
npx playwright test tests/login.spec.ts --debug
```

A browser window will open, navigating to `https://www.saucedemo.com/`. The Playwright Inspector window will also open. The test will pause. Click the **Resume** button or *F8* on your keyboard to continue.

The line `await page.fill('#username-input', 'standard_user');` will be highlighted in the Inspector's source view.

Now, let's walk through the steps to find and apply the correct locator:

1. **Use the locator picker:**
    1. In the Playwright Inspector window, click the **Pick Locator** button.

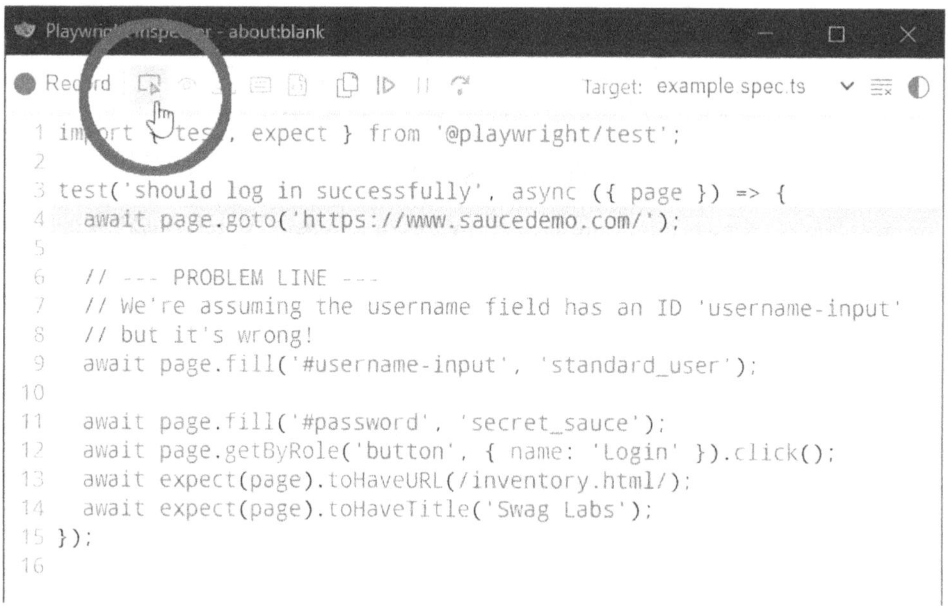

Figure 8.2: The Pick Locator button

    2. Now, move your mouse over the browser window. As you hover over elements, Playwright will suggest locators.
    3. Hover over the actual username input field on the page. As you hover, the Inspector suggests `locator('[data-test="username"]')`.

2. **Validate and refine the locator**:
    1. Click on the username input field in the browser window. The suggested locator will appear in the **Locator** input field within the Inspector:

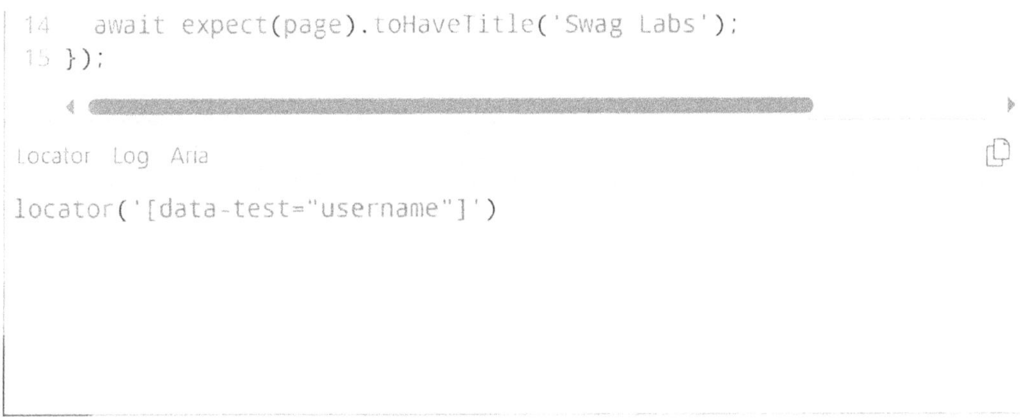

Figure 8.3: Locator tab in the Inspector

    2. In the Inspector's **Locator** field, type your new suggested locator: `locator('[data-test="username"]')`. Just a heads-up: you might see a different locator in this field. That's because Playwright is constantly evolving, and its locator mechanism keeps getting more efficient over time. As you type, Playwright will highlight the matching element(s) in the browser window. This confirms that your new locator correctly identifies the username field.

3. **Copy the corrected locator**: Once you're satisfied with the locator, click the **Copy** button next to the **Locator** field in the Inspector.

4. **Update your test code**: Go back to your `example.spec.ts` file and replace the incorrect locator:

```
import { test, expect } from '@playwright/test';

test('should log in successfully', async ({ page }) => {
  await page.goto('https://www.saucedemo.com/');

  // --- CORRECTED LINE ---
  await page.locator('[data-test="username"]').fill('standard_
user');

  await page.fill('#password', 'secret_sauce');
  await page.getByRole('button', { name: 'Login' }).click();
  await expect(page).toHaveURL(/inventory.html/);
  await expect(page).toHaveTitle('Swag Labs');
});
```

5. **Rerun**: Close the Inspector and the browser, then rerun your test without the `--debug` flag to confirm it passes.

This time, the test should pass successfully!

Inserting await page.pause() in your test code

For targeted debugging, you can insert `await page.pause();` at any point in your test script where you want to pause execution and open the Inspector. This is very useful for isolating problematic sections of your code:

```
test('my debugging test', async ({ page }) => {
  await page.goto('https://example.com');
  // ... some actions
  await page.pause(); // Execution will pause here and open the Inspector
  // ... more actions
});
```

When you run your tests with `page.pause()` present, the Inspector will automatically open at that point, regardless of whether `PWDEBUG` is set.

Suppose you're testing a login page. You could insert `page.pause()` after navigating to the site to examine the state before filling in the form. Once you've verified everything looks correct, you can continue execution. After debugging, simply remove the `pause` statement to return the test to normal.

While the Playwright Inspector is great for stepping through your tests interactively, sometimes you want an even more visual and intuitive way to understand what's happening. That's where Playwright's UI mode comes in.

Exploring UI Mode for debugging

Using **UI Mode** in Playwright makes debugging much more visual. You can actually see what's happening on the page step by step, which helps you quickly pinpoint where things might be going wrong or behaving unexpectedly.

The biggest differentiator from Playwright Inspector is time-travel debugging. You get a full visual timeline of every action, with DOM snapshots at each step. You can scrub through the timeline to see the page state at any past moment, which is invaluable for understanding how the UI evolved during the test.

UI Mode also helps you iterate faster through its **watch mode**. With watch mode, Playwright automatically re-runs your tests whenever it detects code changes. This saves a tremendous amount of time: there's no need to restart tests manually after every edit. You can simply adjust your code and instantly see the results.

Finally, all the important debugging information, such as the DOM, console logs, network requests, errors, and source code, is brought together in one convenient interface.

Launching UI Mode

To start UI Mode, run the following command in your terminal:

```
npx playwright test --ui
```

This will open a dedicated Playwright test runner window in your browser where you can do the following:

- See a list of your tests
- Click to run individual tests or groups

- View real-time logs and execution traces

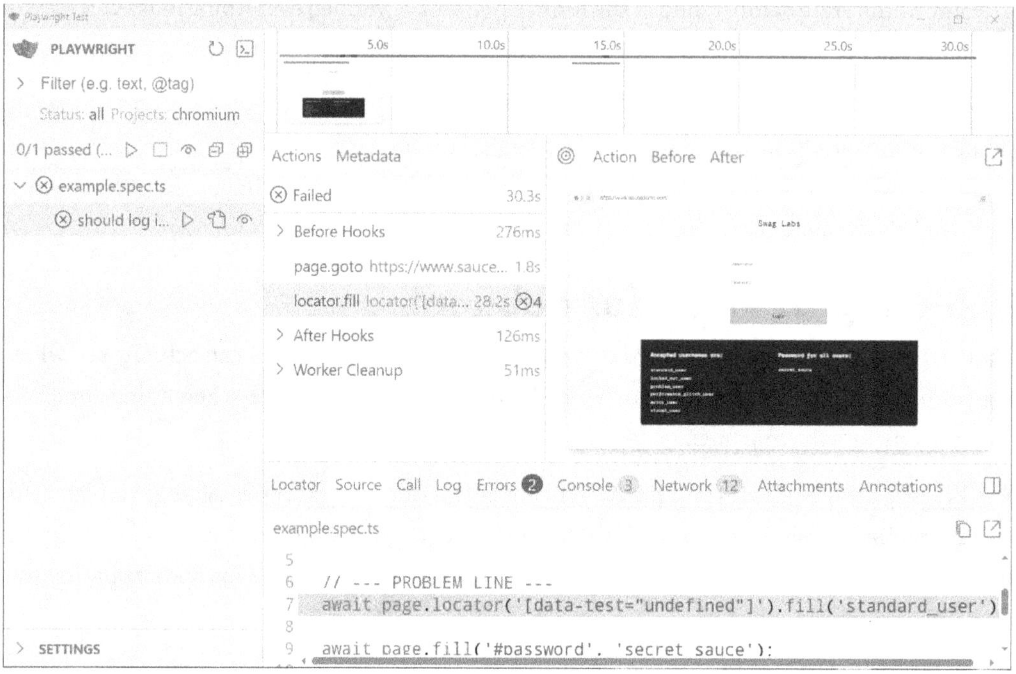

Figure 8.4: Playwright's UI Mode

As your tests run in the browser, you can watch each step unfold live. This real-time view is very helpful for spotting flaky behavior or tricky timing issues that might slip by in headless mode.

You can re-watch individual steps and inspect the state before, during, and after each action using the tabs above the rendered screenshot, which gives you detailed visibility into what's happening under the hood.

Just click through each step to see exactly where things go wrong. It's useful to catch problems with selectors, assertions, or timing that can be hard to pin down otherwise.

One advantage of using UI Mode is how clearly it surfaces dependency-related failures. Now, if a project dependency breaks (say a library update changes an expected behavior), you can immediately see where and why the failure occurred. The visual timeline, console logs, and network traces all highlight the exact point of failure.

Sometimes, even with the best-written tests, things go wrong. When they do, having a visual snapshot of the failure can be a game-changer.

Capturing screenshots for failed tests

Taking screenshots of failed tests is incredibly helpful when it comes to debugging. Instead of just reading through a stack trace, you get a visual snapshot of what the app looked like right when things went wrong, which can make tracking down the issue a whole lot easier.

Let's take a look at how Playwright makes this possible, along with some popular settings and best practices you can use.

Playwright's built-in screenshot-on-failure feature

Playwright Test provides a straightforward way to configure screenshot capture specifically for failed tests. This is done in your `playwright.config.ts` file, within the `use` section:

```
// playwright.config.ts
import { defineConfig } from '@playwright/test';

export default defineConfig({
  use: {
    // Capture screenshot after each test failure.
    screenshot: 'only-on-failure',

    // You can also configure other recording options here,
    // like video or trace, which are also very useful for debugging.
    // video: 'on-first-retry', // Example: record video on first retry
    // trace: 'on-first-retry', // Example: record trace on first retry
  },
});
```

The `screenshot` property allows you to use a few options:

- `'off'` (default): No screenshots are taken automatically.
- `'on'`: Screenshots are taken for every test, regardless of success or failure. This can be useful for visual regression testing or detailed documentation, but it generates many files.
- `'only-on-failure'`: This is the most common and recommended option for debugging failed tests. Playwright will automatically take a screenshot of the page when a test fails. The screenshot will be saved in your `test-results` directory (or wherever you've configured your output directory).

- `'on-first-retry'` (since Playwright 1.49): If you have retries configured for your tests, this option will capture a screenshot only on the first failure of a test, even if it's set to retry multiple times. This helps avoid generating redundant screenshots for every retry attempt of the same failure.

So, instead of trying to mentally reconstruct the test failure from logs, a screenshot provides immediate visual evidence, often pinpointing the root cause much quicker.

Also, when sharing test failure reports with developers or other QA team members, including a screenshot makes it much easier for them to understand and reproduce the issue.

Where are the screenshots saved?

When `screenshot: 'only-on-failure'` (or `'on'` or `'on-first-retry'`) is enabled, Playwright will save the screenshots in the `test-results` directory by default. Within `test-results`, you'll typically find a folder for each test run, and inside that, folders for individual tests. The screenshots will be named descriptively, often including the browser name.

Here's an example path:

`test-results/example-should-log-in-successfully-chromium/test-finished-1.png`

Manual screenshot capture

While the `screenshot: 'only-on-failure'` option is great for general test failures, you might have scenarios where you want more fine-grained control or to capture screenshots at specific points within your test logic, regardless of whether the test ultimately fails.

You can use `page.screenshot()` or `locator.screenshot()` for this:

```
import { test, expect } from '@playwright/test';

test('my custom screenshot test', async ({ page }) => {
  await page.goto('https://playwright.dev/');

  try {
    // Assert something that might fail
    await expect(page.locator('#undefined!')).toBeVisible();
  } catch (error) {
    // If the assertion fails, take a custom screenshot
    await page.screenshot({ path: 'shot.png', fullPage: true });
```

```
        console.error('Test failed, custom screenshot taken!');

        // Re-throw the error to ensure the test is marked as failed
        throw error;
    }
});
```

You can use the following parameters for `page.screenshot()` and `locator.screenshot()`:

- `path` (string): The file path to save the screenshot to.
- `fullPage` (boolean): Whether to take a screenshot of the full scrollable page (`default: false`, takes a screenshot of the viewport).
- `clip` (object): An object defining a rectangular area to clip the screenshot (like `{ x, y, width, height }`).
- `omitBackground` (boolean): Hides the default white background and allows capturing screenshots with transparency.
- `quality` (number): The quality of the image, between 0-100. Not applicable to PNG images.
- `type` (`'jpeg'` or `'png'`): The image format.

Playwright's HTML reporter is excellent for viewing test results, and it automatically embeds the screenshots taken on failure directly into the report, providing a seamless debugging experience.

To open the report run the following:

```
npx playwright show-report
```

This will launch a local server and open your default browser to display the interactive HTML report, where you can click on failed tests to see their details, including the captured screenshots.

Sometimes, even with screenshots and logs, it can be tough to figure out exactly what happened during a test. That's where video recordings come in.

Recording videos of test runs

When a test fails, or even when it passes but you want to visually verify the flow, having a video recording can be incredibly insightful. A video gives you a visual timeline of the user's interactions and the application's responses, which makes it much easier to pinpoint the exact moment and cause of the failure.

Even for successful tests, a video can help you confirm that the test is performing the intended actions and that the UI behaves as expected. Fortunately, Playwright provides a straightforward way to configure video recording.

Configuring video recording

Inside `playwright.config.ts`, add the following:

```
import { defineConfig } from '@playwright/test';

export default defineConfig({
  use: {
    // ... other configurations
    video: {
      mode: 'on',

      // Optional: specify video resolution
      size: { width: 1280, height: 720 },
    },
    // You also need to specify a directory for the videos
    contextOptions: {
      recordVideo: {
        dir: 'test-results/my-videos/', // Output directory
      },
    },
  },
  // ... other configurations
});
```

Let's take a closer look at the parameters:

- `mode`: The `mode` options for video may have the following parameters:
  - `'off'` (default): No video recording.
  - `'on'`: Records a video for every single test run, regardless of success or failure. This can generate a lot of video files.
  - `'retain-on-failure'`: Records a video for each test, but only keeps the video files for tests that fail. Successful test videos are automatically deleted. This is often a good balance.

    - `'on-first-retry'`: Records a video only when a test is retried for the first time. This is useful if you only want videos for flaky tests.
- `size`: You can specify the `width` and `height` for the recorded video. If not specified, Playwright defaults to the viewport size scaled down to fit 800x800. It's often beneficial to set this to match your desired test viewport size for clear recordings.
- `dir` (in `contextOptions.recordVideo`: You can specify the directory where Playwright should save the recorded video files. Playwright will generate unique names for each video. Keep in mind that this isn't required, but is useful if you want a way to view the videos outside of the HTML test report. Without this, the videos are still saved in the `playwright-report` folder based on the video mode option.

In Node.js, you can record the actions within a specific browser context:

```
import { chromium } from 'playwright';

(async () => {
  const browser = await chromium.launch();
  const context = await browser.newContext({
    recordVideo: {
      dir: 'test-results/my-videos/',
      size: { width: 1280, height: 720 },
    },
  });
  const page = await context.newPage();

  // Your automation steps here
  await page.goto('https://playwright.dev/');
  await page.getByText('Get started');
  // ...

  // Important: Videos are saved upon browser context closure.
  // Make sure to close the context and browser.
  await context.close();
  await browser.close();
})();
```

This script automates a browser, records all actions performed within a browser context (including navigation, clicks, etc.) as a video, and then saves that video to the `test-results/my-videos/` directory upon completion of the automation.

In this manual approach, you'll need to explicitly close the `context` to ensure the video file is saved. If your code doesn't record a video, it's likely because a runtime error in your automation script is preventing it from reaching the `context.close()` command. Start by checking the console for error messages to identify issues such as invalid selectors or network errors. Also, make sure the directory for saving the video exists and is writable.

Accessing recorded videos

After a test run (or manual execution), the video files will be located in the directory you specified (such as `test-results/videos/`). Playwright assigns unique names to these files (for example, `128d168173888fb.webm`).

For multi-page scenarios or when you need the path to a specific video, you can access it via the `page.video()` object:

```
import { test } from '@playwright/test';

test('my test with video', async ({ page }) => {
  await page.goto('https://playwright.dev/');
  // ... test steps

  // Get the path to the video file for this page
  const videoPath = await page.video()?.path();
  console.log(`Video saved at: ${videoPath}`);
});
```

Make sure to enable video recording in your `playwright.config.ts` file before running this code.

When recording videos of your tests, it's good to be mindful of file size. Videos can take up quite a bit of disk space, especially for longer test runs or when recording at higher resolutions. To help manage this, you might want to use the `'retain-on-failure'` or `'on-first-retry'` settings, which only save videos when they're really needed.

Recording does introduce a small performance hit. While the impact is usually minimal, it's worth noting, especially if you're working with a large suite of tests.

Also, remember to regularly clean up your `test-results/videos` directory. If you're using the `'on'` mode (which records all test runs), that folder can fill up fast, so a little housekeeping now and then goes a long way.

Lastly, test videos are typically saved in WebM format. The good news is that most modern browsers and media players can handle this format without any trouble, so you should be able to review your recordings easily.

Summary

By now, you've seen how headless mode can speed things up, which is great when you're running a lot of tests or working in a CI pipeline. But when you need to see what's going on visually, headful mode has your back. Playwright makes it easy to switch between headless and headful modes, which gives you flexibility depending on whether you're optimizing for speed or investigating test behavior.

While headless mode offers performance advantages ideal for CI pipelines and large test suites, headful mode shines when visual feedback is needed during development and troubleshooting. Tools such as **Playwright Inspector** and **UI Mode** provide deep insights into test execution.

Additionally, Playwright's ability to **capture screenshots, record videos, and generate detailed reports** lets you track down and document failures more effectively.

With these skills in your toolkit, you're well on your way to writing faster and easier-to-debug tests. Up next, we'll dive into testing for web accessibility.

9

Accessibility Testing with Playwright and axe-core

Creating an inclusive web experience is about making sure that everyone, no matter their abilities, can easily access and enjoy your digital content. In this chapter, we'll dive into the important topic of accessibility testing and walk you through how to build it right into your development process.

We'll show you how to use helpful tools such as **axe-core** for accessibility analysis, so you can catch and fix issues early on. That means smoother, more user-friendly websites that are also more likely to meet legal requirements.

You'll learn how to set up your accessibility testing environment, get a clear understanding of the **Web Content Accessibility Guidelines** (**WCAG**), and start writing automated tests to spot accessibility problems on your site.

Taking this proactive approach not only improves the experience for all your users, it also helps build trust in your brand and keeps you on the right side of accessibility laws.

As such, we will cover the following topics in this chapter:

- Integrating accessibility tools with Playwright
- Understanding WCAG compliance
- Writing automated tests for WCAG compliance
- Fixing common accessibility issues
- Complementing automated tools with manual accessibility testing

Technical requirements

The source code for this chapter is available at `https://github.com/PacktPublishing/Hands-On-Automated-Testing-with-Playwright/tree/main/Chapter09`.

Integrating accessibility tools with Playwright

You can catch accessibility issues early in your development process by integrating tools such as `axe-core` with Playwright. Typically, this kind of testing focuses on meeting standards such as the WCAG. Tools such as `axe-core`, **Lighthouse**, and **pa11y** are often used, with `axe-core` (by Deque Systems) being the most popular in the industry.

Adding these checks to your workflow not only boosts overall user experience but also helps you build more inclusive, user-friendly products right from the start.

Catching accessibility issues early with automation

Manually testing for **accessibility** (**a11y**) can be slow and error-prone. Adding automated checks to your existing **end-to-end** (**E2E**) test suite is a much more reliable way to catch issues.

> What is a11y?
>
> **A11y** is a common shorthand, or numeronym, for the word *accessibility*. The *11* refers to the 11 letters between the first letter, *a*, and the last letter, *y*, in *accessibility*. You'll often see it used by people in tech, design, and web development when they talk about making websites, apps, and digital content easy to use for everyone, no matter their abilities.

By running checks with every code commit, you can find and fix accessibility bugs before they reach production. This saves time and money. While automated tools can't catch everything (manual testing is still necessary for user experience flows), `axe-core` can detect over 50% of WCAG issues without false positives.

The results are provided directly in your test logs and point to the exact elements and rules that failed, which makes debugging straightforward.

Integrating axe-core with Playwright

The key tools we will be using in this chapter are `axe-core` and `@axe-core/playwright`:

- **`axe-core`**: This is a JavaScript library that can be injected into any web page to analyze its content against a comprehensive set of accessibility rules based on WCAG standards.
- **`@axe-core/playwright`**: This is the official community package that provides a seamless bridge between Playwright's browser automation capabilities and the `axe-core` engine. It simplifies the process of injecting axe and retrieving the results within a Playwright test.

Pairing Playwright with `axe-core` makes it easy to run accessibility checks right inside your tests. This way, you can stay on top of key standards such as WCAG, Section 508, and more. By running these checks early, you'll catch common issues such as missing alt text, wrong **Accessible Rich Internet Applications** (**ARIA**) roles, or low color contrast before they ever make it to production.

Plus, it scales well. You can easily integrate `axe-core` into your CI/CD pipelines, so accessibility testing becomes a consistent part of your release process, not an afterthought.

Writing tests that analyze the entire page

To get started, simply add the `@axe-core/playwright` package to your project as a development dependency:

```
npm install @axe-core/playwright --save-dev
```

Now, let's create a new test file, `tests/accessibility.spec.ts`. We will write a test that navigates to `wikipedia.org` and checks it for accessibility violations. This test will analyze the entire page and fail if any violations are found:

```
import { test, expect } from '@playwright/test';
import AxeBuilder from '@axe-core/playwright';

test.describe('Accessibility Tests', () => {
  test('should pass accessibility scan', async ({ page }) => {
    // Navigate to the page
    await page.goto('https://www.wikipedia.org/');

    // Run axe-core accessibility scan
    const results = await new AxeBuilder({ page })
      .withTags(['wcag2aa', 'section508'])
      .analyze();
```

```
    // Log violations for debugging
    if (results.violations.length > 0) {
      console.log('Accessibility violations:', results.violations);
    }

    // Assert no violations
    expect(results.violations).toEqual([]);

  });
});
```

This test passes because `wikipedia.org` doesn't have any accessibility issues. But if you run the test on a site that does have accessibility problems, Playwright will list all the violations right in your console. For example, the results from testing `sweetshop.netlify.app` show several accessibility issues:

```
Accessibility violations: [
  {
    id: 'color-contrast',
    impact: 'serious',
    tags: [
      'cat.color',
      'wcag2aa',
      'wcag143',
      'TTv5',
      'TT13.c',
      'EN-301-549',
      'EN-9.1.4.3',
      'ACT'
    ],
    description: 'Ensure the contrast between foreground and background
colors meets WCAG 2 AA minimum contrast ratio thresholds',
    help: 'Elements must meet minimum color contrast ratio thresholds',
...
```

The core of the accessibility scan process starts with the `AxeBuilder` constructor, which sets up the scan for the Playwright page you're testing. To focus on specific accessibility standards, you can use the `withTags()` method to filter the rules being checked (we'll discuss accessibility standards in a bit). Once everything is configured, calling `analyze()` runs the actual scan and returns a `results` object.

Inside this object, you'll find `results.violations`, which is an array containing any accessibility issues found. Each violation includes useful details such as a description of the issue, the elements affected, and suggestions for how to fix them.

No worries if the code doesn't make complete sense right now. As you continue through the chapter, it'll all become much clearer.

Understanding WCAG compliance

Inclusivity is about making sure everyone can access and use your website, no matter how they interact with it. That includes people who rely on screen readers, use only a keyboard for navigation, or depend on other assistive technologies.

There are also important legal requirements to consider. In many parts of the world, such as the U.S. with *Section 508* and Europe with *EN 301 549*, websites are required to meet accessibility standards such as the WCAG. Staying compliant helps keep your site on the right side of the law.

WCAG, developed by the **World Wide Web Consortium** (**W3C**), provides a framework for making web content accessible, primarily through success criteria organized under four principles: **perceivable, operable, understandable, and robust** (**POUR**).

Beyond regulations, improving accessibility also enhances the overall user experience. Clear navigation, readable text, and thoughtful design benefit all users, not just those with disabilities. It makes your website easier and more enjoyable for everyone to use.

Finally, addressing accessibility can help protect your brand from potential legal issues or negative publicity. Making your content accessible isn't just the right thing to do; it also protects you from legal headaches and helps everyone trust and enjoy what you offer. By putting accessibility first, you're showing your audience you genuinely care.

> The W3C is an international community that develops open standards to support the web's long-term growth and ensure that it works seamlessly across platforms. The WCAG is part of a series of standards published by the W3C's **Web Accessibility Initiative** (**WAI**).

The WCAG structure

WCAG is organized in a hierarchical structure:

- Principles: At the highest level are four foundational principles, often remembered by the acronym POUR:
    - **Perceivable**: Information and user interface components must be presented to users in ways they can perceive. This means providing alternatives for visual and auditory content (such as alt text for images and captions for videos).
    - **Operable**: User interface components and navigation must be operable. This ensures that users can interact with the website, regardless of their input method (such as keyboard navigation and voice commands).
    - **Understandable**: Information and the operation of the user interface must be understandable. This focuses on clear language, predictable functionality, and consistent navigation.
    - **Robust**: Content must be sufficiently robust to be reliably interpreted by diverse user agents, including assistive technologies. This means using web standards correctly so content remains accessible as technology evolves.
- Guidelines: Under each principle are guidelines, which are broader statements of accessibility goals. For example, under *Perceivable*, there's a guideline for *Text Alternatives*. These guidelines are not directly testable but provide the framework for the success criteria.
- Success criteria: These are the specific, testable statements that define what needs to be done to meet the guidelines. They are designed to be technology-neutral, meaning they apply to various web technologies.

Conformance levels

WCAG success criteria are categorized into three conformance levels, which build upon each other:

- **Level A (Minimum)**: This is the most basic level of accessibility. It addresses major barriers that would make a website difficult or impossible for certain users with disabilities to access. Meeting Level A criteria is essential for a website to be considered accessible, but it doesn't remove all barriers.
    - **Example**: Providing text alternatives (alt text) for non-text content such as images (*Success Criterion 1.1.1: Non-text Content*).

- **Level AA (Recommended)**: This is the most commonly aimed-for level and is often required by accessibility laws and regulations (*Section 508* in the US and *EN 301 549* in Europe). Level AA includes all Level A criteria, plus additional criteria that enhance accessibility for a broader range of users and provide a better user experience.
  - **Examples**: Ensuring a minimum contrast ratio for text and images of text (*Success Criterion 1.4.3: Contrast (Minimum)*); making content reflow without requiring two-dimensional scrolling (*Success Criterion 1.4.10: Reflow*).
- **Level AAA (Highest)**: This is the highest and most comprehensive level of conformance. Achieving Level AAA means meeting all Level A and AA criteria, plus additional criteria that provide the maximum level of accessibility. While highly desirable, it's not always practical or achievable for all types of web content, and WCAG itself doesn't recommend it as a general rule.
  - **Examples**: Providing sign language interpretation for prerecorded audio content (*Success Criterion 1.2.6: Sign Language (Prerecorded)*); ensuring a higher contrast ratio for text (*Success Criterion 1.4.6: Contrast (Enhanced)*).

> WCAG (`https://www.w3.org/TR/WCAG22/`) has evolved over time. WCAG 2.0, 2.1, and 2.2 are all current standards, with newer versions adding additional success criteria to address emerging technologies and user needs (such as mobile accessibility and cognitive disabilities). WCAG 2.2 is currently the latest version.

Customizing axe rules

The `withTags()` method in `AxeBuilder` lets you customize your accessibility scans by filtering which rules get applied. By specifying tags, you can limit the scan to rules associated with particular WCAG versions and levels (such as Level A or AA) or other categories such as best practices. This is especially helpful when you're working toward compliance with a specific standard, such as WCAG 2.1 Level AA, which is often a legal or organizational requirement.

Instead of manually figuring out the right tags for compliance, most teams adopt a standard configuration profile. Using profiles makes it easy to maintain consistency and ensure that you are targeting the right level of accessibility:

Profile strategy	Tags to use	When to use this
Standard baseline	`['wcag21aa']`	The default. This targets WCAG 2.1 AA. It is the current legal standard for most organizations and covers both A and AA rules.
Enhanced quality	`['wcag21aa', 'best-practice']`	Recommended. Combines the legal baseline with industry-accepted best practices (such as strict heading hierarchies) that improve the actual user experience.
Future-proof	`['wcag22aa']`	Forward-looking. Targets the newer WCAG 2.2 AA standard. Use this if you want to prepare your application for upcoming regulatory shifts.

Table 9.1: Common tag profiles for AxeBuilder accessibility scans

If you need to build a custom profile, here is what the individual tags represent:

- **`wcag2a`**: Refers to Level A conformance of the WCAG version 2.0 or 2.1. It represents the minimum level of accessibility, addressing essential requirements such as providing text alternatives for non-text content, but it doesn't ensure full accessibility for all users.
- **`wcag2aa`**: Refers to WCAG 2.0 or 2.1 Level AA rules, which include Level A requirements plus additional criteria, such as sufficient color contrast. This is often the target for many organizations as it provides a robust level of accessibility without being as stringent as Level AAA.
- **`wcag21a`**: Specifically targets WCAG 2.1 Level A rules. WCAG 2.1 builds on WCAG 2.0, adding criteria to address mobile accessibility, low vision, and cognitive disabilities.
- **`wcag21aa`**: Targets WCAG 2.1 Level AA rules, combining WCAG 2.1 Level A with additional Level AA requirements.
- **`wcag22aa`**: Targets WCAG 2.2 Level AA rules. WCAG 2.2 is a more recent standard, and `axe-core` (in versions 4.5 and later) includes support for these rules, which is useful for future-proofing accessibility efforts.

- `best-practice`: Refers to rules that are not strictly tied to WCAG success criteria but represent industry-accepted practices that improve accessibility, such as ensuring that every page has an `h1` heading. These are useful for enhancing user experience beyond minimum compliance.

It's important to remember that WCAG levels are cumulative. If you target Level AA, the rules for Level A are automatically included. You do not need to specify both.

Ensuring web accessibility is crucial for creating inclusive digital experiences. As we have seen, the WCAG provides a globally recognized standard for achieving this, but manually checking for compliance can be a time-consuming and error-prone process. This is where the power of automation comes in.

Writing automated tests for WCAG compliance

By integrating Playwright with `axe-core`, you can streamline your WCAG testing. This combination allows you to automatically scan your web applications for a wide range of accessibility issues, directly within your testing pipeline.

Leveraging axe-core for WCAG 2.1 AA accessibility audits

Suppose you're testing a website and want to ensure that it meets WCAG 2.1 Level AA; you could use the following:

```
import { test, expect } from '@playwright/test';
import AxeBuilder from '@axe-core/playwright';

test('Check for WCAG 2.1 A and AA compliance', async ({ page }) => {
  await page.goto('https://amazon.com');

  // Run axe-core accessibility scan
  const results = await new AxeBuilder({ page })
    .withTags(['wcag21a', 'wcag21aa'])
    .analyze();

  // Log violations for debugging
  if (results.violations.length > 0) {
```

```
    console.log('Accessibility violations:', results.violations);
  }

  // Assert no violations
  expect(results.violations).toEqual([]);
});
```

In this code, `withTags(['wcag21a', 'wcag21aa'])` ensures that only rules related to WCAG 2.1 Level A and AA are checked, and the test passes if no violations are found.

Remember, if you check for `wcag21aa` compliance, you're automatically checking for `wcag21a` as well, because Level AA inherently includes all Level A requirements. This means you can omit `wcag21a` from the `.withTags()` method in your code without missing any Level A checks:

```
import { test, expect } from '@playwright/test';
import AxeBuilder from '@axe-core/playwright';

test('Check for WCAG 2.1 A and AA compliance', async ({ page }) => {
  await page.goto('https://amazon.com');

  const results = await new AxeBuilder({ page })
    .withTags(['wcag21aa'])
    .analyze();

  if (results.violations.length > 0) {
    console.log('Accessibility violations:', results.violations);
  }

  expect(results.violations).toEqual([]);
});
```

The outcome is the same.

One nuance to note is that tags such as `wcag2a` and `wcag2aa` may apply to both WCAG 2.0 and 2.1, as WCAG 2.1 is backward compatible with 2.0. However, specifying `wcag21a` or `wcag21aa` ensures that you're focusing on the WCAG 2.1-specific rules. Similarly, `wcag22aa` is relevant for projects targeting WCAG 2.2, which `axe-core` supports in newer versions (4.5 and above).

The `best-practice` tag comes in handy when you want to go above and beyond WCAG requirements by adding extra recommendations that improve accessibility, even though they aren't required for compliance. Just keep in mind that using this tag might highlight things that aren't actual WCAG violations but could still affect the overall user experience.

If your violation list comes up empty when you were expecting to see issues, try a few quick checks: make sure the tag names are correct, confirm the page content actually relates to the rules you're testing, and double-check that the `axe-core` version you're using supports the standards you want.

> When testing dynamic content, make sure everything is fully loaded before scanning. Playwright's `waitForLoadState('networkidle');` method can help with this by ensuring that all content appears before your accessibility checks run.

Scoping the scan

Scoping a scan means telling `axe-core` which parts of the HTML document to analyze or ignore. This is useful for testing a specific component in isolation or excluding elements that are irrelevant to your test, such as third-party ads:

- `.include(selector)`: This method restricts the scan to *only the element(s) matching the provided CSS selector*. In the following example, `.include('form')` tells `axe-core` to analyze only the `<form>` element and its children. All other parts of the page are ignored.
- `.exclude(selector)`: This method scans the entire page *except for the element(s) matching the CSS selector*. In the following example, `.exclude('.ad-banner')` is used to skip any elements with the `ad-banner` class, which might be outside the development team's control.

Here's an example:

```
import { test, expect } from '@playwright/test';
import AxeBuilder from '@axe-core/playwright';

test('should analyze accessibility of the form and exclude the ad banner',
async ({ page }) => {
  await page.goto('https://demoqa.com/automation-practice-form');

  const results = await new AxeBuilder({ page })
    .include('form')        // Only analyze elements within the 'form'
    .exclude('.Google-Ad')  // Skip elements with .Google-Ad class
.analyze();
```

```
  // Log the violations for debugging/reporting
  if (results.violations.length > 0) {
    console.log('Accessibility Violations found:');
    results.violations.forEach(violation => {
      console.log(`- ${violation.id}: ${violation.description}`);
      console.log(`  Help: ${violation.helpUrl}`);
      console.log('  Nodes:', violation.nodes.map(node => node.html).
join('\n'));
      console.log('---');
    });
  }

  // If violations are found, this test will fail and list them.
  expect(results.violations).toEqual([]);
});
```

By calling `.include('form')`, we're telling `axe-core` to focus only on the `<form>` element and everything inside it, while ignoring the rest of the page. Then, with `.exclude('.Google-Ad')`, we fine-tune the scan even more by skipping over any elements with the `Google-Ad` class, even if they're inside the form.

This is handy for avoiding things like ads that developers might not have control over. The `.analyze()` method runs the scan based on those rules and gives us the results. This way, the test stays focused and efficient, checking just the parts of the page that matter most.

In this example, we're also including code that checks whether the `results` object returned by the Axe analysis contains any accessibility violations. If the violations array isn't empty (meaning violations were found), it logs information about each one to the console. This is useful for debugging and reporting because it clearly lists the specific problems that you need to fix.

This part of the code gives you all the details you need, such as the following:

- **The ID of the problem**: This tells you which specific rule was broken (for example, `color-contrast`)
- **A description of the issue**: This gives you a quick summary of what's wrong
- **A link to more help**: `axe-core` is great because it gives you a link you can click to learn more about the violation and how to fix it

- **The specific HTML elements**: It shows you the exact part of the page's code that's causing the problem

So, while the `expect(results.violations).toEqual([]);` line is what officially fails the test, the logging part is what gives you the information you need to actually go and fix the problems.

> You can use an `npm` plugin called the **Playwright Accessibility MCP Server**, which lets you run accessibility checks directly from a chat-enabled IDE using Playwright + Axe. It's especially helpful for exploratory testing, where an MCP-powered editor and chat interface make the process feel quick. But for ongoing, automated coverage, you'll still want to implement scripted Playwright + Axe tests in your code base so they can run consistently in CI and provide continuous feedback.

Using custom rules

You can also control which accessibility rules `axe-core` uses for its analysis. This helps you focus on specific accessibility concerns or temporarily disable rules that are not applicable:

- `.withRules(['rule-name-1', 'rule-name-2'])`: This configures the scanner to run *only the specified rules*. In the following example, `.withRules(['color-contrast', 'image-alt'])` limits the scan to checking only for color contrast issues and missing image alt text. All other accessibility checks are skipped.
- `.disableRules(['rule-to-disable'])`: This is the opposite of `.withRules()`. It runs all of the `axe-core` default rules *except for the ones you specify*. This is useful for ignoring a known issue or a rule that doesn't apply to your project's context.

Here is an example:

```
import { test, expect } from '@playwright/test';
import AxeBuilder from '@axe-core/playwright';

test('should not have accessibility violations on the page', async ({ page
}) => {
  await page.goto('https://www.google.com');

  const results = await new AxeBuilder({ page })
    // Only check for these two specific accessibility rules:
    .withRules(['color-contrast', 'image-alt'])
    .analyze();
```

```
    // You can also log the violations for more detailed
    // debugging if needed

    // Assert that there are no violations.
    expect(results.violations).toEqual([]);
  });
```

In this case, `.withRules(['color-contrast', 'image-alt'])` configures the scanner to check only for color contrast issues (ensuring that text is readable against its background) and missing alt text for images (ensuring that images have descriptive text for screen readers). By doing this, all other accessibility rules that `axe-core` checks typically are skipped, which allows you to focus on specific concerns.

> To keep your standards consistent, consider integrating these tests into your CI/CD pipeline using tools such as GitHub Actions. This way, accessibility remains part of your workflow from start to finish.
>
> You can define a fixture that builds and configures `AxeBuilder`. That way, you avoid duplicating setup across tests, and you get a consistent baseline (tags, excluded selectors, etc.) while still allowing test-specific tweaks such as `include()`. You can see how to set this up at `https://playwright.dev/docs/accessibility-testing#creating-a-fixture`.

The real work of building an accessible website starts after the scan is done. The next section will cover some of the most common issues found in these scans.

Fixing common accessibility issues

Automated tools such as `axe-core`, when paired with Playwright, are fantastic for catching accessibility issues early. But finding those issues is just the first step: fixing them is what truly makes your web app inclusive and user-friendly for everyone.

Let's walk through some of the most common accessibility problems these tools highlight, and look at practical ways to fix them so your site meets WCAG standards:

- **Low color contrast**:
    - **The issue**: Text that blends into the background can be hard to read, especially for people with low vision or color blindness. WCAG 2.1 requires at least 4.5:1 contrast for normal text and 3:1 for large text.

Figure 9.1: Example showing text with low color contrast

-
    - **How to fix**: Make sure your text and background colors have enough contrast to meet accessibility standards. It helps everyone read your content more easily. You can check this using handy tools such as **AccessibleWeb's Contrast Checker** (`https://accessibleweb.com/color-contrast-checker/`). Many design platforms also have built-in contrast checkers, so take advantage of them early and often while designing.
- **Missing labels on form fields**:
    - **The issue**: When input fields such as `<input>`, `<textarea>`, or `<select>` don't have proper labels, screen reader users can't tell what they're supposed to enter.
    - **How to fix**: To connect `<label>` to its input, use the `for` attribute. Set `for` to match the `id` value of the input like this:

```
<label for="username">Username:</label>
<input type="text" id="username">
```

Another option is to wrap the input in a label, though it's used less often. Here is an example:

```
<label>Username: <input type="text" id="username"></label>
```

- **Missing alternative text for images**:
    - **The issue**: When images don't have meaningful alt text or have empty `alt` attributes when they should describe something, screen reader users miss out on important information.

- **How to fix**: Use clear, concise alt text that explains what the image is showing, as in this example:

  ```
  <img src="puppy.jpg" alt="A golden retriever puppy playing
  with a ball.">
  ```

If the image is purely visual and adds no real information, use an empty `alt=""` value to let screen readers skip it, as in this example:

  ```
  <img src="spacer.gif" alt="">
  ```

- For complex images such as charts, use a short `alt` description, and give more detail nearby or link to it. This helps screen reader users get the full picture.

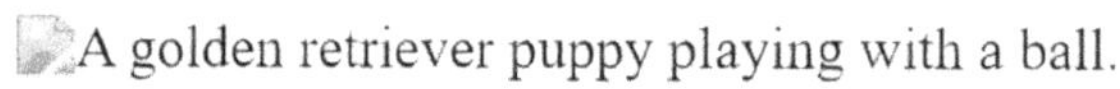

Figure 9.2: An image's alt attribute also provides fallback text if the image doesn't load

- **Keyboard navigation problems**:
  - **The issue**: Not everyone uses a mouse; some rely entirely on keyboards. If your site isn't keyboard-friendly, it's excluding those users.
  - **How to fix**: Make elements focusable. Use proper semantic HTML such as `<button>`, `<a>`, or `<input>`. If using something non-standard, add `tabindex="0"` to make it focusable.

Also, keep the tab order logical. Elements should follow a natural flow. Avoid setting `tabindex` values above `0` because they can mess up navigation.

It's important that users can always tell where they are when navigating with a keyboard. If the browser's default focus style isn't very noticeable, adding your own custom focus styles can make a big difference in visibility. Here's a simple example using CSS:

```
*:focus {
  outline: 2px solid blue;
}
```

The following screenshot demonstrates the resulting effect:

Figure 9.3: A custom focus style helps users clearly see which element is currently active or selected

- **Poor heading structure**:
    - **The issue**: Headings (`<h1>` to `<h6>`) help organize your content and make it easier to navigate, especially for people using screen readers. If headings are missing or out of order, it can be confusing and frustrating to follow the page.
    - **How to fix**: Start with a single `<h1>` heading. This is usually your page's main title. From there, use `<h2>`, `<h3>`, and so on for subsections. Be sure to keep the order logical: don't skip levels, such as jumping from `<h1>` straight to `<h3>`. While it's not a hard rule, it's a good idea to stick with just one `<h1>` heading per page for clarity.
- **Dynamic content isn't announced**:
    - **The issue**: When an application updates content on a page without a full page reload (such as displaying an error message after a user submits a form, showing a *loading* indicator, or a notification popping up), users of screen readers may not be aware of these changes. This is because screen readers often only read the content that is present when the page first loads or when a user navigates to a specific element.
    - **How to fix**: To solve this, you can use a feature called **ARIA** live regions. ARIA is a set of attributes that can be added to HTML elements to improve accessibility for people with disabilities. A live region is a special area on a web page that a screen reader monitors for changes. When content within a live region changes, the screen reader knows to announce it to the user.

      There are two main types of `aria-live` settings you can use to help screen readers announce updates on a page:

        - `aria-live="polite"`: This setting takes a gentle approach. It waits until the screen reader user has finished their current activity (such as reading a paragraph or filling out a form) before announcing the new content. It's great for non-urgent updates, such as a **loading...** message or a simple status change.
        - `aria-live="assertive"`: This one's more urgent. It tells the screen reader to immediately interrupt whatever it's doing to announce the new content. It's best for critical messages, such as errors, that the user needs to know about right away.

You can also pair `aria-live` with specific ARIA roles to give screen readers even more context:

- `role="alert"`: This role is often used with `aria-live="assertive"` to indicate that the content is an important, time-sensitive message (such as a form validation error).
- `role="status"`: Usually used with `aria-live="polite"`, this role signals that the message is a general status update, such as **Your changes have been saved**.

By tackling these common accessibility issues head-on, you're not just checking boxes: you're building a better, more inclusive web experience for everyone.

Automated accessibility tools such as `axe-core` are a great starting point, but they typically only cover about 30–50% of the WCAG criteria. To ensure that your site is truly accessible, it's important to complement automated testing with some manual checks.

Complementing automated tools with manual accessibility testing

As we've seen in this chapter, automated tools are great at spotting straightforward issues such as missing alt text on images, low color contrast, or incorrect HTML attributes (for example, missing ARIA labels). Where they fall short is in areas that need human judgment. For instance, is the link text descriptive enough (**Click here** versus **Learn more about our services**)? Does the reading order make sense for someone using assistive technologies? Are interactive elements easy to use with just a keyboard?

Automated tools can also overlook problems in content that loads dynamically (such as JavaScript-driven interfaces) or in more complex interactions. That's why manual testing is so important. It fills the gaps that automation can't cover, especially when it comes to ensuring compatibility with screen readers.

Test your app using popular screen readers such as the following:

- **NVDA** (**NonVisual Desktop Access**, free for Windows): `https://www.nvaccess.org/`
- **VoiceOver** (built into macOS and iOS): `https://support.apple.com/guide/voiceover/welcome/mac`
- **JAWS** (**Job Access With Speech**, a paid option for Windows): `https://www.freedomscientific.com/products/software/jaws/`

When testing, focus on how clearly the content is conveyed. Make sure that all text, including buttons, links, and form labels, is read aloud in a way that is both clear and meaningful. The screen reader should follow the intended order, moving naturally through headers, paragraphs, and interactive elements so that the experience feels consistent with the design of the page.

Images should include accurate alt text, and hidden elements should not cause confusion or leave gaps in the content.

Using only the *Tab*, *Enter*, and arrow keys, make sure every interactive element can be reached without relying on a mouse so that the site is accessible to people who depend on keyboard navigation.

You'll also want to give some thoughtful attention to managing focus. Active elements should have a clear, visible focus indicator, such as an outline. The movement of focus should feel logical, particularly in dynamic areas of the site such as modals or single-page applications, where navigation can otherwise become confusing.

Finally, review the clarity of the content itself. Text should be straightforward, concise, and free from unnecessary jargon so that it can be easily understood, including by users with cognitive disabilities.

Also, test how your content behaves when zoomed in. According to WCAG guideline *1.4.10 (Reflow)*, your content should still be readable and functional when zoomed to 400%. You can test this using your browser's zoom tools.

If you include any time-based media such as videos, make sure captions are available and accurate to meet guideline *1.2.2*. This helps users who are deaf or hard of hearing follow along with your content.

To make this actionable, use this "smoke test" checklist for a quick pass on any new feature or page:

- **Keyboard navigation (no mouse)**:
    - [ ] **Tab order**: Can you tab through every interactive element (links, buttons, and forms)? Does the order match the visual flow?
    - [ ] **Visible focus**: Can you clearly see which element has focus at all times (such as a ring or outline)?
    - [ ] **No traps**: Can you navigate in and out of all elements (such as modals or video players) using only the keyboard?
    - [ ] **Interaction**: Can you activate buttons with *Enter* or the spacebar, and interact with drop-down menus and sliders using arrow keys?

- **Visual and zoom:**
    - [ ] **400% zoom:** Set your browser zoom to 400% (or a mobile width). Does the content reflow into a single column without requiring horizontal scrolling?
    - [ ] **Color and contrast:** Are there any error messages or states conveyed only by color (such as a red border with no text label)?
- **Screen reader quick pass (NVDA/VoiceOver):**
    - [ ] **Meaningful sequence:** Turn on the screen reader and tab through. Do the announcements make sense?
    - [ ] **Images:** Do meaningful images have descriptive text, and are decorative icons ignored?
    - [ ] **Dynamic content (live regions):** If a status updates (such as a **Form Submitted** message), does the screen reader announce it automatically?
- **Media:**
    - [ ] **Captions:** If there is video, can you toggle captions on, and are they accurate?

It's best to start running accessibility tests early in the development process. Don't wait until the release stage. This helps you save time down the line.

Summary

In this chapter, we explored just how valuable it can be to bring accessibility testing into your development workflow, especially when combining the automation power of Playwright with the auditing strength of `axe-core`. This approach helps you catch accessibility issues early on, which not only saves time and effort but also makes sure your web applications are usable by everyone.

We also took a closer look at accessibility standards such as the WCAG, breaking them down from broad principles to specific success criteria, and the different conformance levels (*A*, *AA*, and *AAA*). Understanding this structure gives you the tools you need to create truly inclusive digital experiences.

Through hands-on examples using `AxeBuilder` and methods such as `withTags()`, `include()`, and `exclude()`, you've seen how to tailor your accessibility scans to focus on specific requirements such as meeting WCAG 2.1 Level AA compliance.

At the end of the day, making accessibility a priority isn't just about following regulations. It's about creating better experiences for everyone, strengthening your brand, and showing a real commitment to inclusion.

In the next chapter, we'll look at visual regression testing in Playwright, which involves setting up tests to compare screenshots, handling differences, and ensuring visual consistency.

10

Setting Up Visual Regression Testing

Modern web applications are constantly evolving, and even the smallest code change can unintentionally affect the **user interface** (**UI**). Traditional tests check whether your app *works*, while visual regression testing checks whether it still *looks* the way it should. It's a powerful technique to catch unexpected UI changes, such as a misaligned button or a missing icon, before they slip into production.

In this chapter, you'll learn how to use Playwright to capture and compare screenshots of your application, manage acceptable visual differences, and integrate visual testing into your development workflow. When you're fixing bugs or releasing new features, visual tests help ensure that your app stays visually consistent and polished across updates.

As such, we will cover the following topics in the chapter:

- Getting started with visual testing
- Capturing and comparing screenshots
- Managing acceptable visual differences
- Automating visual regression workflows
- How to keep visual tests stable and predictable

Technical requirements

The source code for this chapter is available at `https://github.com/PacktPublishing/Hands-On-Automated-Testing-with-Playwright/tree/main/Chapter10`.

Getting started with visual testing – capturing and comparing screenshots

Visual regression testing is a quality assurance process that checks for unintended visual changes in an application's UI. Instead of just testing functionality (such as *does this button work?*), it verifies that the UI looks the same as it did before.

Playwright has powerful, built-in tools to make this process seamless. The core idea is as follows:

- **Capture a screenshot**: You use the `page.screenshot()` method to take a screenshot of a specific element or the entire viewport
- **Compare with a baseline**: Playwright automatically compares this new screenshot with a baseline image that you've previously approved
- **Generate a diff image**: If there's a difference between the two images, Playwright generates a *diff* image, which is a visual overlay that makes differences between images easy to spot
- **Report the failure**: The test fails, and the test runner provides a clear report, including links to the new, baseline, and diff images

Before we can detect visual changes, we first need to capture what the UI looks like. Playwright makes this easy by allowing you to take screenshots of entire pages, specific elements, or custom regions. These images become the foundation for visual comparisons in future test runs. It helps you make sure your app still looks the way it's supposed to, especially after changes to your code.

Let's explore how to take high-quality screenshots, compare them with baselines, and understand when and why tests fail due to visual differences.

Simple screenshot capture (for debugging)

Sometimes you just want to take a screenshot for manual inspection or debugging. For this, you use the `page.screenshot()` method. This method saves a screenshot of the current viewport to a specified path.

Create a file called `tests/example.spec.ts` and add this:

```
import { test, expect } from '@playwright/test';

test('take a simple screenshot for debugging', async ({ page }) => {
  await page.goto('https://playwright.dev/');
```

```
  // Take a screenshot and save it as 'playwright_homepage.png'
  await page.screenshot({
    path: 'test-results/playwright_homepage.png'
  });
});
```

This code should capture a screenshot of `https://playwright.dev/` and save it to your `test-results` folder. By default, it captures only the viewport, but you can set `fullPage: true` to include the full scrollable content.

Here is an example:

```
import { test, expect } from '@playwright/test';

test('take a simple screenshot of header', async ({ page }) => {
  await page.goto('https://playwright.dev/');

  // Take a screenshot of the entire page
  await page.screenshot({
    path: 'test-results/playwright_homepage.png',
    fullPage: true
  });
});
```

You can also take a screenshot of a specific element instead of the entire page. This is great for testing individual components:

```
import { test, expect } from '@playwright/test';

test('take a simple screenshot of header', async ({ page }) => {
  await page.goto('https://playwright.dev/');

  // Take a screenshot of just the header element
  const element = page.locator('header');
  await element.screenshot({
    path: 'test-results/element-screenshot.png'
  });
});
```

This code will save a screenshot like this in the `test-results` folder:

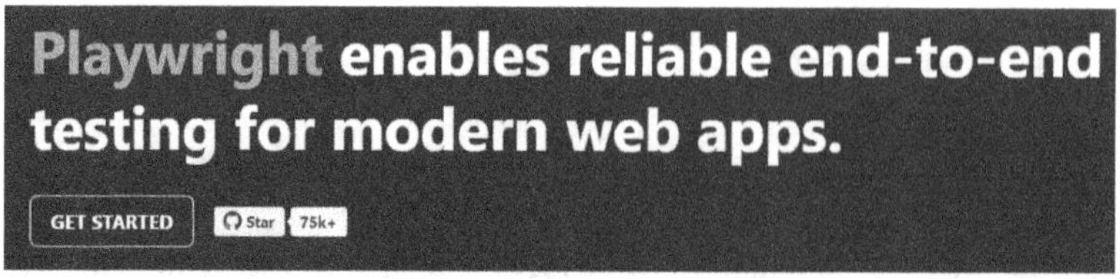

Figure 10.1: A screenshot of just the header element from playwright.dev

When you're writing tests, it's a good idea to focus on element-level screenshots, especially for smaller, isolated components. They help your tests run faster and make it easier to spot exactly where a visual change happened. Full-page screenshots can still be helpful in certain situations, but they're usually a bit more fragile and tougher to troubleshoot.

> Simply running `page.screenshot()` will put a nice image in your test report, but it provides zero test coverage. If you want Playwright to automatically catch visual regressions (layout shifts, broken CSS, or color changes), you must use the assertion method:
>
> ```
> await expect(page).toHaveScreenshot();
> ```
>
> We'll dive deeper into `toHaveScreenshot()` later in this chapter.

When using `page.screenshot()`, you have handy options to customize your screenshot.

Customizing your screenshot

Playwright provides a variety of arguments to customize the screenshot, from the file path and format to the specific area to be captured.

Core arguments

The following core arguments control where the screenshot is saved, its format, and the basic capture options:

- `path`: A string specifying the file path to save the screenshot. The file extension (such as `.png` or `.jpeg`) will determine the image format. If you don't provide a `path` option, Playwright will return a buffer containing the image data instead of saving it to a file.
- `type`: Specifies the image format. It can be `'png'` or `'jpeg'`. This is often inferred from the `path` extension, but you can set it explicitly.

- `fullPage`: A Boolean value. When set to `true`, Playwright will take a screenshot of the entire scrollable page, not just the visible viewport. The default is `false`, which captures only what's currently displayed.
- `quality`: An integer between 0 and 100. This option is only applicable to `jpeg` screenshots and controls the compression quality. A higher number means a higher-quality image but a larger file size.

Clipping and masking

These options allow you to capture specific parts of a page or hide sensitive or dynamic content during the screenshot process:

- `clip`: An object that specifies a rectangular area of the page to capture. It must contain the following properties:
    - `x`: The *x* coordinate of the top-left corner of the clip area
    - `y`: The *y* coordinate of the top-left corner of the clip area
    - `width`: The width of the clip area
    - `height`: The height of the clip area

  For example, you can use the `clip` option to capture the top-left corner of a page like this:

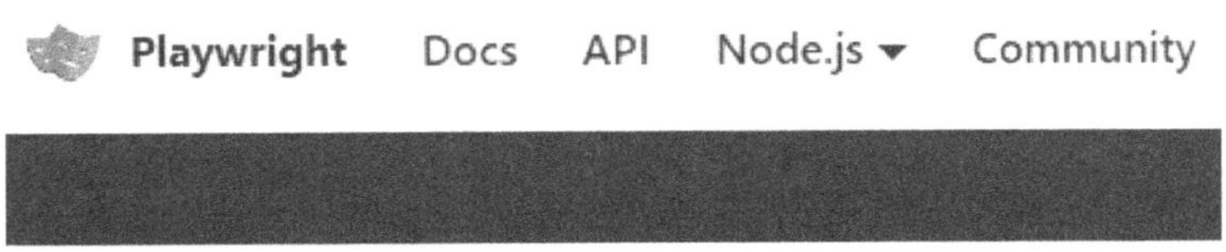

Figure 10.2: In this case, we're using clip: {x:0, y:0, width:500, height:100} to capture part of the Playwright home page

- `mask`: An array of `Locator` objects. Any elements matching these locators will be covered with a pink overlay when the screenshot is taken. This is useful for masking out dynamic or volatile content, such as ads or timestamps, to make your screenshots more consistent for visual testing.

Advanced customization

For more control, these arguments let you adjust background, scaling, timing, and behavior during the screenshot:

- `omitBackground`: A Boolean value. When set to `true`, Playwright will hide the default white background, allowing you to capture a screenshot with a transparent background. This is only supported for `png` images.
- `scale`: This argument controls the scaling of the screenshot:
    - `'css'`: The screenshot will have one pixel per CSS pixel on the page. This is useful for keeping file sizes small on high-resolution displays.
    - `'device'`: The screenshot will have one pixel per physical device pixel. This will result in a higher-resolution image on high-DPI screens. The default value is `'device'`.
- `timeout`: A number in milliseconds. It sets the maximum time Playwright will wait for the page to be ready before taking the screenshot. The default is `30` seconds.
- `animations`: This argument can be set to `'disabled'` to stop CSS animations, CSS transitions, and web animations before taking the screenshot. The default is `'allow'`.
- `caret`: Can be set to `'hide'` to hide the text caret (cursor) in input fields.

You can combine these arguments to create highly specific and controlled screenshots for a variety of use cases. For example, to create a lightweight, high-speed screenshot of a specific element that needs a transparent background and should not be affected by any active animations, you could combine them like this:

```
await page.locator('#my-element').screenshot({
    omitBackground: true,    // Transparent background
    scale: 'css',            // Smaller file size
    animations: 'disabled', // Freeze all animations
    timeout: 5000            // Wait a maximum of 5 seconds
});
```

The Playwright team often adds more nuanced and powerful options over time to address more advanced use cases. Playwright's documentation is always the best place to find the most current and comprehensive list of arguments, as it's kept up to date with each new release: `https://playwright.dev/docs/api/class-page#page-screenshot`.

Comparing screenshots (visual regression testing)

Comparing screenshots is a great way to catch visual changes. Let's walk through a simple example step by step. Here, we'll use `https://practicesoftwaretesting.com/` and compare it with its buggy version: `https://with-bugs.practicesoftwaretesting.com/#/`.

Step 1: the first run (creating the golden snapshot)

Create a file called `tests/example.spec.ts` and add this:

```
import { test, expect } from '@playwright/test';

test('Homepage should look the same', async ({ page }) => {
  await page.goto('https://practicesoftwaretesting.com/contact');

  // This is the magic line!
  await expect(page).toHaveScreenshot('homepage.png');
});
```

The `toHaveScreenshot()` assertion makes screenshot comparisons easy with almost no setup. Here's what happens the *first* time you run it (since there's no baseline image yet):

1. Playwright takes a screenshot.
2. It saves it in a special snapshots folder.
3. It fails the test (on purpose, since there's nothing to compare it to yet).

Now, you could run the test with the following:

```
npx playwright test
```

You'd see something like this in the output:

```
Running 1 test using 1 worker
✓ tests/example.spec.ts:4 ' Homepage should look the same (5s)
› Error: A snapshot doesn't exist at tests\example.spec.ts-snapshots\
homepage-chromium-win32.png, writing actual.
```

The filename includes both the browser (`chromium`) and your operating system (`win32` for Windows, in this case). That way, your snapshots are always compared against the right environment.

> Use clear and descriptive names for your snapshots. Instead of something vague, such as `test1.png`, go with something such as `checkout-summary-error.png`. This makes it much easier to understand what each snapshot represents, especially when you're reviewing test results or reports with your team.

Step 2: subsequent runs (the comparison)

Now that you have a golden snapshot, run the test again:

```
npx playwright test
```

From now on, every run will do the following:

- Take a new screenshot in memory
- Compare it pixel by pixel with the corresponding golden snapshot on disk
- Pass the test if they match (or if the differences are small enough to fit the threshold you've set)

Step 3: handling failures (when the UI changes)

If your UI looks different from the baseline, the test will fail, and Playwright will tell you exactly what changed.

For example, you might see a message like this:

```
9301 pixels (ratio 0.02 of all image pixels) are different.
```

Let's update our test to use the buggy site so we can see this in action. In `tests/example.spec.ts`, change it to the following:

```
import { test, expect } from '@playwright/test';

test('Homepage should look the same', async ({ page }) => {
  await page.goto('https://with-bugs.practicesoftwaretesting.com/#/
contact');

  await expect(page).toHaveScreenshot('homepage.png');
});
```

Now, run the `report` command:

```
npx playwright show-report
```

The HTML report will show you three images side by side:

- The **expected** image (your golden snapshot)
- The **actual** image (the new screenshot)
- The **diff** image, with differences highlighted

Try using the visual slider in the report to drag between **Expected** and **Actual**. This gives you a concrete feel for how Playwright spots changes:

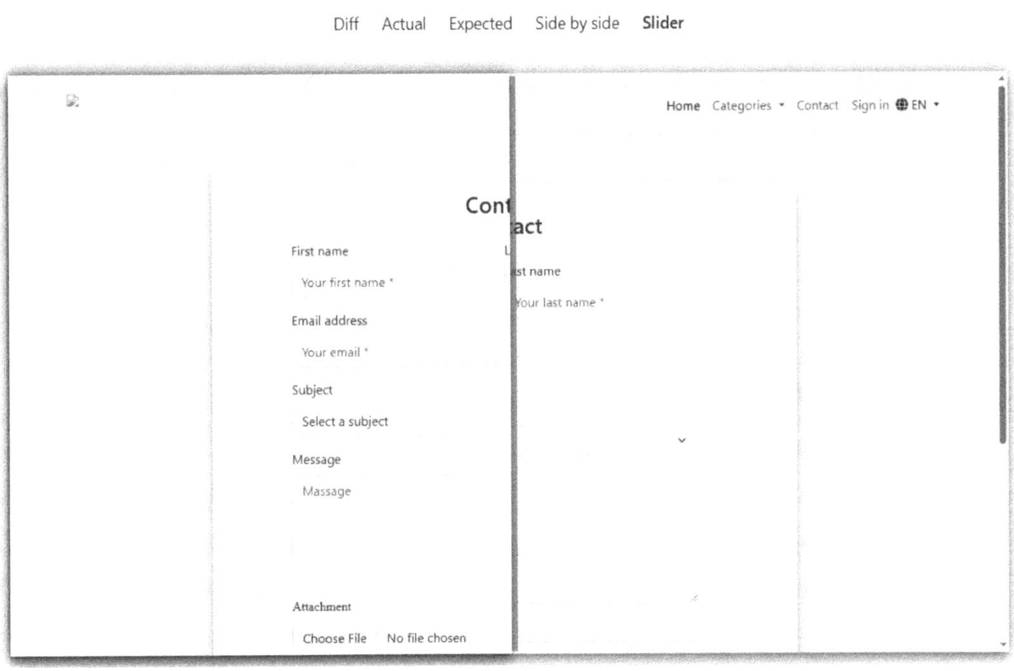

Figure 10.3: The visual slider lets you drag between the "expected" and "actual" versions

> Because visual snapshots are part of your test baseline, you should commit them to your version control system (such as Git). This allows your team to track intentional UI changes and review visual diffs alongside code changes.

Step 4: updating the golden snapshot

If the UI change was intentional (for example, you changed a button's color), you need to update the golden snapshot. You do this by running the `test` command with the `--update-snapshots` flag:

```
npx playwright test --update-snapshots
```

This command tells Playwright to overwrite the old golden snapshots with the new versions. After running this, you should commit the updated snapshots to your Git repository.

> If you need more control, or if you're not using Playwright Test, you can manually compare screenshots with libraries such as pixelmatch (`https://github.com/mapbox/pixelmatch`).

Sometimes, tiny differences in screenshots, such as subtle font rendering changes or anti-aliasing quirks, can cause tests to fail, even though nothing's actually broken. That's where managing acceptable visual differences comes in.

Managing acceptable visual differences

Playwright gives you flexible tools to control how strict your visual comparisons are. You can set thresholds to allow minor pixel changes or mask out dynamic elements such as timestamps to make your tests more reliable across different environments. In this section, you'll learn how to fine-tune these settings so your tests only flag meaningful visual changes and ignore the noise.

Configuring thresholds

Pixel-perfect comparisons can sometimes be too strict, especially due to minor anti-aliasing differences across machines. You can relax the comparison rules using the following options:

- `maxDiffPixels`: The maximum number of pixels that are allowed to be different.
- `threshold`: A number between `0` and `1`. This is a per-pixel color tolerance. A value of `0.2` means a pixel's color can differ by up to 20% to still be considered a match.

You can set these options per-assertion or globally in `playwright.config.ts`. Per-assertion configuration is useful when you need custom tolerances for specific screenshots.

Let's say we set the `maxDiffPixels` option to a very high value while testing the buggy site. That way, Playwright won't complain about the pixel differences:

```
import { test, expect } from '@playwright/test';

test('Homepage should look the same', async ({ page }) => {
  await page.goto('https://with-bugs.practicesoftwaretesting.com/#/
contact');

  await expect(page).toHaveScreenshot('homepage.png', {
```

```
    maxDiffPixels: 10000, // allow up to 10000 differing pixels
  });
});
```

You can also use global configuration (`playwright.config.ts`) to reduce repetition across tests:

```
import { defineConfig } from '@playwright/test';

export default defineConfig({
  expect: {
    toHaveScreenshot: {
      threshold: 0.2,         // 20% pixel ratio difference allowed
      maxDiffPixels: 100      // max pixels allowed to differ
    },
  },
  // other options ...
});
```

This global config applies unless overridden in individual assertions.

Don't forget to include your snapshots in version control. By committing them alongside your code, you create a clear project history that shows when and why visual changes were made. This makes rollbacks and reviews simpler and helps maintain a stable and predictable UI over time.

Masking dynamic elements

Your page might contain dynamic content such as ads, timestamps, or animations that will always cause screenshot tests to fail. You can *mask* these elements, telling Playwright to ignore them during the comparison.

The following is an example:

```
await expect(page).toHaveScreenshot('homepage.png', {

  // Pass an array of locators to mask
  mask: [page.locator('.dynamic-timestamp'),
         page.locator('.user-avatar')]
});
```

The `{ mask: [...] }` options object customizes how the screenshot is taken. Inside the `mask` array, you can include elements that you want to hide during the screenshot. Playwright will "mask" those elements, so they won't show up when capturing or comparing the screenshot.

Just keep in mind that everything else on the page still needs to match the reference image (`homepage.png`) for the test to pass.

Once you've mastered capturing and comparing screenshots, the next step is to make visual testing part of your everyday development process. Manual testing is helpful during development, but automation is what truly unlocks the power of visual regression testing.

Automating visual regression workflows

Visual regression testing becomes most powerful when it's seamlessly integrated into your development and deployment workflows. Automating these tests ensures that any unintended UI changes are caught early, ideally before they ever reach production.

The core idea is to make visual testing a standard, automated check, just like unit or integration tests.

Overview of the automated workflow

Here's how the automated workflow typically operates within a Git and CI/CD environment:

1. **Baseline screenshots**: Your project repository contains a set of *golden* or baseline screenshots. These are the approved, correct versions of your application's UI components or pages.
2. **Developer makes a change**: A developer modifies the code (for example, changes a CSS style or refactors a component) and pushes it to a new branch, creating a pull request.
3. **CI pipeline triggers**: The push automatically triggers a CI pipeline. This pipeline executes a series of jobs, including your Playwright tests.
4. **Playwright executes tests**: Inside the CI environment, Playwright performs the following steps for each visual test:

    - It navigates to the specified page or component
    - It takes a new screenshot
    - It compares this new screenshot pixel by pixel with the corresponding baseline screenshot stored in the repository

5. **Results and feedback**:
   - **No differences found**: If the new screenshots perfectly match the baselines, the test passes. The CI check shows a green checkmark, which signals that the UI is visually unchanged and the pull request is safe to merge from a visual standpoint.
   - **Differences found**: If Playwright detects any visual mismatch, the test fails. The CI check shows a red X. The pipeline generates a report that includes the *baseline* image, the *new (actual)* image, and a *diff* image that highlights the exact differences. This immediately alerts the developer that their change had an unintended visual side effect.
6. **Review and update**:
   - **If it's a bug**, you fix the code and push again, re-running the workflow.
   - **If the change is intentional** (such as a planned button color change), you run a command locally (`npx playwright test --update-snapshots`) to update the baseline screenshots, commit these new baselines to their branch, and push. The CI will then run again, and this time the tests will pass because the new baseline matches the new UI.

Example with GitHub Actions

Integrating this into a CI/CD pipeline is straightforward. Here is a simple example of a GitHub Actions workflow file that automates this process:

```
# .github/workflows/playwright.yml

name: Playwright Tests

on:
  push:
    branches: [ main, master ]
  pull_request:
    branches: [ main, master ]

jobs:
  test:
    runs-on: ubuntu-latest
    steps:
```

```
      - uses: actions/checkout@v4

      - name: Install Node.js
        uses: actions/setup-node@v4
        with:
          node-version: lts/*

      - name: Install dependencies
        run: npm ci

      - name: Install Playwright Browsers
        run: npx playwright install --with-deps

      - name: Run Playwright tests
        run: npx playwright test

      - name: Upload test report
        # This step runs only if tests fail to upload the diffs
        if: failure()
        uses: actions/upload-artifact@v4
        with:
          name: playwright-report
          path: playwright-report/
          retention-days: 30
```

We've already touched on integrating Playwright tests into CI/CD workflows earlier in *Chapter 7, Integrating Workflows with CI/CD Pipelines*, but here's a quick refresher on the key steps involved in the automation script.

First, there's the `actions/checkout@v4` step. This checks out your code, including any baseline screenshots, so everything needed for testing is available in the CI environment.

Next up is `npm ci`, which installs your project's dependencies in a clean and reliable way. This ensures the testing environment is consistent every time the workflow runs.

Then, the `npx playwright install --with-deps` command installs all the necessary browsers and operating system-level dependencies within the CI runner. This step is essential for making sure there are no rendering differences between your local machine and the CI system.

After that, we have `npx playwright test`. This runs your Playwright tests and automatically enters comparison mode. If any mismatches are found, the tests will fail, which helps you catch visual regressions early.

Finally, if the tests do fail, `actions/upload-artifact@v4` comes into play. It uploads the Playwright report, including baseline, actual, and diff images, as an artifact. This way, you can easily download and review the visual differences directly from the GitHub pull request.

> Run visual tests early and often (ideally on every pull request). This helps you catch visual bugs before they make it into your main branch and ensures your UI stays consistent throughout development.
>
> Modern apps often support multiple themes. Visual tests should verify active themes because color/contrast differences can hide or reveal layout issues. You can test themes by doing the following:
>
> - Toggling the UI control
> - Setting cookies or `localStorage` keys that the app reads
> - Using saved `storageState`
> - Injecting an attribute/CSS before the page loads
>
> Each approach will be decided by the system you are testing and will have different trade-offs. The most realistic is toggling the UI, while `storageState` is often the most stable for CI.

Visual tests are great for catching UI issues, but they can be surprisingly fragile. To get the most out of them and avoid chasing down false positives, it's important to create a stable, consistent testing setup.

How to keep visual tests stable and predictable

Visual tests can be a bit picky. They tend to break when even small details in the test setup change. Things such as a different operating system version, screen resolution, or browser engine can cause tests to fail, even if your app is working just fine.

These unpredictable failures are often called *flaky* because they're inconsistent and tricky to reproduce. One of the best ways to avoid flaky visual tests is to standardize your testing environment. For example, always using the same browser (such as a specific version of Chromium) across all tests helps prevent issues caused by differences in how browsers render pages. Even tiny changes, such as a Chrome update, can alter how fonts, colors, or layouts appear, which might trip up your tests.

If you generate your baseline screenshots (those golden reference images) on a local Windows or Mac machine, they often embed operating system-specific details or subtle rendering quirks that don't match up with CI environments, such as GitHub Actions running on Ubuntu.

This can result in a mismatch, where your tests pass locally but fail in CI, or vice versa, even across different browser types. To sidestep this, it's smart to generate or update your baselines directly in a Docker container that replicates your CI setup, ensuring everything from the operating system to the browser behaves identically (we have covered Docker in more detail in *Chapter 7, Integrating Workflows with CI/CD Pipelines*).

You can achieve this by running your tests inside an official Playwright Docker image. Start by pulling an image based on Ubuntu, such as `mcr.microsoft.com/playwright:v1.56.1-noble`, for standard setups, or the ARM64 variant for M1 Macs (you can find a list of images at `https://mcr.microsoft.com/en-us/artifact/mar/playwright/`).

Then, use a command such as this to mount your project, install dependencies, and update snapshots:

```
docker run --ipc=host --shm-size=1gb --rm --network host -v $(pwd):/work/
-w /work/ -it mcr.microsoft.com/playwright:v1.56.1-noble /bin/bash
```

Once inside the container, run the following:

```
npm ci && npx playwright install --with-deps && npx playwright test
--update-snapshots
```

This setup takes snapshots in a Linux environment that matches CI, so you don't have to worry about those annoying operating system quirks: your visual tests stay consistent. If you're working with specific browsers or different architectures, just tweak the Docker image as needed. A little effort up front saves you a lot of headaches later.

Another helpful tip is turning off animations and transitions during tests. Things such as fade-ins or sliding menus can make your screenshots inconsistent, especially if the test happens to catch an animation mid-motion. By adding a simple CSS rule like the following, you can make sure everything stays still and fully rendered when screenshots are taken:

```
* {
  transition: none !important;
  animation: none !important;
}
```

This leads to much more stable and reliable test results. The more predictable you can make your test environment and app behavior, the fewer false alarms you'll get from your visual tests.

> When dealing with dynamic content such as multi-language applications, text length changes (such as German versus English) can trigger false positives in visual tests. Instead of masking these areas (which might hide real bugs), the best approach is to segment your tests using Playwright projects in your `playwright.config.ts` file. By creating a specific project for each locale, you generate separate, stable baselines for every language.

Summary

Visual regression testing is an essential layer of quality assurance that helps ensure your application's UI stays consistent and reliable even as the code evolves. With Playwright's built-in tools, capturing and comparing screenshots becomes a straightforward process, whether you're testing an entire page or a single element.

In this chapter, you learned how to take and compare screenshots, manage acceptable visual differences, and automate these tests within a CI/CD pipeline. By combining these practices with thoughtful test design and stable environments, you can confidently catch unintended UI changes before they reach your users.

As you continue building modern, visually rich applications, visual testing will become a key part of your toolkit, which helps you ship changes faster, with fewer surprises.

In the next chapter, we'll focus on testing mobile web experiences by simulating devices and handling responsive designs.

11

Testing Mobile Web Experiences

As more and more people browse the web on their phones and tablets, mobile testing has become an important part of the testing strategy. Whether someone's scrolling on an iPhone, tapping through on Android, or relaxing with a tablet in hand, your app should look great and run great on every screen. That's exactly what mobile testing helps make happen.

In this chapter, we'll explore how easy Playwright makes it to test your site on mobile devices, even if you don't have any actual phones or tablets lying around. You'll learn how to use built-in device presets, create your own custom setups, and simulate real-world conditions such as slow network speeds, different locations, and screen rotations.

We'll also cover how to test mobile-specific interactions such as taps, and show you how to debug when things don't go quite as expected. By the end, you'll be well-equipped to make sure your app works beautifully for every user, no matter what device they're using.

As such, we will cover the following topics in the chapter:

- Understanding emulation versus real devices
- Configuring Playwright for mobile emulation
- Simulating real-world scenarios with Playwright emulations
- Debugging mobile-specific issues
- Common mobile-specific issues and solutions

Technical requirements

The source code for this chapter is available at

`https://github.com/PacktPublishing/Hands-On-Automated-Testing-with-Playwright/tree/main/Chapter11`.

Understanding emulation versus real devices

Before diving into this chapter, it's important to understand the environment you're testing in. There are two main ways to test mobile experiences with Playwright:

- **Mobile emulation**: This is Playwright's default and most common approach. It uses desktop versions of Chrome, Firefox, and WebKit to simulate the properties of a mobile device, including its viewport size, user agent, touch capabilities, and device scale factor. Emulation is fast, cheap, and excellent for catching layout, CSS, and responsive design issues.
- **Real devices**: For issues related to specific hardware, OS-level integrations, or carrier networks, testing on real physical devices is necessary. Playwright can connect to the Chrome browser on an Android device via the **Android Debug Bridge** (**ADB**) or run tests against mobile browser farms in the cloud. However, for most day-to-day debugging of web application behavior, emulation is your first line of defense.

In this chapter, we focus on debugging within Playwright's emulation context, as this is where you'll spend most of your development time.

Configuring Playwright for mobile emulation

One of the best things about Playwright is how easy it makes mobile testing. It comes with a built-in library of device descriptors, which are basically ready-to-go profiles for popular devices, including iPhones, Android phones, iPads, and more.

These profiles are pre-configured with all the details you'd need to simulate a real mobile device: screen size, user agent, touch support, and even the device's scale factor. It's a quick way to see how your site will look and behave on devices without needing the physical hardware.

Using built-in device descriptors

To use one of these device profiles, you can simply import the `devices` object from the Playwright library. When you create a new browser context, you can spread the properties of a specific device descriptor from the `devices` object. This configures the new context with all the relevant settings for that device.

Let's walk through an example using the `'iPhone 15 Pro Max'` descriptor to test how your layout looks on that device:

```
import { test, expect, devices } from '@playwright/test';

test.describe('Responsive layout on mobile', () => {
  test('should display the mobile navigation menu on iPhone 15 Pro Max',
async ({ browser }) => {

    const iPhone15PM = devices['iPhone 15 Pro Max'];

    // Create a new browser context with iPhone 15 Pro Max settings
    const context = await browser.newContext({
      ... iPhone15PM ,
    });
    const page = await context.newPage();

    await page.goto('https://github.com');

    const mobileMenuButton = page.getByRole('button', { name: 'Toggle
navigation' });
    await expect(mobileMenuButton).toBeVisible();

    // Clean up the context
    await context.close();
  });
});
```

In this example, we import the `devices` object from the playwright library. We then access the `'iPhone 15 Pro Max'` descriptor and spread its properties into the `newContext()` method. This single line of code configures the browser context to behave like an iPhone, with the right user agent and viewport settings included:

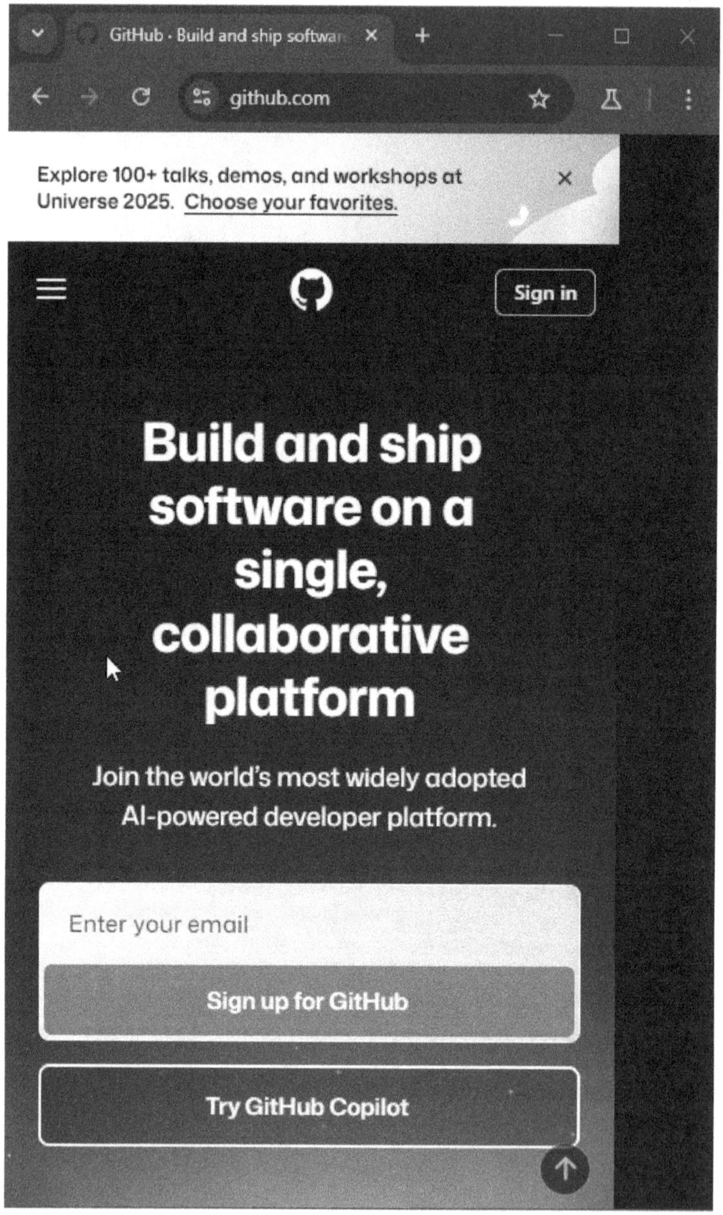

Figure 11.1: Verifying the visibility of the navigation menu on iPhone mobile view

You can also choose from other devices (such as Pixel 5, Galaxy S9+, iPad Pro 11, etc.). To see the list of built-in emulated devices, you can use the following:

```
import { devices } from 'playwright';
console.log(Object.keys(devices));
```

This will print an array of all built-in device descriptors:

```
[
  'iPhone 15',
  'iPhone SE',
  'Pixel 5',
  'Galaxy S9+',
  ...
]
```

Using a Playwright configuration file

You can also specify a device in your Playwright configuration file (`playwright.config.ts`) using the `projects` section. This creates a dedicated testing project for that device. For example, to run tests on a Pixel 5 and an iPhone 12, your config would look something like this:

```
import { defineConfig, devices } from '@playwright/test';

export default defineConfig({
  projects: [
    {
      name: 'Mobile Chrome',
      use: {
        ...devices['Pixel 5'],
      },
    },
    {
      name: 'Mobile Safari',
      use: {
        ...devices['iPhone 12'],
      },
    },
  ],
});
```

In the first project, `use: { ...devices['Pixel 5'] }` pulls in the predefined settings for a Pixel 5 from the `devices` object. The spread operator (`...`) unpacks all the device-specific settings, such as the viewport size (393 x 851 for Pixel 5) and the browser's user agent, so Playwright can emulate that device exactly.

Similarly, the second project uses the settings for an iPhone 12, which would include details like its smaller viewport (390 x 844) and Mobile Safari's user agent.

Customizing viewport and device properties

While device descriptors are convenient, you might need to test a specific screen size or a custom device configuration that isn't included in Playwright's default list. In such cases, you can manually configure the viewport and other device properties.

With the `newContext()` method, you have several options to fine-tune your emulation settings. For mobile testing, the most commonly used properties include the following:

- `viewport`: An object that specifies the width and height of the browser's viewport in pixels.
- `deviceScaleFactor`: The device's pixel density. For example, a Retina display would have a `deviceScaleFactor` of 2.
- `isMobile`: A Boolean that, when set to `true`, enables touch events and ensures the meta-viewport tag is respected.
- `userAgent`: A string that identifies the browser and device to the web server.

You've already seen these properties in action back in *Chapter 3, Browser-Agnostic Testing Across Chromium, Firefox, and WebKit*. As a quick refresher, here's an example of how to set up a custom mobile device configuration:

```
import { test } from '@playwright/test';

test('Custom mobile emulation test', async ({ browser }) => {
  const context = await browser.newContext({
    viewport: { width: 375, height: 667 },
    deviceScaleFactor: 2,
    isMobile: true,
    userAgent: 'Mozilla/5.0 (iPhone; CPU iPhone OS 13_5 like Mac OS X)
AppleWebKit/605.1.15 (KHTML, like Gecko) Version/13.1.1 Mobile/15E148
Safari/604.1',
  });
```

```
    const page = await context.newPage();

    // This test's purpose is only to generate a screenshot using
    // a custom mobile emulation setup.
    await page.goto('https://www.whatsmybrowser.org');
    await page.screenshot({ path: 'custom-mobile-emulation.png' });

    await context.close(); // closes all pages as well
  });
```

This script simulates browsing from an iPhone by customizing the browser context with specific mobile-like settings. It sets the viewport size, device pixel ratio, and user agent string to match those of an iPhone running iOS 13.5. These parameters help the target website (in this case, `whatsmybrowser.org`) think that the visit is coming from a real mobile device.

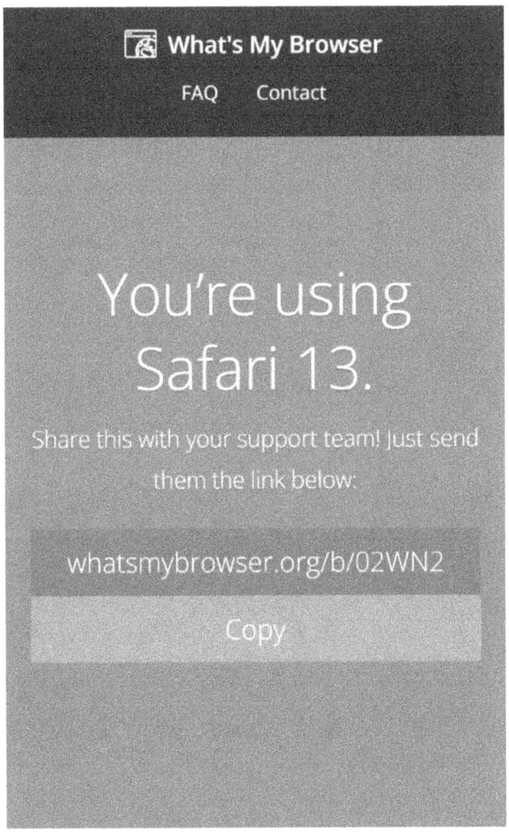

Figure 11.2: WhatIsMyBrowser.com detects the browser as Safari

The test wraps up by closing the browser context, cleaning up any open tabs and resources. This kind of test is handy when you want to verify responsive behavior or browser detection logic for mobile users.

For accurate emulation, use the full device descriptor instead of tweaking individual settings one by one, as websites may respond to user agents or other settings beyond just viewport size. Opt for custom descriptors when testing specific or unsupported devices.

Testing responsive layouts across devices

Running the same functional test across multiple viewports can lead to code duplication. A better approach is to parameterize your tests or create a loop that runs the same set of assertions for different screen sizes.

Here is an example of how you can write a single test that verifies a feature across a range of defined viewports:

```
import { test, expect } from '@playwright/test';

const viewports = [
  { name: 'Mobile', width: 390, height: 844 },
  { name: 'Tablet', width: 768, height: 1024 },
  { name: 'Desktop', width: 1920, height: 1080 },
];

for (const viewport of viewports) {
  test(`should render correctly on ${viewport.name}`, async ({ page }) =>
{
    await page.setViewportSize({
      width: viewport.width,
      height: viewport.height
    });
    await page.goto('https://www.whatsmybrowser.org/');
    await expect(page).toHaveScreenshot({ fullPage: true });
  });
}
```

This looping strategy keeps your test code **DRY** (short for **Don't Repeat Yourself**) and makes it easy to add or remove viewports from your test suite as your requirements evolve.

Here, we're using the `toHaveScreenshot()` method instead of the `screenshot()` method from the earlier example. `screenshot()` captures a screenshot manually and saves it to a specific file path you choose. It happens immediately when that line runs.

`toHaveScreenshot()`, on the other hand, is an assertion: it checks that the current page's visual output matches a previously stored baseline screenshot. Playwright also handles where that baseline lives, and the `fullPage: true` option tells it to capture the entire scrollable page for comparison.

Using projects with tags

Instead of just running tests against default browsers, we can define specific *visual* projects that override the viewport settings. This setup allows us to separate our standard functional tests from our heavier visual regression tests.

We use two key Playwright concepts to achieve this:

- **Projects:** In the `playwright.config.ts` file, projects allow us to define different environments under one roof
- **Tags:** We use tags such as `@visual` to mark specific tests, and then tell our projects to exclusively run (or ignore) tests with those marks

Here is the configuration setup:

```
// playwright.config.ts
export default defineConfig({
  // ... other global config options ...
  projects: [
    // Standard Functional Project
    {
      name: 'chromium',
      use: {
        ...devices['Desktop Chrome'],
      },
      // IMPORTANT: Set standard projects to ignore visual tests
      grepInvert: /@visual/,
    },
```

```
    // Visual Regression Projects
    // These projects exist ONLY to run tests tagged with @visual
    {
      name: 'visual-mobile',
      use: {
        viewport: { width: 390, height: 844 },
      },
      // Only run tests matching this tag
      grep: /@visual/,
    },
    {
      name: 'visual-tablet',
      use: {
        viewport: { width: 768, height: 1024 },
      },
      grep: /@visual/,
    },
    {
      name: 'visual-desktop',
      use: {
        viewport: { width: 1920, height: 1080 },
      },
      grep: /@visual/,
    },
  ],
});
```

The three `visual-*` projects will only execute tests that contain the string `@visual` in their title or description. The `grepInvert: /@visual/` property tells our default `chromium` project to skip any test tagged as visual. This prevents double-testing and keeps your fast functional tests separate from slower visual ones.

Now that the configuration is handling the *where* and *how big*, the test file itself can be simple:

```
// tests/visual.spec.ts
import { test, expect } from '@playwright/test';

// The @visual tag connects this block to the projects in the config.
test.describe('Visual regression @visual', () => {
```

```
  test('homepage should look correct', async ({ page }) => {
    await page.goto('https://www.whatsmybrowser.org/');
    await expect(page).toHaveScreenshot({ fullPage: true });
  });
});
```

By adding `@visual` to the `test.describe()` block, every test inside it inherits that tag. When this single test runs, Playwright essentially clones it three times. It runs once disguised as a phone, once as a tablet, and once as a 1080p desktop browser, taking a full-page screenshot for each.

Modern users don't browse the web in perfect lab conditions: they're on spotty coffee shop Wi-Fi, traveling across time zones, and switching between devices on the fly. Testing for that kind of chaos is where Playwright's emulation tools shine.

Simulating real-world scenarios with Playwright emulations

When testing web applications, you want to make sure they hold up in the messy, unpredictable real world. Fortunately, Playwright's emulation features let you recreate these scenarios without leaving your desk.

In this section, we'll dive into how you can use Playwright to mimic network conditions, geolocation, and device orientation to ensure your app delivers a seamless experience, no matter the circumstances.

Emulating network conditions

Playwright allows you to emulate different network conditions. The following script will use the **Chrome DevTools Protocol** (**CDP**) to throttle the network. This method gives you fine-grained control, but it only works with Chromium-based browsers such as Google Chrome and Microsoft Edge. Browsers such as Safari (WebKit) or Firefox don't support CDP, so if you try this there, it won't work.

It's a good idea to add a `skip` condition in your tests when using CDP. This way, tests that aren't compatible will be automatically bypassed. Here's an example:

```
import { test, expect } from '@playwright/test';

// Define the network conditions for a slow 3G connection
```

```
const slow3G = {
  downloadThroughput: 500 * 1024 / 8, // 500 kbps
  uploadThroughput: 500 * 1024 / 8,   // 500 kbps
  latency: 400, // 400ms
  offline: false,
};

test.describe('Emulate Slow Network Conditions', () => {
  // This test is specifically for Chromium as it uses the CDP session.
  // You can also define a custom project in your config so the tests
  // run only in Chromium.
  test.skip(
    ({ browserName }) => browserName !== 'chromium',
    'This feature is currently only supported on Chromium.'
  );

  test('should emulate a slow 3G connection', async ({ page }) => {
    const client = await page.context().newCDPSession(page);
    await client.send('Network.emulateNetworkConditions', slow3G);

    console.log('Slow 3G network conditions have been enabled.');

    // Navigate to a website. The loading time will be noticeably
    // longer due to the emulated network conditions.
    const startTime = Date.now();
    await page.goto('https://playwright.dev');
    const loadTime = Date.now() - startTime;

    console.log(`Page loaded in ${loadTime}ms under slow 3G conditions.`);

    // You can now perform your tests as usual.
    // All subsequent network requests on this page will be throttled.
    await expect(page).toHaveTitle(/Playwright/);

    // You can also disable the emulation if needed by setting the
    // values back to default (or 0 for no throttling).
    await client.send('Network.emulateNetworkConditions', {
```

```
      offline: false,
      latency: 0,
      downloadThroughput: -1, // -1 disables throttling
      uploadThroughput: -1,   // -1 disables throttling
    });

    console.log('Network emulation has been disabled.');
  });
});
```

This code checks how your website handles slower or unreliable internet connections, something that happens more often than we'd like in real life. By intentionally slowing down the network, you can see whether your site still loads quickly, if images are properly optimized, and whether any features start acting up when the connection isn't great.

The core of the script works by using the CDP. We first define the characteristics of a slow 3G network, including low download/upload speeds and high latency. Then we establish a CDP session with the browser and send a command (`Network.emulateNetworkConditions`) to tell the browser to throttle its network capabilities according to those predefined settings.

Once throttling kicks in, the script heads over to `https://playwright.dev` and tracks how long the page takes to load. Unsurprisingly, it'll be slower than usual, which helps see how your site performs under pressure. When the test wraps up, the script turns off the network emulation and gets everything back to normal.

Emulating geolocation

When developing applications that rely on location data, it's useful to test how they behave in different geographic scenarios. Playwright lets you emulate geolocation within a browser context, which makes it easy to simulate being anywhere in the world.

Here's an example:

```
// tests/geolocation.spec.ts
import { test, expect, devices } from '@playwright/test';

test.use({
  ...devices['Pixel 5'],  // Emulate a Pixel 5 device
  geolocation: {
    latitude: 41.889938,  // Mock latitude (Rome, Italy)
```

```
    longitude: 12.492507  // Mock Longitude (Rome, Italy)
  },
  permissions: ['geolocation'],
});

test('should mock @geolocation to Rome on Pixel 5', async ({ page }) => {

  await page.goto('https://www.openstreetmap.org/');

  // Click the Locator button
  await page.getByRole('button', { name: /Show My Location/i }).click();

  // Wait for URL to contain Rome coordinates
  await expect(page).toHaveURL(/41\.88/);
});
```

This example creates a browser context for a Pixel 5 device and sets a specific geolocation with a latitude of `41.889938` and a longitude of `12.492507` (which points roughly to Rome, Italy).

It also grants the browser permission to access geolocation data. This emulation is useful for testing location-based features, such as showing nearby restaurants or tailoring content based on a user's location.

Emulating device orientation

This is useful for testing how your website or app responds to different screen orientations. For example, does the layout adjust correctly when a user rotates their phone?

Normally, you emulate a device in portrait mode like this:

```
const context = await browser.newContext({
  ...devices['iPhone 12'],
  screen: {
    width: 390,  // Portrait width
    height: 844  // Portrait height
  }
});
```

If you want to emulate landscape mode, you'd swap the width and height:

```
const context = await browser.newContext({
  ...devices['iPhone 12'],
  screen: {
    width: 844,  // Landscape width
    height: 390  // Landscape height
  }
});
```

By combining these tools, Playwright makes it easier to catch issues early and deliver a polished experience.

Emulating tap gestures

A large portion of your users will interact with your application on a touchscreen. This means your testing strategy must go beyond simple clicks and keyboard inputs. You need to validate that touch-based interactions may trigger different code paths than traditional mouse events. And if they're not tested properly, you risk frustrating a portion of your audience.

The most fundamental touch gesture is the **tap**, which is the mobile equivalent of a click. While `page.click()` often works on mobile-emulated pages, the dedicated `page.tap()` method is more explicit and reliable for simulating a true touch interaction. It finds an element and taps it in the center.

Here's an example:

```
import { test, expect, devices } from '@playwright/test';

// Use a built-in mobile device
const iPhone15 = devices['iPhone 15'];

test.use({
  ...iPhone15,
  viewport: iPhone15.viewport,
  userAgent: iPhone15.userAgent,
});
```

```
test('Wikipedia search field interaction on mobile', async ({ page }) => {
  // Navigate to Wikipedia
  await page.goto('https://www.wikipedia.org/');

  // Tap the search input field
  await page.tap('input[name="search"]');

  // Type something
  await page.fill('input[name="search"]', 'Playwright');

  // Tap the search button
  await page.tap('button[type="submit"]');

  // Assert that a new page loads
  await expect(page).toHaveURL(/.*Playwright.*/);
});
```

This test ensures that the search field works correctly in a mobile environment. It sets the viewport and user agent to match iPhone 15, navigates to Wikipedia's homepage, taps the search input, enters the `Playwright` query, taps the submit button, and then verifies that the browser navigates to a results page whose URL contains the search term. By tapping elements instead of clicking, the test better reflects how people actually use touchscreens.

Even the most carefully written mobile tests can hit unexpected snags. These quirks can be tricky to reproduce and diagnose without the right approach. Next up, we'll dive into how to tackle tricky mobile-specific bugs.

Exploring tools for debugging mobile-specific issues

Debugging is an inevitable part of test automation. When targeting mobile devices, the process introduces unique challenges, from varying viewports and touch interactions to network inconsistencies. Fortunately, Playwright is packed with great tools designed to make debugging mobile web apps a more manageable process.

We've already touched on some of these tools in earlier chapters, but let's take a moment to review them again so you know exactly what's in your toolbox.

The Trace Viewer

The **Trace Viewer** is one of Playwright's most useful debugging tools, especially handy when working with mobile tests. It gives you a detailed snapshot of your entire test run, which makes it helpful for tracking down issues that show up in headless mode or on a CI/CD pipeline.

To use it, you'll need to enable tracing in your `playwright.config.ts` file. A good tip is to turn it on only for the first retry of a failed test. That way, you get the debugging info you need without cluttering your logs from successful runs:

```
// playwright.config.ts
import { defineConfig } from '@playwright/test';

export default defineConfig({
  // ... other configs
  use: {
    trace: 'on-first-retry', // 'on', 'off', 'retain-on-failure'
  },
});
```

After a test fails and is retried, a `trace.zip` file will be saved in your test output directory. To view it, simply run the following:

```
npx playwright show-trace path\to\trace.zip
```

This opens a rich web application that lets you scrub through the test's timeline. For each action, you get the following:

- **Action details:** The exact locator, timings, and logs for each step.
- **DOM snapshots:** A "before" and "after" snapshot of the DOM for every action. You can fully inspect the HTML and CSS as it existed at that exact moment. This is awesome for understanding why an element was not visible or clickable.
- **Console logs:** Any messages logged to the browser console.
- **Network requests:** A complete log of all network activity, which is important for debugging assets that fail to load or API calls that return errors on mobile.
- **Source code:** The corresponding line in your test script is highlighted.

The Trace Viewer's visual timeline makes it very easy to spot when a mobile layout shifts unexpectedly or when an animation hides an element you're trying to interact with.

> You can find a deeper look at Trace Viewer in *Chapter 6, Test Parallelization and Performance Optimization*.

The Playwright Inspector

The **Inspector** is a GUI tool that lets you step through your test execution line by line. It's the best tool for live debugging when a test isn't behaving as expected. You can launch it by running the `test` command with the `--debug` flag, like this:

```
npx playwright test --debug
```

When you run this, Playwright will open a browser window alongside the **Inspector** window. The test execution is paused at the first line, allowing you to do the following:

- **Step over**: Execute the current line and move to the next.
- **Resume**: Continue running the test until the next breakpoint or the end.
- **Explore selectors**: Use the **Pick Locator** tool to hover over elements in the browser and see the recommended Playwright locator for it. This is invaluable for fixing broken or unreliable selectors.
- **See the DOM in action**: Watch as your script interacts with the page, helping you spot timing issues or unexpected pop-ups that only appear on smaller viewports.

> We covered the Playwright Inspector in more detail back in *Chapter 8, Headless Testing and Debugging*.

The page.pause() method

For a quick *in-the-moment* debugging session, you can insert `await page.pause()` directly into your test script.

Here's an example:

```
import { test, expect, devices } from '@playwright/test';

test('Google autocomplete shows suggestions', async ({ browser }) => {
  const iPhone15PM = devices['iPhone 15 Pro Max'];

  const context = await browser.newContext({
    ... iPhone15PM ,
  });
  const page = await context.newPage();

  await page.goto('https://www.google.com');

  // Type a query into the search box
  const searchBox = await page.getByRole('textbox');
  await searchBox.fill('playwright');

  // Pause execution here to inspect the page state
  await page.pause();

  const suggestions = page.locator('ul[role="listbox"] li');
  await expect(suggestions.first()).toBeVisible();

  // Check that at least one suggestion contains "playwright"
  const suggestionTexts = await suggestions.allTextContents();
  expect(suggestionTexts.some(text => text.toLowerCase().
includes('playwright'))).toBeTruthy();

  // Clean up the context
  await context.close();
});
```

When Playwright hits `page.pause()`, it puts the script on hold and brings up a handy interactive window where you can poke around the browser.

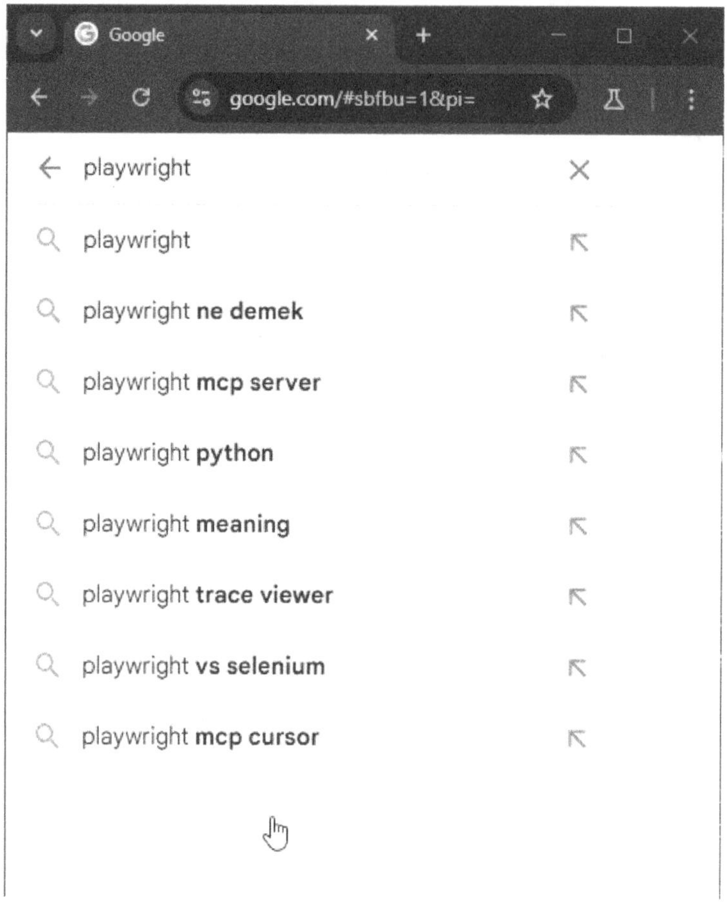

Figure 11.3: Pausing the script to check the page elements

You can click around the page, inspect elements, or even run some code to see what's going on. The script will remain suspended until you're ready to hit **Resume** and let it keep going.

Playwright shines in mimicking mobile environments, but there are some common issues you might run into.

Common mobile-specific issues and solutions

When you shift from desktop testing to mobile simulation, the game changes a bit. Mobile devices bring their own quirks: tiny screens, touch-only interactions, stricter performance budgets, and browsers that don't always play by desktop rules. Playwright can handle these challenges well, but knowing what to expect (and how to fix it) will save you from a lot of "why isn't this working?" moments.

Handling touch events

Mobile devices rely on gestures such as taps, swipes, or pinches, which don't exist in desktop testing. As we learned in this chapter, Playwright supports touch events through methods such as `page.touchscreen.tap()`, but you might find that a click doesn't trigger the same behavior as a tap in a mobile test.

This can happen if a web application has event listeners specifically tied to touch events (such as `touchstart` and `touchend`) that don't respond to mouse events or if the application's logic differentiates between touch and click handlers. For example, a button might have a `touchstart` listener for mobile users but rely on a `click` listener for desktop, and triggering one might not fire the other. This is a real issue in cross-device testing.

If the tap fails, inspect the element's event listeners in the browser's dev tools to confirm it's wired up for touch. Sometimes, you'll need to dispatch a sequence of touch events (such as `touchstart` and `touchend`) manually using the `page.evaluate()` method to simulate more complex gestures.

For swipes, Playwright doesn't have a direct swipe API, but you can simulate it by combining `touchstart`, `touchmove`, and `touchend`. This can get tricky, so test thoroughly and consider libraries such as Playwright's `dragTo` for simpler drag-like interactions (see `https://playwright.dev/docs/input#drag-and-drop`).

> Before interacting with an element that you suspect is off-screen, you can explicitly scroll it into view using the `scrollIntoViewIfNeeded()` method. Here's an example:
>
> ```
> await page.locator('#my-element').scrollIntoViewIfNeeded();
> ```
>
> Note that this method has limited browser support, and may change or be removed in the future (see `http://mdn.io/scrollIntoViewIfNeeded`). If the element is consistently off-screen, it's safer to rely on the widely supported `scrollIntoView()` method instead.

Managing viewport and orientation issues

Mobile browsers can be a bit tricky when it comes to viewport sizes and orientation changes. A common issue is that elements may appear off-screen or behave differently in portrait versus landscape mode. While Playwright's device emulation helps with setting the viewport size, you'll still want to test orientation changes manually when needed.

You can update the page to switch orientations:

```
// iPhone 15 Landscape
await page.setViewportSize({ width: 852, height: 393 });
```

If you notice elements not responding, try using `page.locator()` along with `waitFor()` to make sure they're visible and ready before interacting.

Here's an example:

```
await page.locator('#submit-button').waitFor({ state: 'visible' });
await page.locator('#submit-button').tap();
```

This helps prevent flaky tests when elements load slowly or are initially off-screen.

Also, keep an eye out for mobile-specific CSS such as `position: fixed` or `overflow: hidden`, as they can interfere with scrolling. To test scroll behavior, you can use `mouse.wheel()` or simulate touch scrolling with `page.evaluate()`.

> Turning on `isMobile` can also make a site load different layouts, elements, or even completely different content than the desktop version. That means your tests could behave in unexpected ways. So, double-check that the page is showing up the way you expect.

Dealing with mobile pop-ups and dialogs

On mobile, pop-ups can show up in a few different ways. The simplest ones are the built-in browser dialogs, such as JavaScript's `alert()`, `confirm()`, or `prompt()`. These usually look like native system pop-ups, styled to match the phone's operating system, so they might look slightly different on iOS versus Android.

Then there are custom pop-ups made with HTML, CSS, and JavaScript. These are often used for things such as cookie consent notices, login forms, or promotional banners. On mobile, they often depend on touch gestures such as tapping outside the dialog or swiping to close them.

Also, some web apps trigger system-level permission pop-ups, such as when asking for your location or to send notifications. These also look and behave differently depending on the browser and mobile OS. Mobile screens are smaller, so pop-ups can easily cover important content or act unpredictably if the viewport isn't managed properly. While Playwright's mobile emulation is helpful, it's still important to keep these differences in mind to avoid flaky tests.

Playwright makes handling browser-native dialogs (such as alerts, confirms, and prompts) pretty straightforward using the `page.on('dialog', ...)` event listener. When one of these JavaScript dialogs appears, Playwright can catch it for you. From there, you can inspect things such as the dialog's type, message, or default value and either accept or dismiss it programmatically.

Figure 11.4: You can handle a Confirm dialog like this by using page.on('dialog', dialog => dialog.accept())

For a practical example of working with browser-native alerts and confirmation dialogs, see *Chapter 2, Advanced Selectors and Handling Dynamic Content.*

Now, things get a bit more complex when you're dealing with custom pop-ups. Many mobile websites use modals built with HTML and CSS instead of native dialogs to create a more customized experience. These modals might need a tap on a **Close** button, a swipe down, or even a tap outside the modal to dismiss them. Since these aren't browser-native dialogs, Playwright's dialog event won't catch them: they're just regular DOM elements. That means if your script tries to interact with something hidden behind a modal, it might fail.

To handle this, you'll want to inspect the modal's DOM structure and use Playwright's `page.locator()` and touch-specific actions to interact with it. For example, if a site shows a cookie consent banner with a **Got it** button, you could tap it like this:

```
await page.locator('#cookie-consent-accept').waitFor({ state: 'visible'
});
await page.touchscreen.tap('#cookie-consent-accept');
```

Using `waitFor()` makes sure the modal is fully visible before you try to tap it. This is especially important on mobile, where things can take a bit longer to load due to network speed or rendering time.

If the modal doesn't have a dedicated close button (such as if it closes when you tap outside of it), you can mimic that by tapping somewhere outside the modal, like this:

```
await page.touchscreen.tap(10, 10); // Taps near the top-left corner
```

This assumes the top-left corner isn't covered by the modal, so double-check your page layout first.

System-level permissions dialogs

Mobile web apps often trigger system-level permissions dialogs, such as requests for geolocation, camera access, or notifications. These are browser-specific and can vary between mobile OSes. Playwright lets you predefine permissions in the context (or in the Playwright config) to avoid these dialogs altogether:

```
const context = await browser.newContext({
  ...devices['iPhone 13'],
  permissions: { 'geolocation': 'grant', 'notifications': 'deny' },
});
```

This grants geolocation access and denies notifications, so the dialogs won't appear during testing. If you need to test the dialog itself, you can allow it to appear and handle it as a native dialog (if it's implemented that way) or as a custom modal. Although the examples in this chapter use built-in permissions (such as allowing access to geolocation) to keep things simple, it's good to remember that not every browser shows permission prompts as native system dialogs. Some display them directly on the page instead. In real testing, you don't want to skip these custom flows. Users will run into them, and your automated tests should be ready to recognize and handle them.

Addressing mobile performance challenges

Mobile devices just don't have the same horsepower as desktops: slower processors, less memory, and spotty network connections. This can lead to all sorts of problems, such as pages that take forever to load or animations that stutter and jerk.

Playwright has some handy tools to help you out here. For example, you can use `context.setOffline()` or `context.route()` to simulate things such as a slow 3G connection or even no internet at all. That's great for seeing how your app holds up when the network's not cooperating. But here's the catch: these simulations don't always tell the whole story. A page might seem fine in your tests but still choke on a real phone because of something such as limited memory or other device-specific quirks that an emulator just can't mimic.

To get a more accurate sense of performance, Playwright's trace viewer is a lifesaver. You can spot things such as a large image slowing down the load time or some heavy JavaScript hogging resources.

Honestly, nothing beats testing on actual devices when you can. Real phones will show you problems such as thermal throttling or memory limits that emulators might gloss over. By mixing Playwright's simulation tools, Trace Viewer insights, and real-device testing, you'll be in a much better spot to make sure your app runs smoothly for mobile users, no matter how tough the conditions get.

Summary

In this chapter, we built on what we already knew about testing across different browsers and saw just how easy Playwright makes it to emulate mobile devices. You learned how to set up these emulations, whether you're coding them directly or using a config file, and even how to tweak settings for a specific device.

We also got into simulating real-world situations, such as faking slow internet, pretending to be in a different location, and even flipping your phone around. Plus, we covered how important it is to handle mobile gestures such as taps so your tests really act like a human user.

When things went wrong (because they always do), we checked out Playwright's great debugging tools, such as the Trace Viewer and the Inspector, and how `page.pause()` can be a lifesaver for quick checks. Finally, we looked at common mobile headaches, such as weird touch events, slow performance, screen layout issues, and annoying pop-ups, with some practical fixes.

By now, you should feel pretty confident writing solid, reliable mobile tests with Playwright. This means your web apps will look and feel great, no matter what device or situation your users are in.

In the next chapter, we will explore testing form interactions, including inputs, validations, and specialized fields, to ensure robust handling of user inputs.

12

Testing Forms

Forms are the backbone of user interaction on the web, from simple login pages to complex multi-step wizards. In testing, they're also one of the most critical (and sometimes finicky) parts of an application to get right. This chapter takes you through Playwright's toolkit for interacting with all sorts of form elements: text fields, dropdowns, checkboxes, radio buttons, date pickers, and even custom widgets.

You'll see how to mimic real user actions, handle tricky UI behaviors, and validate that your forms respond correctly to both valid and invalid input.

By the end of this chapter, you'll be able to simulate real user interactions and verify that your forms handle both success and failure cases gracefully.

The chapter is structured into the following main sections:

- Interacting with text inputs and dropdowns
- Testing checkboxes and radio buttons
- Handling date pickers and custom fields
- Testing form validation logic

Technical requirements

The source code for this chapter is available at `https://github.com/PacktPublishing/Hands-On-Automated-Testing-with-Playwright/tree/main/Chapter12`.

Interacting with text inputs and dropdowns

Working with text inputs and dropdowns in Playwright is pretty simple. To enter text, you'll mostly use `fill()` or `pressSequentially()`, and when it comes to standard dropdowns, `selectOption()` does the trick.

Interacting with text inputs

You have two main methods for entering text into an input field such as `<input type="text">` or `<textarea>`:

- `locator.fill()`
- `locator.pressSequentially()`

When using `locator.fill()`, Playwright first finds the target element and waits for it to be **actionable**, meaning it's visible, enabled, and ready for input. It automatically wipes out any text that's already in the field, then instantly types in the new string you've provided. This whole process helps make sure your text comes out clean and dependable for almost any form you're filling out.

When working with an input element, you first need to locate it on the page. You can use locators such as `page.getByLabel()`, which is particularly handy for inputs as they are often associated with a `<label>` element for accessibility.

Here's an example of filling out username and password fields:

```
// Fills the input
await page.getByLabel('Username').fill('my_user');

// Fills the input with a placeholder attribute
await page.getByPlaceholder('Enter your password').fill('S3cr3tP@
ssw0rd!');
```

The `locator.pressSequentially()` method, on the other hand, simulates actual keyboard presses. This method operates by locating the element, waiting until it's actionable, and then placing the cursor's focus on it. Unlike `fill()`, it does not clear existing content. Instead, it simulates a user typing by sending individual keypress events for each character in the string.

This does a better job of imitating how a real person types, which is especially useful when testing interactive features that react to keystrokes, such as search suggestions or automatic input formatting.

Here's an example of typing into a search box on Wikipedia:

```
import { test, expect } from '@playwright/test';

test('should search for "Playwright testing"', async ({ page }) => {
  // Navigate to Wikipedia
  await page.goto('https://en.wikipedia.org');

  // Locate the search box
  const searchBox = page.getByRole('searchbox', { name: /Search
Wikipedia/i });

  // Clear the input first if needed
  await searchBox.clear();

  // Type character by character
  await searchBox.pressSequentially('Playwright testing');

  // Submit the search by pressing Enter
  await searchBox.press('Enter');

  // Verify the page title contains the search term
  await expect(page).toHaveTitle(/.*Playwright testing.*/);

});
```

This script does a few key things. First, it heads over to Wikipedia's English home page and finds the search box by its role and name. It then clears out anything that might already be in there and types `Playwright testing` one letter at a time, just like a real person would. Next, it gives the *Enter* key a press to run the search. Finally, to make sure everything worked as expected, it checks that the new page's title contains the search term.

Interacting with dropdowns (<select>)

Playwright's `selectOption()` method is your go-to tool for handling drop-down elements, and it's designed to be flexible, letting you select options in multiple ways (by value, label, or index), while also supporting single- and multi-select dropdowns:

- **By value**: This targets the value attribute of an `<option>` tag, such as `<option value="US">United States</option>`. You'd call `await countryDropdown.selectOption('US')` to select it. This is ideal when you know the exact value, as it's precise and unaffected by display text changes (for example, if *United States* is later shown as *USA*).
- **By label**: This selects an option based on its visible text, such as `await countryDropdown.selectOption({ label: 'United Kingdom' })`. It's great for scripts that mimic user behavior, since users typically see and choose options by their displayed text. However, be cautious as the text might change due to localization or updates.
- **By index**: This selects an option based on its position in the dropdown, starting at `0` for the first option. For example, `await countryDropdown.selectOption({ index: 2 })` picks the third option. This is useful when values or labels are dynamic or unpredictable, but it's fragile as the dropdown's order could change.

Here's an example of selecting a country from a dropdown:

```
const countryDropdown = page.getByLabel('Country');

// Select by value ('DE' for Germany)
await countryDropdown.selectOption('DE');

// Select by label (visible text)
await countryDropdown.selectOption({ label: 'United Kingdom' });

// Select by index
await countryDropdown.selectOption({ index: 2 });
```

Now, what about multi-select dropdowns, which have `multiple` attributes, such as `<select multiple>`? These allow users to pick more than one option, like choosing multiple toppings for a pizza. With `selectOption()`, you can pass an array of values, labels, or even a mix of both to select multiple options in one go.

Take the following example:

```
const toppingsDropdown = page.getByLabel('Toppings');

// Select multiple toppings by their values
await toppingsDropdown.selectOption([
  'pepperoni',
  'mushrooms',
  'onions'
]);

// Or by labels
await toppingsDropdown.selectOption([
  { label: 'Pepperoni' },
  { label: 'Mushrooms' },
  { label: 'Onions' }
]);
```

Note that you need to ensure that the `<select>` element actually supports multiple selections. If it doesn't, passing an array will throw an error, as single-select dropdowns only accept one option.

Handling custom dropdowns (non-<select>)

Many modern websites use custom dropdowns built from `<div>`, `<ul>`, and other elements. You cannot use `selectOption()` on these. Instead, you must replicate a user's actions:

1. Click the element that opens the drop-down menu.
2. Click the desired option from the list that appears.

Here is an example:

```
import { test, expect } from '@playwright/test';
test('State dropdown functionality', async ({ page }) => {
  // Navigate to the form page
  await page.goto('https://demoqa.com/automation-practice-form');

  // Locate the state dropdown
  const stateDropdown = page.locator('#state');

  // Click state dropdown to open it
```

```
    await stateDropdown.click();

    // Select a state ("Haryana")
    const stateOption = page.getByText('Haryana');
    await expect(stateOption).toBeVisible();
    await stateOption.click();
  });
```

This code first clicks the state dropdown to open it. Then it selects a state from the list that is now visible.

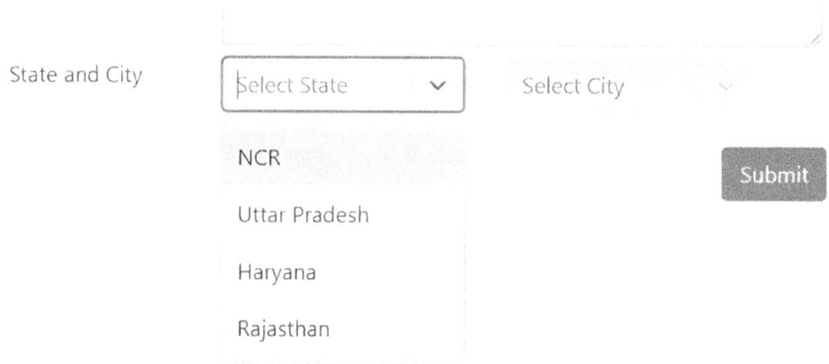

Figure 12.1: Selecting a state from the dropdown

Custom dropdowns can sometimes have delays or animations when opening. In those cases, it's a good idea to add a short wait (for example, `await page.toBeVisible()`) so the options have time to appear before you click.

If the dropdown is loading its options on the fly (such as from an API call), you might also want to wait for the network activity to finish; `page.waitForResponse()` can help make sure everything's ready before you interact with it.

Understanding the distinction between .fill(), .press(), and .pressSequentially()

The `page.press()` method lets you simulate pressing a single key or a combination of keys on the keyboard, directed at a specific element. It's a precise tool that mimics a user physically hitting a key and triggers events such as `keydown`, `keypress`, and `keyup`. This is particularly handy for testing specific keyboard interactions, such as hitting the *Enter* key to submit a form or using arrow keys to navigate. For example, you could use `page.press('input[name="search"]', 'Enter')` to mimic pressing the *Enter* key in a search field to trigger a search.

Unlike `page.fill()`, `page.press()` doesn't set or modify the value of an input field directly: it only sends a key event, and any change to the input's value depends on how the web application handles that keypress.

If you're filling a text field with a long string, `page.fill()` is the go-to choice because it's faster and more straightforward. However, if you need to simulate incremental typing (for example, to trigger autocomplete suggestions after each keypress), you might use `page.pressSequentially()`, which simulates typing character by character.

Additionally, `page.press()` supports special keys (such as *Tab*, *Esc*, or *Ctrl* + *A*), which `page.fill()` cannot handle since it's not designed for key events.

Playwright also provides the `.type()` method, which is higher-level and just inserts text into an element character by character with an optional delay, while `.pressSequentially()` literally presses each key in sequence, firing all the corresponding `keydown`, `keypress`, and `keyup` events as if a real user were typing. That makes `.type()` great for quickly filling inputs, but `.pressSequentially()` is more accurate when you need to test behaviors that depend on actual key events, such as shortcuts, input masks, or custom `onKeyDown` logic.

Here's a comparison of how different Playwright input methods behave:

Feature	`page.fill()`	`page.press()`	`page.pressSequentially()`
Purpose	Sets the entire value of an input field	Simulates pressing a specific key	Simulates realistic typing
Clears field?	Yes	No	No
Triggers input events?	Yes	No (only key events)	Yes
Triggers key events?	No	Yes	Yes
Typing simulation	No (instant value set)	No	Yes (character-by-character)
Use case	Quickly setting full values	Submitting forms, keyboard navigation	Mimicking human-like typing
Speed	Fast (instant)	N/A (single key)	Slower (based on typing speed)

Table 12.1: Comparing the .fill(), .press(), and .pressSequentially() methods

While text fields and dropdowns are about gathering user input, checkboxes and radio buttons are all about making choices. They may look simple, but in testing, they come with their own quirks, such as ensuring the right options stay selected, others get deselected when they should, and states persist as expected.

Testing checkboxes and radio buttons

When testing checkboxes, you often need to select or deselect them programmatically and then verify their state. In Playwright, the `page.check()` method is used to select a checkbox, while `page.uncheck()` deselects it.

Radio buttons are a bit different because they belong to a group where only one option can be selected at a time, defined by sharing the same name attribute in the HTML. Let's look at how we can deal with these elements.

Working with checkboxes

Let's say you have a checkbox for something such as accepting terms and conditions. To check it (just like a user would click to agree), you can use the `check()` method:

```
// Check a checkbox
await page.get_by_label("I agree to the terms").check();
```

The nice thing about `check()` is that it's idempotent, meaning if the checkbox is already selected, it won't try to click it again. This makes it a safe and reliable way to ensure the box is checked.

If you need to make sure the box is *not* selected, you can use `uncheck()` instead:

```
// Uncheck a checkbox
await page.uncheck('#accept-terms');
```

This method will only click the checkbox if it's currently checked, making sure it ends up unchecked. In this case, we're using the `uncheck()` method directly on the page object, and passing it a selector (`'#accept-terms'`) as the argument. This is just another way of locating the element.

Both `check()` and `uncheck()` are smart about waiting for the element to be ready (visible and enabled) before interacting with it. That helps make your tests more stable and less flaky.

Testing radio buttons

You also use `page.check()` to select a radio button, but there's no equivalent `uncheck()` method since deselecting one radio button happens automatically when another in the same group is selected.

For instance, if you have a radio button group with the name `color` and values such as `red` and `blue`, you can select the `red` option like this:

```
await page.check('input[value="red"]')
```

Playwright makes sure the right radio button gets selected, and it automatically takes care of deselecting any other option in the group for you. When you're testing radio buttons, keep in mind that they're designed to be **mutually exclusive**: one gets picked and the others get unchecked. It's a good idea to test this behavior to make sure your app is working as expected.

Here's an example of how to test a radio button group:

1. Check one radio button.
2. Assert that it is checked.
3. Check another radio button in the same group.
4. Assert that the new radio button is checked.
5. Assert that the previous radio button is now unchecked.

Asserting the state of checkboxes and radio buttons

Now, asserting the state of these elements is where `toBeChecked()` comes in. This is part of Playwright's expect API, used to verify whether a checkbox or radio button is in the checked state.

For example, after checking a checkbox with `await check()`, you can assert its state with `toBeChecked()`:

```
const termsCheckbox = page.locator('#accept-terms');
await termsCheckbox.check();
await expect(termsCheckbox).toBeChecked();
```

This passes if the checkbox is checked and fails otherwise. If you need to verify that a checkbox or radio button is *not* checked, you can use this:

```
await expect(page.locator('#accept-terms')).not.toBeChecked();
```

This is particularly useful for ensuring a checkbox is unchecked after calling `page.uncheck()` or confirming that a radio button outside the selected group is not checked.

> If you're testing a complex form, you might encounter scenarios where elements are dynamically loaded or hidden. Playwright's auto-waiting behavior helps here, but you can also use `page.toBeVisible()` to ensure the element is present before interacting with it. For assertions, `toBeChecked()` is robust, but if you need to verify other properties (such as whether the element is enabled), you can combine it with other expect matchers, such as `toBeEnabled()`.

A practical example

Let's consider a practical example to tie this together. Imagine a form where you can check boxes to pick your hobbies and choose your gender from a set of radio buttons.

Your test might look like this:

```
import { test, expect } from '@playwright/test';

test.describe('DemoQA Automation Practice Form', () => {
  test.beforeEach(async ({ page }) => {
    await page.goto(
      'https://demoqa.com/automation-practice-form',
      { waitUntil: 'domcontentloaded' }
    );
  });

  test('should interact with gender radio buttons', async ({ page }) => {
    const maleRadio = page.locator('#gender-radio-1');
    const femaleRadio = page.locator('#gender-radio-2');
    const otherRadio = page.locator('#gender-radio-3');

    await expect(maleRadio).not.toBeChecked();
    await expect(femaleRadio).not.toBeChecked();
    await expect(otherRadio).not.toBeChecked();

    await maleRadio.check({ force: true });
    await expect(maleRadio).toBeChecked();
    await expect(femaleRadio).not.toBeChecked();
```

```
    await expect(otherRadio).not.toBeChecked();

    await femaleRadio.check({ force: true });
    await expect(maleRadio).not.toBeChecked();
    await expect(femaleRadio).toBeChecked();
    await expect(otherRadio).not.toBeChecked();
  });

  test('should interact with hobbies checkboxes', async ({ page }) => {
    const sportsCheckbox = page.locator('#hobbies-checkbox-1');
    const readingCheckbox = page.locator('#hobbies-checkbox-2');
    const musicCheckbox = page.locator('#hobbies-checkbox-3');

    await expect(sportsCheckbox).not.toBeChecked();
    await expect(readingCheckbox).not.toBeChecked();
    await expect(musicCheckbox).not.toBeChecked();

    await sportsCheckbox.check({ force: true });
    await expect(sportsCheckbox).toBeChecked();
    await expect(readingCheckbox).not.toBeChecked();
    await expect(musicCheckbox).not.toBeChecked();

    await readingCheckbox.check({ force: true });
    await expect(sportsCheckbox).toBeChecked();
    await expect(readingCheckbox).toBeChecked();
    await expect(musicCheckbox).not.toBeChecked();

    await sportsCheckbox.uncheck({ force: true });
    await expect(sportsCheckbox).not.toBeChecked();
    await expect(readingCheckbox).toBeChecked();
    await expect(musicCheckbox).not.toBeChecked();
  });
});
```

This script is about making sure the gender radio buttons and hobbies checkboxes on the `DemoQA` form page work just right: clicking, unclicking, and behaving as they should. To keep things consistent, we have a `test.beforeEach` hook that kicks in before each test. It takes the browser straight to the form page, so every test starts from the same spot.

The form includes multiple kinds of inputs, but for our purposes, we're focusing on the radiobuttons:

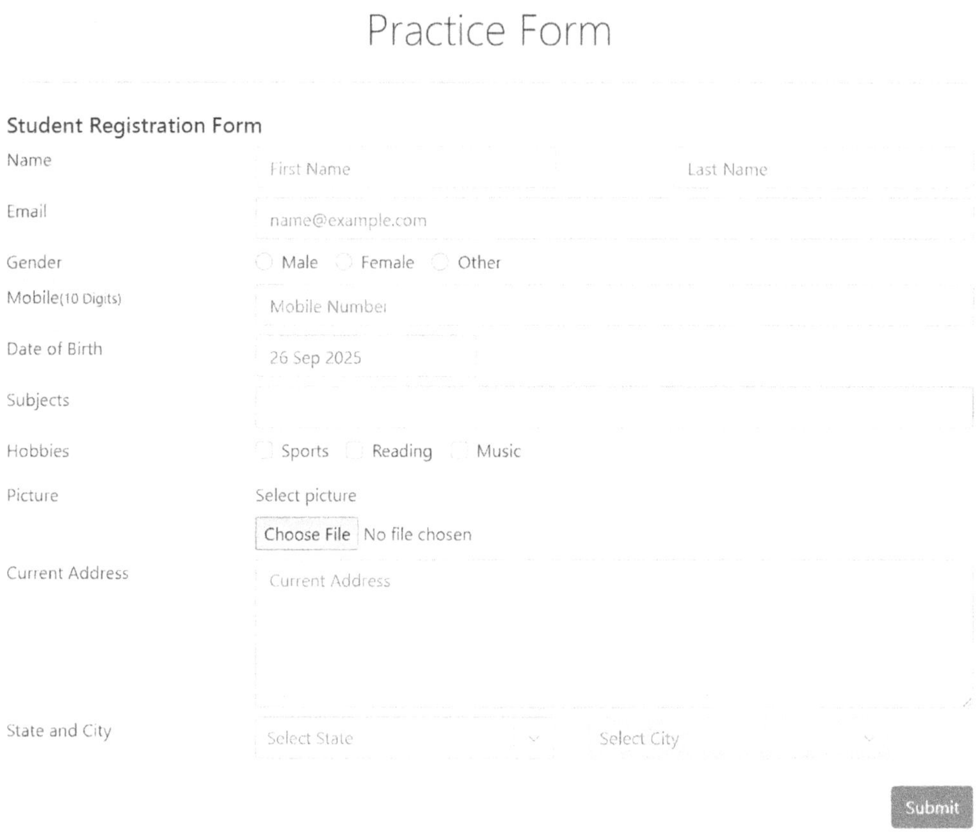

Figure 12.2: The DemoQA form page

The script is organized into two test cases: one for radio buttons and another for checkboxes. The first test case focuses on the three gender radio options: **Male**, **Female**, and **Other**. The test starts off by checking that none of these buttons are selected at the start, using the `toBeChecked()` assertion to confirm.

Then, it simulates clicking the **Male** radio button and makes sure only **Male** is selected, while **Female** and **Other** stay unchecked. To double-check, it does the same for the **Female** radio button, ensuring that picking one option automatically deselects the others, just like radio buttons are supposed to work.

The second test focuses on the hobbies checkboxes: **Sports**, **Reading**, and **Music**. It first ensures that none of the checkboxes are selected at the start. Then, it checks the **Sports** checkbox and verifies that only **Sports** is selected.

Next, it checks the **Reading** checkbox, which confirms that both **Sports** and **Reading** are now selected, as checkboxes allow multiple selections. Finally, it unchecks the **Sports** checkbox and verifies that only **Reading** remains checked. This ensures the checkboxes can be independently toggled on and off.

Notice the `{ force: true }` argument we pass to the `check()` method. Sometimes, using `{ force: true }` can be useful to tell Playwright to bypass its normal actionability checks and perform the action even if the element is hidden, covered, or disabled. That might smooth over flaky timing issues during tests, but keep in mind that it also means the test no longer reflects what a real user can do. If a Google ad or any other overlay is covering the radio button, the forced check will still succeed, even though a person wouldn't be able to click it. This makes the test look healthy while a genuine UI problem is hiding underneath. It's usually safer to wait for the control to become actionable or deal with the overlay directly instead of forcing the interaction.

> `page.check()` and `page.uncheck()` throw an error if the element isn't a checkbox or radio button, or if it's disabled or not found.

Not all form elements are created equal. Some play nice, and others not so much. Date pickers and custom input fields often fall into the latter category. They might look simple on the surface, but behind the scenes, they can be built with complex markup.

Handling date pickers and custom fields

Working with date pickers and custom fields in Playwright can feel a bit like solving a puzzle, since every web app seems to have its own unique way of building these components. Thankfully, Playwright gives you handy tools to tackle them, and with a little know-how, you can handle them like a pro. Let's walk through some practical tips and tricks for dealing with these elements.

Handling date pickers

Date pickers are common in web forms, but their structure can differ significantly: some are simple input fields, while others are complex widgets with calendars, dropdowns, or custom formats. The key is to inspect the date picker's HTML structure to determine the best way to interact with it.

If the date picker is a basic text input (such as `<input type="date">` or a text field), you can often set the value directly using Playwright's `fill` method. For example, if the input expects a specific format such as `YYYY-MM-DD`, you can pass the date as a string:

```
await page.fill('input[type="date"]', '2025-08-08');
```

This works well for native HTML date inputs or text fields that don't trigger additional JavaScript events. But you should verify the expected format by inspecting the input field because some fields might require formats such as `MM/DD/YYYY` or `DD-MM-YYYY`.

> When you're working with `calendar` elements, you might notice their classes or IDs can change quite a bit. To keep things smooth, try focusing on stable attributes such as `data-date` or `aria-label` for your selectors. They're much more dependable.
>
> A lot of date pickers are designed with accessibility in mind, so they often come with handy **ARIA** (short for **Accessible Rich Internet Applications**) attributes. You can use these to make your automation rock-solid, such as clicking on something with `page.click('[aria-label="Next month"]')`.

Some date pickers open a little calendar when you click them, often powered by libraries such as jQuery UI, Bootstrap, or Material UI. The usual flow is simple: click the input, browse to the right date, and pick it. With Playwright, you can handle this using `click()` and `selectOption()`, along with `toBeVisible()`, to make sure everything's ready before you move on.

Here is an example:

1. Use `locator.click('selector')` to activate the date picker.
2. Then, navigate to the date by identifying the calendar's elements (day, month, and year dropdowns or buttons). You might need to click arrows to change months or select a specific day.

Here's a hypothetical example for a calendar picker where you select a year, month, and day:

```
// Define locators
const datePickerInput = page.locator('#date-picker-input');
const calendar = page.locator('.calendar');
const yearDropdown = page.locator('.year-dropdown');
const monthSelectorAugust = page.locator('.month-selector[data-
month="August"]');
const daySelector8 = page.locator('.day-selector[data-day="8"]');

// Open the date picker
await datePickerInput.click();

// Wait for the calendar to appear
await calendar.waitFor({ state: 'visible' });

// Select year (dropdown)
await yearDropdown.selectOption('2025');

// Select month (clicking a month button)
await monthSelectorAugust.click();

// Select day
await daySelector8.click();
```

The exact selectors you'll need depend on how the calendar's HTML is set up. Open your browser's DevTools and look for stable hooks such as IDs, classes, or data attributes.

Remember, if the calendar loads its content dynamically, `waitFor({ state: 'visible' })` is your friend: it makes sure the element is ready before you try to interact with it.

Handling custom fields

Date pickers in modern frameworks such as React, Vue, or Angular can be a bit tricky to automate. They often come with fancy animations, custom event listeners, and dynamic DOM updates that don't always get along with Playwright's usual click-and-type approach. A simpler approach is to skip the UI altogether and set the input's value directly with JavaScript. It's faster and saves you a lot of headaches.

Take this example:

```
await page.evaluate((date) => {
  document.querySelector('#date-picker-input').value = date;

  // trigger change event
  const event = new Event('change', { bubbles: true });
  document.querySelector('#date-picker-input').dispatchEvent(event);
}, '2025-08-08');
```

First, directly setting the `value` property in JavaScript lets you instantly update the input to the date you want, so no clicking around in the UI is required.

Next, firing a change event (as in the example) might be important. Many modern frameworks (React's controlled components, for example) depend on events such as change or input to update the app's state. If you skip this step, the app might not notice the new date, even if it looks correct in the field.

The code uses `{ bubbles: true }`, so the event travels up the DOM, just like it would if a real person made the change. Depending on your date picker, you might also need to send an input event or even a blur event to fully imitate actual user behavior.

Here is an example:

```
await page.evaluate((date) => {
  const input = document.querySelector('#date-picker-input');
  input.value = date;
  input.dispatchEvent(new Event('input', { bubbles: true }));
  input.dispatchEvent(new Event('change', { bubbles: true }));
}, '2025-08-08');
```

There are a couple of things worth keeping in mind. Not every date picker is built using a standard `<input>` element. Some use `<div>` or other non-input elements to show the selected date, so you'll want to make sure you're targeting the right element before trying to update it.

Also, keep in mind that skipping the UI can sometimes skip built-in validation. For example, if the date picker normally prevents you from selecting certain dates or requires a specific format, directly setting the value might ignore those rules, meaning your test might not reflect what a real user would experience. To avoid that, it's a good idea to double-check the app's behavior afterward: look for error messages or make sure the UI updates the way it should.

If you want to make your test extra reliable, you can pair this approach with Playwright's built-in checks. Here is an example:

```
await page.evaluate((date) => {
  const input = document.querySelector('#date-picker-input');
  input.value = date;
  input.dispatchEvent(new Event('change', { bubbles: true }));
}, '2025-08-08');

await expect(page.locator('#date-picker-input')).
toHaveValue('2025-08-08');
```

Here, after setting the value, we verify that the input's value is correct or confirm that the application's state changed as expected.

> If the custom field is inside a shadow DOM (common in web components), use `page.locator('>> css=selector')` to pierce the shadow root. See *Chapter 2, Advanced Selectors and Handling Dynamic Content.*

Now, even the best-looking form isn't worth much if it accepts bad data or fails silently when something goes wrong. Your forms should protect both data integrity and the user experience.

Testing form validation logic

Whether it's a simple login page or a complex signup process, making sure that form validation works correctly is important to create a smooth user experience. When you're testing form validation, the goal is to mimic real-world user behavior. This means filling out form fields, submitting the form, and checking for things such as error messages, field highlights, or successful submissions.

Testing unsuccessful form submission

Suppose you have a login form with username and password fields. You'd write a test to fill the form with invalid data and check whether the expected error message appears. Playwright's page object is your main tool here. You can use methods such as `locator.fill()` to input text into fields, `locator.click()` to submit the form, and `locator.locator()` to target specific elements and check their state:

```
import { test, expect } from '@playwright/test';

test('Login with invalid credentials shows error message', async ({ page
}) => {
  await page.goto('https://www.saucedemo.com/');

  // Auto-waiting locators
  const usernameField = page.getByPlaceholder('Username');
  const passwordField = page.getByPlaceholder('Password');
  const loginButton = page.getByRole('button', { name: 'Login' });
  const errorContainer = page.locator('[data-test="error"]');

  // Fill + submit
  await usernameField.fill('invalid_user');
  await passwordField.fill('wrong_password');
  await loginButton.click();

  // Assert error is visible and has exact text
  await expect(errorContainer).toBeVisible();
  await expect(errorContainer).toContainText(
    'Epic sadface: Username and password do not match any user in this
service'
  );
});
```

After submission, you'd check whether an error message such as **Please enter a valid email** appears. You can target the error message element by its `data-test` attribute, then use `expect(locator).toBeVisible()` or `expect(locator).toHaveText()` to assert that the error shows up.

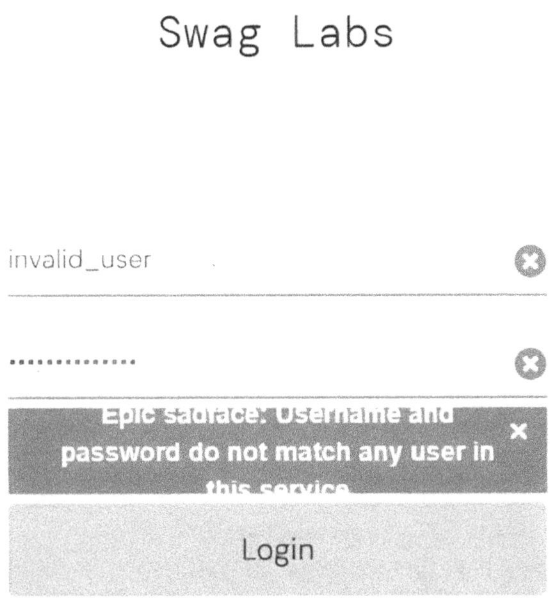

Figure 12.3: The error message on Swag Labs

If your form uses client-side validation, you might also check whether the email input has a red border or a specific class, such as `is-invalid`, using the following code:

```
page.locator('input#email').getAttribute('class').
```

One thing to keep in mind is handling dynamic content. Forms often show error messages or update the UI asynchronously, so you need to ensure Playwright waits for these changes. Methods such as `page.toBeVisible()` or `page.waitForTimeout()` can help, but Playwright's auto-waiting feature usually handles this automatically by waiting for elements to be actionable before interacting with them.

> When you're testing forms, don't forget about accessibility. Forms are one of the main ways people interact with your site, so you'll want to make sure that things such as validation messages work well with screen readers. With Playwright, you can check ARIA attributes or bring in tools such as `@axe-core/playwright` to run accessibility audits right alongside your validation tests. See *Chapter 9, Accessibility Testing with Playwright and axe-core.*

Testing successful form submission

So far, we've tested failure cases, but what about when the user provides valid data? Let's write a test to ensure the form submits successfully and, for example, redirects to a confirmation page:

```
import { test, expect } from '@playwright/test';

test('valid form submission redirects to confirmation', async ({ page })
=> {
  await page.goto('https://www.saucedemo.com/');

  const usernameField = page.getByPlaceholder('Username');
  const passwordField = page.getByPlaceholder('Password');
  const loginButton = page.getByRole('button', { name: 'Login' });

  await usernameField.fill('standard_user');
  await passwordField.fill('secret_sauce');
  await loginButton.click();

  // Verify redirection to confirmation page
  await expect(page).toHaveURL('https://www.saucedemo.com/inventory.
html');
});
```

In this test, we fill in valid data for all fields, submit the form, and check that the browser redirects to the expected URL. If your form doesn't redirect but shows a success message on the same page, you could instead check for that message using `expect(page.locator('.success-message')).toBeVisible()`.

> If interactions fail, use `page.screenshot()` or `page.pause()` to debug the state of the page.
>
> Organizing tests for maintainability is important, especially for larger projects. You can group related tests using `test.describe()` and use `beforeEach()` to set up common preconditions, such as navigating to the form page.

Summary

Testing forms isn't just about clicking buttons and filling fields. It's about ensuring every part of the user's journey works as expected, from the first keystroke to the final confirmation. By combining Playwright's methods such as `fill()`, `type()`, `check()`, and `selectOption()`, as well as custom scripting for more complex elements, you can reliably simulate real user interactions and verify that your forms handle both success and failure cases gracefully.

Along the way, you've seen how to work with native inputs, custom components, validation logic, and dynamic UI changes without introducing flaky tests. Keep these techniques in your toolkit, and you'll be well equipped to build automated tests that make your forms not just functional but rock-solid under real-world conditions.

In the next chapter, we'll learn about uploading files, downloading and verifying content, and managing different file types.

13

Handling File Uploads and Downloads

In modern web applications, the ability to upload and download files is a core part of the user experience. Whether it's sharing images, submitting documents, or generating downloadable reports, these features need to work seamlessly for users while remaining reliable under the hood. For testers and developers, that means ensuring uploads and downloads are not only functional but also resilient to real-world quirks, from slow networks to unexpected file formats.

In this chapter, we'll explore how to automate these workflows with Playwright, cutting out the manual tedium and making our tests both faster and more dependable. You'll learn how to simulate file uploads without wrestling with OS-level dialogs, verify that downloads happen exactly as expected, and handle a variety of file types (from PDFs to CSVs) with confidence. Along the way, we'll cover edge cases and look at best practices for keeping your test environment clean.

The chapter is structured into these parts:

- Automating file upload workflows
- Handling file downloads in tests
- Keeping your test environment clean

Technical requirements

The source code for this chapter is available at `https://github.com/PacktPublishing/Hands-On-Automated-Testing-with-Playwright/tree/main/Chapter13`.

Automating file upload workflows

Uploading files is one of the most common interactions in web applications. In manual testing, this often means clicking a **Choose File** button, navigating through your system's file picker, and selecting the right file. In automation, however, we can bypass those OS-level dialogs entirely and work directly with the underlying `<input type="file">` element.

Automating file uploads in tests

In most web apps, file uploads are handled through an HTML `<input type="file">` element: you click a button, a file picker pops up, and you choose a file from your computer.

When you're automating this with Playwright, you don't have to pretend to be a human clicking through that dialog. Instead, Playwright's `setInputFiles()` method lets you attach files directly to the input element, which skips the whole pop-up process. It's quicker and more reliable, and saves you from wrestling with those native OS dialogs that are a pain to automate.

To upload a file using Playwright, you start by finding the `<input type="file">` element on the page with a locator. Even if the input is hidden, Playwright can still work with it, which is handy. Once you have the element, you use the `setInputFiles()` method to simulate a user selecting a file from their system.

You just pass the file path as a string if you're uploading one file, or an array of paths if you're handling multiple files. For example, if you have a file called `document.pdf` sitting in a `tests` folder in your project, you'd point to that path, and Playwright takes care of the rest:

```
import { test, expect } from '@playwright/test';
import path from 'node:path';

test('should upload a single file', async ({ page }) => {
  // Navigate to the page with the file input
  await page.goto('https://demoqa.com/automation-practice-form');

  // Build an absolute path to the file you want to upload
  const filePath = path.join(__dirname, 'document.pdf');
```

```
    // Locate the input element and set the file
    await page.locator('input[type="file"]').setInputFiles(filePath);

    // Confirm the file input reflects the selected file
    await expect(page.locator('#uploadPicture')).toHaveValue(/document\.
  pdf$/);

    // You can also click the submit button and
    // add assertions to verify the upload was successful
  });
```

This script defines the path to the file to be uploaded. It uses `path.join(__dirname, 'document.pdf')` to build that path in a way that works no matter which OS you're on. The `__dirname` variable returns the absolute path of the directory that contains the current script, and `path.join` combines that with the filename while automatically using the correct type of slashes for each OS (forward slashes on Linux/Mac, backslashes on Windows). This is important because Playwright needs the exact, absolute file path to successfully locate and upload the file. In this case, the code assumes there's a file called `document.pdf` sitting right next to your script.

The main event here is the file upload. The script finds the file input on the page by looking for an `<input>` tag with `type="file"` using `page.locator('input[type="file"]')`. Once it has that, it calls `setInputFiles` and hands over the file path we just built. That's basically the code's way of *pretending* a user picked the file from a file chooser.

You could build on this, such as clicking a submit button and using `expect` to check that the upload actually worked (we'll cover that shortly), but that part's not implemented here.

Clearing the file selection

When you're testing file uploads, there are times when you'll want to check what happens if no file is selected or if you need to reset a file input back to its empty state. This can be helpful for catching edge cases, such as making sure a form throws the right error if a required file is missing, or confirming that everything works fine when the file is optional.

You can clear a file input just by calling the `setInputFiles()` method on the locator for that input and passing in an empty array.

For example, if your file input has an ID of `upload`, you can reset it like this:

```
await page.locator('#upload').setInputFiles([]);
```

That one line of code wipes out the file selection, so it's as if the user never picked anything.

Handling multiple file uploads

The goal is to automate the process of selecting and uploading multiple files through a web form, which is a common task in testing scenarios such as submitting forms with attachments.

In a typical web form, multiple file uploads are enabled by an `<input type="file" multiple>` element, which allows users to select more than one file at a time. Fortunately, the `setInputFiles()` method is versatile and can handle both single and multiple file uploads, depending on what you pass to it.

For multiple files, you pass an array of file paths or file-like objects to the `setInputFiles()` method. The files must exist on your local filesystem, as Playwright will read them and simulate uploading their contents to the browser.

You'd write code that looks something like this:

```
import { test, expect } from '@playwright/test';

test('should upload multiple files successfully', async ({ page }) => {
  // Navigate to the file upload page.
  await page.goto('https://filebin.net/');

  // Locate the file input element
  const fileInput = page.locator('input[type="file"]');

  // Set multiple files for upload.
  // Ensure these files exist in your test directory.
  await fileInput.setInputFiles([
    'tests/sample1.jpg',
    'tests/sample2.jpg',
    'tests/sample3.jpg'
  ]);

  // Wait for the shareable link to appear,
  // indicating upload has finished
```

```
  await expect(page.getByRole('link', { name: '? Download files' })).
toBeVisible();

  // Verify that the file names are displayed in the UI
  await expect(
    page.getByRole('link', { name: 'sample1.jpg' }).first()
  ).toBeVisible();
  await expect(
    page.getByRole('link', { name: 'sample2.jpg' }).first()
  ).toBeVisible();
  await expect(
    page.getByRole('link', { name: 'sample3.jpg' }).first()
  ).toBeVisible();
});
```

This script ensure that multiple files can be uploaded to `filebin.net` and that the website displays them correctly. It navigates to the site, uploads three sample images, waits for a download link to confirm the upload, and then checks that the file names appear in the UI.

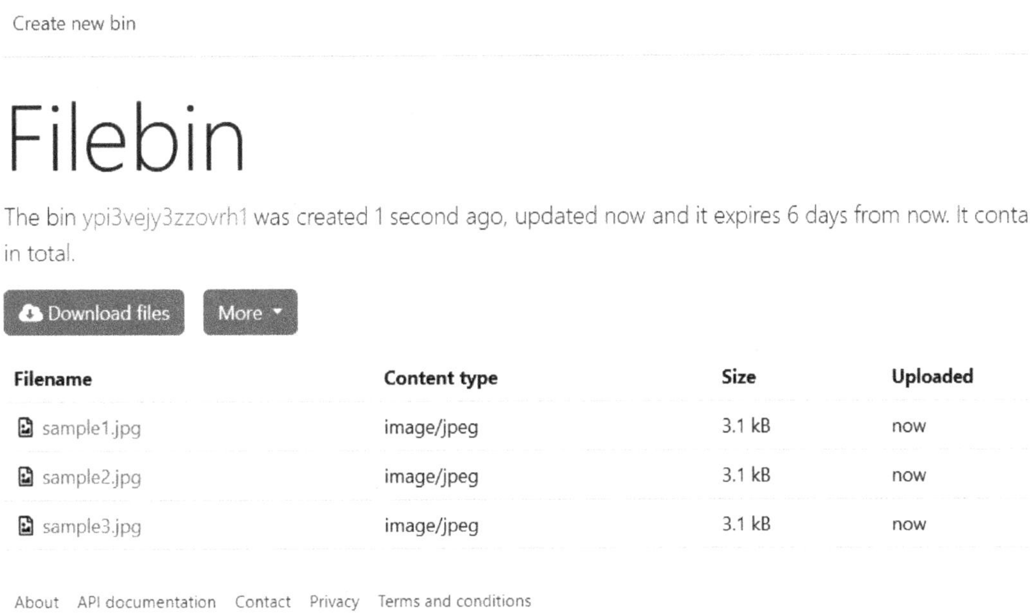

Figure 13.1: Filenames appear in the Filebin UI after upload

The `setInputFiles()` method takes care of reading the files and passing their contents to the browser, mimicking what a user would do when selecting files through a file picker dialog.

One thing to watch out for is ensuring the input element supports multiple files. If the `<input>` tag doesn't have the `multiple` attribute, Playwright will throw an error when you try to upload more than one file. You can check this in your test by inspecting the element's attributes or handling errors gracefully with a `try-catch` block.

> If you're running tests in a CI/CD environment, make sure the file paths you provide are accessible in that environment. Hardcoding local paths such as `/Users/you/file.jpg` might work on your machine but fail in a containerized setup. Use relative paths or generate files dynamically to keep things portable.

Creating file-like objects in memory

Sometimes when you're testing file uploads with Playwright, you don't want to mess around with actual files on your computer. Maybe you just want to create some files on the fly for your tests. That's where creating file-like objects in memory comes in handy. You can make Playwright think you're uploading real files without ever needing to save anything to disk.

You can do that by creating an array of objects that act like files. Each object needs a name, a mime type (to tell the browser what kind of file it is, such as `text/plain` for a text file), and a buffer (the actual content of the file, made with Node.js's `Buffer.from` method).

Here's a quick example of how you'd make and upload a couple of text files:

```
await page.locator('input[type="file"]').setInputFiles([
  {
    name: 'file1.txt',
    mimeType: 'text/plain',
    buffer: Buffer.from('Hey, this is the first file's content!')
  },
  {
    name: 'file2.txt',
    mimeType: 'text/plain',
    buffer: Buffer.from('Yo, this is the second file's content!')
  }
]);
```

In this code, you're creating two text files right in memory. The `mimeType` says they're plain text files, and the `buffer` turns your strings into binary data that Playwright can use as file content. When you pass this to `setInputFiles`, it's like you picked those files from your computer.

This trick is great because you can make any kind of file content you want, such as CSVs, JSONs, or even images, without cluttering up your system with test files. It's perfect for when you need to try out different file sizes, formats, or data to make sure your app handles uploads properly. Plus, you don't have to delete files afterward.

Handling multiple file types (such as PDF and CSV)

Since Playwright's `setInputFiles()` method doesn't really care about the file type (it just hands the file path over to the browser), your job is to make sure the test logic accounts for how each format should be handled, validated, and processed by your app.

In a real app, a PDF upload might pop open a preview, while a CSV upload could get parsed into a table. Those are completely different behaviors, and you want your tests to check that each one works as expected. That means not only simulating the uploads but also making sure the app's responses match your expectations.

Let's say your app has an `<input type="file">` element that allows both `.pdf` and `.csv` files, maybe with an `accept=".pdf,.csv"` attribute. As we have seen, uploading them is as simple as calling `setInputFiles()` with the file paths:

```
await page.locator('#upload').setInputFiles([
  'path/to/document.pdf',
  'path/to/data.csv'
]);
```

You'll either include sample PDF and CSV files in your project or generate them dynamically. Creating test files dynamically is often the better approach, especially for CSVs, which are easy to generate programmatically. PDFs are trickier, but you can use a library such as `pdfkit` in Node.js to create simple ones (`https://www.npmjs.com/package/pdfkit`).

Once the files are uploaded, you'll want to verify that the application handles them correctly. This depends on what your app does with PDFs and CSVs. For instance, if the app displays a preview of the PDF or renders the CSV as a table, you can use Playwright's assertions to verify the UI, like this:

```
expect(page.locator('selector')).toBeVisible();
// or
expect(page.locator('selector')).toContainText('Expected Text');
```

Handling different file types also means testing edge cases. For example, what happens if you upload a DOCX when only CSVs are allowed? Or a corrupted CSV? You can test these scenarios by creating invalid files or files with unexpected formats and checking for error messages.

If your application has specific validation logic (such as checking CSV headers or PDF metadata), you'll need to tailor your test files to trigger those cases. For example, create a CSV with missing headers or a PDF with specific metadata and check the app's behavior. Playwright can't parse these files itself, but you can use Node.js libraries (`csv-parse` for CSVs or `pdf-parse` for PDFs) to validate file content in your test setup or assertions.

If your app uses drag-and-drop for uploads, the same principles apply. If the dropzone is backed by an `<input type="file">` element, use `setInputFiles` with your PDF and CSV paths. If it's a custom dropzone, you might need to simulate drag events, but this is rare and usually unnecessary if an input element is present.

Downloads are just as important as uploads in today's web apps. Your users want them to start quickly, finish smoothly, and deliver exactly what they were expecting. And that brings us to our next section.

Handling file downloads in tests

Downloading files in a web app can be as easy as clicking a link, or as tricky as creating and sending custom reports on the fly. When it comes to testing, the challenge isn't just about starting the download but making sure the right file actually shows up, in the correct format, and with the content you expect.

Luckily, Playwright makes this a breeze by letting you catch download events, grab all the file details, and check everything from filenames to file size.

Triggering and verifying downloads

If your web app lets users download files (such as generating reports or grabbing uploaded content), being able to automate and verify those downloads in Playwright is a useful skill. Playwright makes it pretty straightforward. You can kick off the download, catch the event when it happens, and then check that the file looks exactly how you expect.

In a real app, downloads usually start when a user does something: clicks a link (such as `<a href="file.pdf" download>`), submits a form, or hits a button that makes the server send a file back. When you're automating this with Playwright, you're basically recreating those same actions: trigger the download, grab it when it's ready, and then make sure it passes your checks, whether that's the filename, file size, or what's inside. Playwright's `download` event and APIs let you do all this smoothly.

To start, you need to set up your Playwright test to listen for the `download` event before triggering the action that initiates the download. Playwright's page object emits a `download` event when a file download starts, and you can use `page.waitForEvent('download')` to capture it.

Here's an example where clicking a button triggers a file download:

```
import { test, expect } from '@playwright/test';

test('Trigger and verify CSV download', async ({ page }) => {
  // Navigate to the famous art download page
  await page.goto('https://www.nga.gov/artworks/106382-self-portrait');

  // Wait for the download event
  const downloadPromise = page.waitForEvent('download', { timeout: 30000
});

  // Locate and click the primary download button
  await page.getByRole('link', { name: 'Download', exact: true }).click();

  // Wait for the download to start
  const download = await downloadPromise;

  // Verify the download file
  const fileName = download.suggestedFilename();

  // Match expected downloaded file name
  expect(fileName).toMatch(/self-portrait_1998.74.5.jpg/);
  console.log(`Downloaded file: ${fileName}.`);
});
```

This script automates the process of going to the National Gallery of Art site, clicking the download button, and confirming that a valid image file is downloaded:

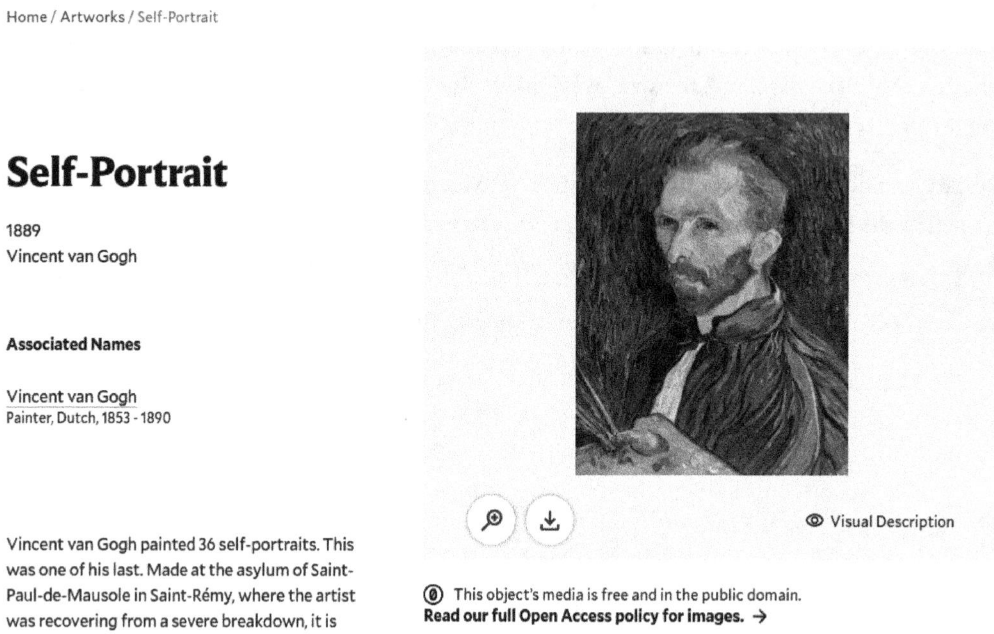

Figure 13.2: The script automates downloading and verifying the image file.

First, we set up a promise to wait for the download event with `page.waitForEvent('download', { timeout: 30000 })`. This tells Playwright to listen for a file download and gives it up to 30 seconds to start. The timeout is important because downloads can sometimes take a moment, especially if the network is slow or the site is doing some processing. Then, we trigger the download by finding and clicking a download button. The `click()` method simulates a user clicking that link to start the download.

Once the download starts, the promise (`downloadPromise`) resolves, giving us a `download` object that contains details about the file. We grab the suggested filename with `download.suggestedFilename()` and check whether it matches the expected image name using the following:

```
expect(fileName).toMatch(/self-portrait_1998.74.5.jpg/);
```

Sometimes, you may want to save the downloaded file to a specific location for further inspection or to keep it after the test. You can use `download.saveAs()` to copy the file to a desired path:

```
import { test, expect } from '@playwright/test';

test('Trigger and verify CSV download', async ({ page }) => {
  // Navigate to the famous art download page
  await page.goto('https://www.nga.gov/artworks/106382-self-portrait');

  // Wait for the download event
  const downloadPromise = page.waitForEvent('download', { timeout: 30000
});

  // Locate and click the primary download button
  await page.getByRole('link', { name: 'Download', exact: true }).click();

  // Wait for the download to start
  const download = await downloadPromise;

  // Verify the download file
  const fileName = download.suggestedFilename();

  // Match expected downloaded file name
  expect(fileName).toMatch(/self-portrait_1998.74.5.jpg/);

  // Save the downloaded file to verify it later (for CI environments)
  await download.saveAs(`./downloads/${fileName}`);

  // Verify the download path exists
  const downloadPath = await download.path();
  expect(downloadPath).not.toBeNull();

  console.log(`Downloaded file: ${fileName} at ${downloadPath}`);
});
```

If you want to make your tests more robust, especially in CI environments where you might want to poke around the file later, you can have the script save the downloaded file into a `downloads` folder using the following:

```
await download.saveAs(`./downloads/${fileName}`);
```

This isn't strictly required for verification, but it's helpful for debugging or running extra checks afterward. Just remember that the target folder (such as `downloads/`) has to exist beforehand, or Playwright will throw an error.

Once that's sorted, we make sure the download actually happened by checking its path with `download.path()`. The assertion confirms that Playwright successfully tracked the file and that it exists on your system:

```
expect(downloadPath).not.toBeNull()
```

For extra clarity, we also log the filename and path to the console.

Validating downloaded content

If you want to check what's inside a downloaded file, you can read it from the path returned by `download.path()`. Since Playwright saves the file straight to your disk, Node.js's `fs` module makes it easy to take a peek at the contents.

First, import the `fs` module like this:

```
const fs = require('fs').promises;
```

Then, you can read the file and check what's inside:

```
const content = await fs.readFile(filePath, 'utf8');
await expect(content).toContain('Expected text in file');
```

This works great for text-based files (such as CSV, JSON, or plain text) where you can directly search for certain strings. For binary files, such as PDFs or images, you'd probably check things such as file size, or use a library that knows how to parse them.

For example, to check the file size in our image example, we can use the following:

```
import { test, expect } from '@playwright/test';
const fs = require('node:fs').promises;

test('Trigger and verify CSV download', async ({ page }) => {
  // Navigate to the famous art download page
```

```
  await page.goto('https://www.nga.gov/artworks/106382-self-portrait');

  // Wait for the download event
  const downloadPromise = page.waitForEvent('download', { timeout: 30000
});

  // Locate and click the primary download button
  await page.getByRole('link', { name: 'Download', exact: true }).click();

  // Wait for the download to start
  const download = await downloadPromise;

  // Verify the download file
  const fileName = download.suggestedFilename();

  // Match expected downloaded file name
  expect(fileName).toMatch(/self-portrait_1998.74.5.jpg/);

  // Save the downloaded file to verify it later (for CI environments)
  await download.saveAs(`./downloads/${fileName}`);

  // Verify the download path exists
  const downloadPath = await download.path();
  expect(downloadPath).not.toBeNull();

  // Verify the file size
  const stats = await fs.stat(downloadPath);

  // Convert bytes to MB
  const fileSizeInMB = stats.size / (1024 * 1024);

  // Ensure file size is reasonable (>100KB)
  expect(fileSizeInMB).toBeGreaterThan(0.1);

  // Ensure file size isn't unrealistically large (<100MB)
  expect(fileSizeInMB).toBeLessThan(100);
```

```
  console.log(`Downloaded file: ${fileName} at ${downloadPath}, Size: ${fileSizeInMB.toFixed(2)} MB`);
});
```

This code should output something such as this to the console:

```
Downloaded file: self-portrait_1998.74.5.jpg at C:\Users\faraz\AppData\
Local\Temp\playwright-artifacts-iq3qYg\4018e28f-9c04-4db2-bb9d-
bf6c814a1036, Size: 6.15 MB
```

Playwright will automatically accept downloads for you; so, as long as your test environment supports downloads, you're good to go. Since Playwright runs browsers in a clean context by default, downloads usually work right away. The only exception is if your app starts the download in a new tab or window. In that case, you'll need to take care of handling that new page yourself. Remember, the target folder has to exist beforehand, or the test will fail.

Handling failure

Sometimes downloads don't go as planned: maybe the server throws an error, or the file you're trying to grab just isn't there. Playwright has you covered for these situations. The `download` object's `failure()` method lets you catch and handle these issues gracefully. If the download fails, this method returns an error message that you can check.

For example, if a server error such as 404 (resource not found) or 403 (forbidden access) occurs, the `failure()` method will capture the specific error message, which lets you inspect it and respond appropriately in your code.

To check for a failed download, you can use this method in an asynchronous operation. For instance, you might write code such as this:

```
const error = await download.failure();
await expect(error).toContain('404');
```

In this example, calling `await download.failure()` grabs the error message from the failed download. Then, the `expect` statement checks whether that message contains `404` to confirm that the failure was due to a `not found` error. This approach comes in handy when you're testing tricky edge cases such as broken links, missing files, or attempts to access something without permission.

Keep in mind that in real test environments, network conditions can fluctuate and filesystems may introduce delays. Playwright won't always treat these as standard download failures, so it's useful to widen your checks.

One approach is to apply a dedicated timeout to the download itself. That way, if the server stalls and the download never begins, the test fails quickly instead of idling until the overall test timeout.

You can do this by passing a timeout value to the event waiter. If no download starts within that period, you can catch the error and verify that the application responds appropriately to slow or unstable network conditions:

```
try {
  // Wait for the download with a short 5-second timeout
  const downloadPromise = page.waitForEvent(
    'download',
    { timeout: 5000 }
  );
  await page.getByText('Download Large File').click();
  await downloadPromise;
} catch (error) {
  // Verify that the error is a timeout, confirming the app didn't crash
  expect(error.message).toContain('Timeout');
}
```

When working with downloads in Playwright, it's worth thinking about how you'll manage the files so your test environment doesn't get messy.

Keeping your test environment clean

By default, when a download completes, Playwright's `download.path()` gives you the file path to a temporary location. These temp files are usually cleaned up automatically by Playwright, so you don't have to worry about them piling up in the background.

But there's a catch: if you use the `saveAs()` method to put the file somewhere specific, it's no longer considered temporary and Playwright won't delete it for you. In that case, it's up to you to tidy things up.

A simple way to do this is with Node.js's `fs.unlink()` function, which removes a file after your test finishes:

```
await fs.unlink(downloadedFilePath);
```

You can put it in an `afterAll` hook so that every test run starts with a clean slate:

```
let downloadedFilePath;

afterAll(async () => {
  if (downloadedFilePath) {
    await fs.unlink(downloadedFilePath);
  }
});
```

This way, any files you explicitly saved with `saveAs()` get removed once the suite wraps up. In a CI/CD environment, this usually isn't an issue as the container is wiped after the run. But for local testing, it is good practice to delete these artifacts to prevent your hard drive from filling up with thousands of test reports.

Summary

File uploads and downloads might seem simple at first glance, but in practice, they involve a surprising amount of nuance, especially when you need to test them reliably across different browsers, file types, and environments. With Playwright's powerful APIs, such as `setInputFiles()`, and its built-in download handling, you can skip the OS-level dialogs, directly control the file life cycle, and validate every step from selection to cleanup.

We've covered how to upload single and multiple files, generate test files in memory, verify download integrity, handle failures gracefully, and keep our environment tidy. By automating these tasks, we not only speed up our testing process but also gain confidence that our application can handle real-world scenarios, whether it's a user uploading a multi-page PDF, downloading a generated report, or accidentally selecting the wrong file.

Ultimately, robust file-handling tests are about more than just "does it work?" They're about ensuring that every user, in every browser, gets a smooth, predictable experience.

In the next chapter, we'll look at ways to automate authentication scenarios with Playwright.

14

Security and Authentication

Authentication is the front door to most web applications, and testing it thoroughly is important for ensuring both security and usability. Whether a user is logging in, logging out, switching roles, or authenticating through a third-party provider, each step in the process needs to work flawlessly. Even a single slip-up can lead to anything from an annoying user experience to a serious security breach.

In this chapter, we'll look at ways to automate authentication scenarios with Playwright. We'll kick things off by testing the core login and logout flows that almost every app depends on. Then, we'll dive into saving and reusing authentication states to make tests faster and cut down on repetitive steps.

You'll see how to manage multiple user roles without logging in over and over, plus how to keep credentials secure in your testing setup. We'll wrap up by tackling trickier cases such as **OAuth** and **single sign-on** (**SSO**), showing you how to handle them smoothly in automated tests. By the end, you'll have a complete toolkit for testing authentication.

The chapter is structured into these sections:

- Testing login and logout flows
- Managing session persistence and efficiency
- Managing multiple user roles in tests
- Securing and handling complex authentication methods

Technical requirements

The source code for this chapter is available at

`https://github.com/PacktPublishing/Hands-On-Automated-Testing-with-Playwright/tree/main/Chapter14`.

Testing login and logout flows

Login and logout are key parts of almost every web app. Testing these flows helps catch bugs such as incorrect redirects, session persistence, and UI glitches. With Playwright, you can automate these tests to run consistently and catch issues early.

We've already covered how to handle logging in correctly in *Chapter 12, Testing Forms,* so now let's focus on logging out the right way. When a user signs out, you'll want to confirm that their session really ends and that they can't wander back into protected areas without logging in again.

Since logging out requires an active session, we'll start by logging in first. Once that's done, we'll trigger the logout by simulating a click on the **Logout** button or link. After logging out, we'll verify that the session has ended by checking that the user is redirected to the login page and can no longer access any protected routes.

Consider this code:

```
import { test, expect } from'@playwright/test';

test('should successfully log out from Swag Labs', async ({ page }) => {
  // Navigate to the login page
  await page.goto('https://www.saucedemo.com/');

  // Log in with valid credentials
  await page.getByPlaceholder('Username').fill('standard_user');
  await page.getByPlaceholder('Password').fill('secret_sauce');
  await page.getByRole('button', { name: 'Login' }).click();

  // Verify successful login by checking for inventory page
  await expect(page).toHaveURL('https://www.saucedemo.com/inventory.
html');
  await expect(page.locator('.inventory_list')).toBeVisible();

  // Open the menu and click logout
```

```
  await page.getByRole('button', { name: 'Open Menu' }).click();
  await page.getByRole('link', { name: 'Logout' }).click();

  // Verify redirection to login page
  await expect(page).toHaveURL('https://www.saucedemo.com/');
  await expect(page.getByRole('button', { name: 'Login' })).toBeVisible();

  // Verify the session cookie named 'session-username' no longer exists
  await expect.poll(async () =>
    (await page.context().cookies()).some(
      cookie => cookie.name === 'session-username'
    )
  ).toBeFalsy();

  // Attempt to access a protected route (inventory) to confirm logout
  await page.goto('https://www.saucedemo.com/inventory.html');
  await expect(page).toHaveURL('https://www.saucedemo.com/');
  await expect(page.getByRole('button', { name: 'Login' })).toBeVisible();
});
```

To log in, we use Playwright's `getByPlaceholder()` method to find the `username` and `password` fields and fill them with a test account. Then, we locate the **Login** button using `getByRole('button', { name: 'Login' })` and click it. The `getByRole()` method is great here because it looks for a button with the accessible name `Login`, which makes the script more robust than relying on fragile CSS selectors.

After logging in, we need to confirm that the login worked before testing the logout. We check two things:

- First, we make sure that the browser's URL is now `https://www.saucedemo.com/inventory.html`, which is the product listing page you see after a successful login. We use `expect(page).toHaveURL()` for this.
- Second, we verify that the inventory list (the grid of products) is visible on the page using `expect(page.locator('.inventory_list')).toBeVisible()`. This ensures that we're really logged in and on the right page. We had to use a CSS selector (`.inventory_list`) here because there's no clear `getBy*` method that matches this element's attributes, but it's a stable choice since it's a key part of the page's structure.

Now comes the logout part. Swag Labs has a hamburger menu (those three lines in the corner) that you need to open to access the logout option:

Figure 14.1: Swag Labs' hamburger menu to access the logout option

We find the hamburger menu button with `getByRole('button', { name: 'Open Menu' })` and click it. This opens the sidebar. Then, we use `page.getByRole('link', { name: 'Logout' })` to find and click the logout link.

To make sure the logout worked, we check two things again:

- First, we confirm that the app cleared the user's authentication data. Sometimes logout logic runs asynchronously, or the UI updates faster than the cookie is actually removed, which can lead to flaky tests. But verifying that the cookie is removed only tells you that the client-side session data is cleared: it doesn't confirm that the server or application properly blocks unauthorized access.
- Second, we want to ensure that the session is truly ended, so we try to access a protected route (the inventory page) directly by navigating to `https://www.saucedemo.com/inventory.html`. If the logout was successful, the site should redirect us back to the login page. We check this by confirming that the URL is `https://www.saucedemo.com/` and that the login button is still visible.

This double-checks that the user can't sneak back into the protected area without logging in again.

> Keep in mind that if the logout functionality invalidates the saved storage or user state that another test relies on, you'll end up frustrated because your test runs will be flaky.
>
> A best practice is to ensure that the user you log out with is a dedicated test user, not your saved user, so it doesn't affect other test runs. The same applies to clearing cookies.

After establishing the basics of logging in and out, the next step is making those processes faster and more efficient.

Managing session persistence and efficiency

Keeping your authentication sessions alive between tests can save a lot of time and cut out repetitive steps. Instead of logging in before every single scenario, you can simply capture and reuse session data so your tests kick off already logged in. This includes cookies, local storage, and, as of version 1.51, `IndexedDB` snapshots (when enabled with `indexedDB: true`. See `https://playwright.dev/docs/release-notes#storagestate-for-indexeddb.`).

Not only does this speed up your whole suite, but it also helps prevent login-related issues from sneaking into tests that don't even involve logging in. In this section, we'll walk through how to save your auth data, reuse it across runs, and keep your session management rock-solid over time.

> There's one edge case to be aware of: if your authentication is stored in session storage, `storageState()` won't capture it. In that situation, you'll need to add a small helper script to save and reload that data yourself. It's a bit of extra work, but you can abstract the logic into a clean helper function so it doesn't clutter your tests. Playwright's docs show a good example of this approach:
>
> `https://playwright.dev/docs/auth#session-storage.`

Saving authentication data

When your tests involve logging in multiple times, Playwright makes things easier by letting you save and reuse authentication data with storage states. Instead of logging in for every test, you can log in once, store the session details (such as cookies and local storage) in a file, and then reuse that state across your tests.

Following Playwright's best practices, we'll use a dedicated setup project to handle authentication and store the session data in a `.auth/` folder, which should be added to your `.gitignore` file to prevent sensitive data from being committed.

Creating the authentication setup test

Create a file named `tests/auth.setup.ts` to handle the login process and save the session storage. This file will act as a setup test that runs before your other tests:

```
// tests/auth.setup.ts
import { test as setup, expect } from '@playwright/test';

setup('authenticate as standard_user', async ({ page }) => {
  // Navigate to the login page
  await page.goto('https://www.saucedemo.com/');

  // Log in with valid credentials
  await page.getByPlaceholder('Username').fill('standard_user');
  await page.getByPlaceholder('Password').fill('secret_sauce');
  await page.getByRole('button', { name: 'Login' }).click();

  // Verify successful login
  await expect(page).toHaveURL('https://www.saucedemo.com/inventory.
html');
  await expect(page.locator('.inventory_list')).toBeVisible();

  // Save the storage state to a file
  await page.context().storageState({ path: '.auth/standard_user.json' });
});
```

Here, the `setup` alias (imported as `test as setup`) is used to define the authentication process. After logging in with the `standard_user` credentials, the `storageState` method saves the browser context's session data to `.auth/standard_user.json`. The `.auth/` folder keeps authentication files organized.

Configuring the setup project

Update `playwright.config.ts` to include a setup project that runs the `auth.setup.ts` file before other tests. This makes sure the authentication state is prepared before any dependent tests run:

```
// playwright.config.ts
import { defineConfig } from '@playwright/test';

export default defineConfig({
  projects: [
    {
      name: 'setup',
      testMatch: /.*\.setup\.ts/,
    },
    {
      name: 'e2e-tests',
      dependencies: ['setup'],
      use: {
        storageState: '.auth/standard_user.json',
      },
    },
  ],
});
```

Here, the `setup` project uses `testMatch: /.*\.setup\.ts/` to include any files ending with `.setup.ts`, including `tests/auth.setup.ts`. The `e2e-tests` project lists `setup` as a dependency, which makes sure the `setup` project runs first and must pass before the `e2e-tests` project executes. The `use` option in the `e2e-tests` project applies the saved `.auth/standard_user.json` state. This allows tests to run in an authenticated state without repeated logins.

Writing tests using the authenticated state

With the `setup` project in place, your tests can reuse the authenticated state:

```
// tests/inventory.test.ts
import { test, expect } from '@playwright/test';

test('should access inventory page with authenticated state', async ({
page }) => {
  // No need to log in,
```

```
  // the storage state is applied from .auth/standard_user.json
  await page.goto('https://www.saucedemo.com/inventory.html');

  // Verify the inventory page is accessible
  await expect(page).toHaveURL('https://www.saucedemo.com/inventory.
html');
  await expect(page.locator('.inventory_list')).toBeVisible();

  // Perform an action on the inventory page
  await expect(page.locator('.inventory_item').first()).toBeVisible();
  await page.getByText('Add to cart').first().click();
  await expect(page.locator('.shopping_cart_badge')).toHaveText('1'); });
```

Here, the browser context starts as if the user is already logged in. The test checks that the inventory page loads smoothly and shows adding an item to the cart, so we can see that everything works properly while logged in.

Adding .auth/ to .gitignore

To prevent sensitive authentication data from being committed, create a `.auth/` folder in your project root (or wherever you save the storage state files) and add it to your `.gitignore` file:

```
.auth/
```

This ensures that files such as `.auth/standard_user.json` are not tracked by Git.

Now, the `.auth/standard_user.json` file can be reused across multiple test suites, which reduces login overhead. You can create additional setup tests for different user roles in separate `.setup.ts` files, each saving its own storage state, such as `.auth/admin_user.json`.

Ways to reuse the authentication data

You can apply the storage state globally in the Playwright configuration file (`playwright.config.ts`) or individually in a test using the `test.use()` method or `browser.newContext()`. When the storage state is applied, the browser context starts with the authenticated session, so you can navigate directly to protected routes without logging in again.

In the following example, you'll see how you can use the `test.use()` method to load the `standard_user.json` file we saved in the previous section:

```
import { test, expect } from '@playwright/test';

// Use the saved storage state to bypass login
test.use({ storageState: './.auth/standard_user.json' });

test('should access inventory page with saved storage state', async ({
page }) => {
  // Navigate directly to the inventory page
  await page.goto('https://www.saucedemo.com/inventory.html');

  // Verify the inventory page is accessible without redirection
  await expect(page).toHaveURL('https://www.saucedemo.com/inventory.
html');
  await expect(page.locator('.inventory_list')).toBeVisible();

  // Example: Perform an action on the inventory page
  await expect(page.locator('.inventory_item').first()).toBeVisible();
  await page.getByText('Add to cart').first().click();
  await expect(page.locator('.shopping_cart_badge')).toHaveText('1');
});
```

The line `test.use({ storageState: './.auth/standard_user.json' })` tells Playwright to apply the saved storage state to the test, so the browser context starts as if the user is already logged in.

You can also configure it in the `playwright.config.ts` file:

```
const config = {
  projects: [
    {
      name: 'authenticated',
      use: {
        storageState: './.auth/standard_user.json',
      },
```

```
    },
  ],
  // other settings
};

export default config;
```

With this setup, you can run tests with the authenticated state by specifying the project:

```
npx playwright test --project=authenticated
```

Sometimes sessions can time out, or the way you log in might change, so it's a smart move to refresh your storage state every now and then just to keep everything running smoothly.

You can save multiple storage states for different roles. This makes it easier to test with various signed-in users. Check out the Playwright docs for an example: `https://playwright.dev/docs/auth#multiple-signed-in-roles`.

When applications use **role-based access control** (**RBAC**), testing only with a single user account isn't enough. That leads us to the next section.

Managing multiple user roles in tests

When you're running Playwright tests, sometimes you need to test your app from the perspective of different kinds of users, such as admins, editors, viewers, and so on. This comes up a lot in apps that use RBAC.

In real-world apps, different users don't just have different permissions: they often see completely different parts of the UI, follow different workflows, and can do (or not do) certain actions. An admin might be able to delete a record, while a regular user can only look at it. To make sure your tests cover all those scenarios, you'll need a way to switch between roles without constantly logging in and out.

The main trick here is browser contexts. You can spin up one context for your admin, another for your regular user, and run them side by side without any conflicts. Each one stays logged in with its own credentials, and they won't step on each other's toes.

To set this up, you typically start by creating a browser instance and then spawning multiple contexts from it. Here's an example to illustrate:

```
import { test, expect, BrowserContext } from "@playwright/test";

let standardContext: BrowserContext;
let lockedoutContext: BrowserContext;

test.afterAll(async () => {
  await standardContext.close();
  await lockedoutContext.close();
});

test("Standard vs Locked Out Permissions", async ({ browser }) => {
  // Create separate contexts for standard and locked out user
  standardContext = await browser.newContext();
  lockedoutContext = await browser.newContext();

  const standardPage = await standardContext.newPage();
  const lockedoutPage = await lockedoutContext.newPage();

  // Standard Login
  await standardPage.goto("https://www.saucedemo.com/");
  await standardPage.getByPlaceholder("Username").fill("standard_user");
  await standardPage.getByPlaceholder("Password").fill("secret_sauce");
  await standardPage.getByRole("button", { name: "Login" }).click();

  // Verify standard user can access inventory page
  await expect(standardPage).toHaveURL(
    "https://www.saucedemo.com/inventory.html"
  );

  await expect(standardPage.locator(".title")).toHaveText("Products");

  // Locked_out_user Login
  await lockedoutPage.goto("https://www.saucedemo.com/");
  await lockedoutPage.getByPlaceholder("Username").fill("locked_out_
user");
```

```
    await lockedoutPage.getByPlaceholder("Password").fill("secret_sauce");
    await lockedoutPage.getByRole("button", { name: "Login" }).click();

    // Verify locked out user gets error message
    const errorMessage = lockedoutPage.locator('[data-test="error"]');
    await expect(errorMessage).toBeVisible();
    await expect(errorMessage).toHaveText(
      "Epic sadface: Sorry, this user has been locked out."
    );
  });
```

In this example, two contexts are created: one for the standard user and one for the locked-out user. Each context gets its own page, and you log in with different credentials. The test then checks that the standard user can see the inventory page, while the locked-out user cannot. Since contexts are isolated, the sessions don't interfere with each other.

One thing to watch out for is resource management. Each context consumes memory, so spawning too many contexts in a single test run can strain your system, especially in CI environments. To optimize, close contexts and pages when they're no longer needed.

> When tests fail, it's helpful to know which role's context caused the issue. Playwright's tracing feature is a lifesaver here. You can enable tracing for each context to capture screenshots, network requests, and actions, which makes it easier to pinpoint whether the standard or locked-out context encountered a problem. Use `context.tracing.start()` and `context.tracing.stop()` to capture traces, and view them with Playwright's trace viewer.

Now that we've walked through testing basic authentication, keeping sessions running smoothly, and handling different user roles, it's time to dive into the more advanced side of authentication.

Securing and handling complex authentication methods

These days, most web apps use more than just a simple username and password to log in. From multi-step **OAuth** to SSO processes, authentication can quickly turn into a tricky puzzle for automated testing.

In this section, we're going to explore ways you can keep your credentials safe and secure, whether that means storing them in environment variables, using a dedicated secrets manager, or other techniques. We'll also talk about how to automate more advanced login flows, so you can protect your information.

Storing credentials securely

A simple and safe way to store your credentials in Playwright is by using **environment variables**. While Playwright doesn't come with its own built-in secrets manager, environment variables are great for keeping sensitive information secure. Environment variables are basically little key-value pairs that live outside your code base. They are usually managed by your operating system or at runtime.

The goal is to keep passwords, tokens, and other private details out of your scripts, and instead, load them only when your tests run. Since Playwright runs in a Node.js environment, you can easily grab these values using `process.env`.

To get started, you can set environment variables in a few ways, depending on your setup. If you're running tests locally, you can define them in your terminal before executing your Playwright script.

On Linux or macOS, in your terminal, run the following:

```
export USERNAME="standard_user"
export PASSWORD="secret_sauce"
```

On Windows, use this:

```
set USERNAME=standard_user
set PASSWORD=secret_sauce
```

Once set, you can use them in your Playwright scripts without ever hardcoding your secrets.

In your Playwright script, you can access these variables like this:

```
import { test, expect } from '@playwright/test';

const username = process.env.USERNAME;
const password = process.env.PASSWORD;

test.beforeAll(() => {
  if (!username || !password) {
```

```
    throw new Error('ERROR: USERNAME or PASSWORD not defined in
environment variables.');
  }
});

test('should successfully log out from Swag Labs', async ({ page }) => {
  // Navigate to the login page
  await page.goto('https://www.saucedemo.com/');

  // Log in with valid credentials
  await page.getByPlaceholder('Username').fill(username);
  await page.getByPlaceholder('Password').fill(password);
  await page.getByRole('button', { name: 'Login' }).click();
});
```

Here, the credentials are pulled from the environment variables at runtime, so they're never hardcoded in the script. This is a simple but effective way to keep things secure, especially for small projects or local development.

If you're working on a bigger project or collaborating with a team, it's a good idea to keep things organized by using a `.env` file for your environment variables. In Node.js, the `dotenv` package makes this easy.

First, install it with the following:

```
npm install dotenv
```

Then, in your project's root folder, create a `.env` file and add the following:

```
USERNAME=standard_user
PASSWORD=secret_sauce
```

This way, your sensitive info stays out of your code. Now, in your Playwright script, load the `.env` file by adding `import dotenv from 'dotenv';` at the top:

```
import { test, expect } from '@playwright/test';
import dotenv from 'dotenv';

dotenv.config();

test('login to example.com', async ({ page }) => {
```

```
    const username = process.env.USERNAME;
    const password = process.env.PASSWORD;

    // Go to login page
    await page.goto('https://www.saucedemo.com/');

    // Log in with valid credentials
    await page.getByPlaceholder('Username').fill(username);
    await page.getByPlaceholder('Password').fill(password);
    await page.getByRole('button', { name: 'Login' }).click();

    await expect(page).toHaveURL('https://www.saucedemo.com/inventory.
  html');
  });
```

To keep your `.env` file from sneaking into version control, just add it to your `.gitignore` file. That way, sensitive data stays local or is managed separately in a secure way.

If you're working in a CI/CD environment such as GitHub Actions or Jenkins, you can configure environment variables directly in the CI platform's settings, so the `.env` file isn't needed in the repository at all.

> It's usually best to pull your variables from the Playwright config file so they load just once instead of being fetched in every single test. We walk through this in *Chapter 16, Real-World Project – Testing an E-commerce Website.*

For an extra boost of security (especially in cloud environments), it's worth using a secrets management tool. Services such as AWS Secrets Manager, HashiCorp Vault, or Azure Key Vault can safely store your credentials and let you access them through APIs or SDKs. In Playwright, you'd just grab these secrets programmatically before your tests run. It might be a bit much for small projects, but for enterprise-level setups with strict security needs, it's a smart move.

> If you're looking for more examples, a good one would be to use the actual API call on the Sauce Demo to save the storage state for use in your setup files. Here's a practical example: `https://github.com/playwrightsolutions/playwright-practicesoftwaretesting.com/blob/main/lib/datafactory/login.ts`.

Handling OAuth and SSO scenarios

Handling OAuth and SSO scenarios in Playwright can be a bit tricky because these authentication flows often involve complex redirects, external **identity providers** (**IdPs**), and session management.

OAuth lets you log in to one account (such as Google or Facebook) and then give another app permission to use certain information from that account, without ever handing over your password. Instead of sharing your password, OAuth works with something called **access tokens**. When you give permission, the first service (called the **authorization server**) sends the other app a token. This token acts like a temporary key: it only unlocks the specific things you've allowed, and only for as long as it's valid.

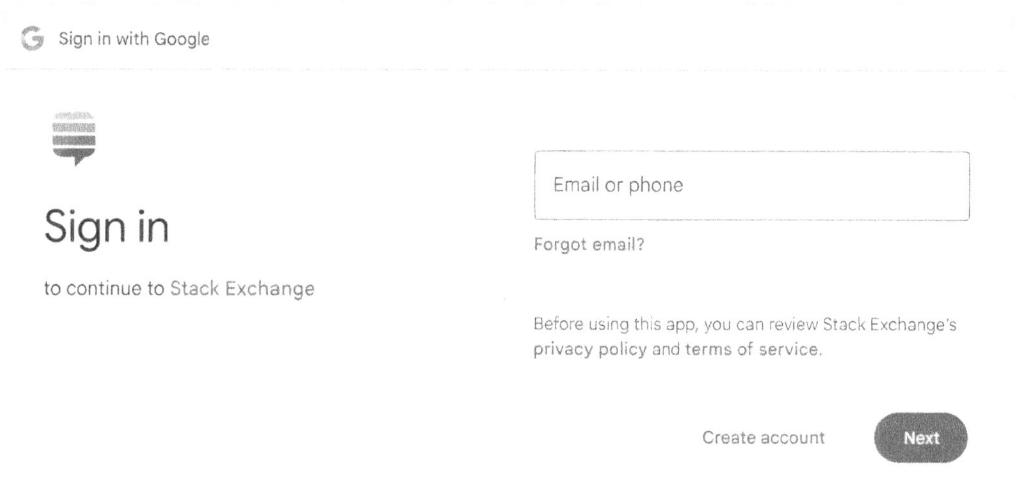

Figure 14.2: Google OAuth lets users sign in to apps or websites without giving away their password

SSO is a handy way to log in just once and get access to multiple apps or websites without juggling different usernames and passwords. For example, when you sign in to Google with your Gmail account, you can get right into YouTube or Google Drive without having to log in again. In Playwright, handling SSO can be a bit tricky because it often means dealing with external login pages, pop-ups, or tokens that change on the fly.

To automate OAuth and SSO in Playwright, you can simulate a user's actions: filling forms, clicking buttons, and navigating redirects through the IdP. However, **CAPTCHAs** or **multi-factor authentication** (**MFA**), such as **time-based one-time passwords** (**TOTPs**), can complicate full automation.

Here are some practical ways to handle these cases:

- **Manual login with session storage**:
    - Launch a Playwright browser with a persistent context to save the session.
    - Navigate to the login page, manually complete the SSO flow (such as sign in with Google), and save cookies and local storage to a file in your project folder.
    - Reuse the saved state in subsequent tests to bypass the login process.

  This method works really well for complex or stable SSO flows, so you don't have to deal with writing complicated authentication scripts.

- **Bypassing CAPTCHAs**: In testing environments, CAPTCHAs can often be bypassed by configuring the test environment to disable them or using mock responses. Consult your IdP's documentation for test-specific configurations, such as disabling CAPTCHAs for specific test accounts.
- **Handling TOTP-based MFA**: For MFA using TOTP, automation is possible if you have access to the TOTP secret key. By storing the key, you can generate valid TOTP codes programmatically during login. Playwright can integrate with libraries such as OTPAuth in Node.js to generate these codes. For detailed guidance, see `https://playwrightsolutions.com/playwright-login-test-with-2-factor-authentication-2fa-enabled/`.
- **Automating email or SMS-based MFA**: For MFA codes sent via email or SMS, tools such as Mailosaur (`https://mailosaur.com/`) provide APIs to programmatically retrieve codes from test email accounts or phone numbers.
- **Direct token or cookie injection**: If your application supports OAuth token authentication or direct cookie setting, you can bypass browser-based SSO flows. For test environments with API access or test users, inject an OAuth access token into the browser's local storage or set cookies directly to authenticate without navigating the full login flow.

Aim for a pragmatic mix: fast, stable tests that cover day-to-day behavior, plus a few carefully scoped full-flow tests to validate the real OAuth/SSO integration. That balance gives you confidence without making your test suite a maintenance burden.

Summary

Authentication sits at the core of application security, and testing it thoroughly is non-negotiable. In this chapter, we learned how to verify login and logout flows, save and reuse authentication states to speed up test execution, and manage multiple user roles without constant re-authentication. We also explored safe ways to manage credentials, along with tips for automating trickier setups such as OAuth and SSO.

The techniques here aren't just about getting tests to pass: they're about making authentication tests faster and easier to maintain over time. As you grow your automation coverage, keep fine-tuning your approach along the way. Regularly refresh stored sessions, adapt to evolving authentication flows, and keep sensitive data secure.

With these practices in place, your authentication testing will be ready to handle whatever changes your application or its security requirements throw at it.

The next chapter is about writing clean, maintainable test code to complement this chapter.

15

Best Practices for Test Maintainability

Testing web applications can be frustrating because modern apps are complex, ever-changing, and full of surprises. In *Chapter 14, Security and Authentication*, we dive into the art of crafting Playwright tests that are not just functional but also clean, readable, and easy to maintain. This chapter is your guide to building a test suite that's less like a tangled mess of code and more like a well-organized story, with a clear beginning, middle, and end.

We'll explore how to structure your tests, leverage the **Page Object Model** (**POM**) to keep things tidy, and manage test data to prevent those frustrating, flaky failures. Whether you're testing a simple login page or a sprawling e-commerce platform, these best practices will help you write tests that are scalable and easy to work with.

The chapter is structured into the following parts:

- Writing clean and readable test code
- Implementing page objects for better test organization
- Managing test data effectively to reduce maintenance

Technical requirements

The source code for this chapter is available at

`https://github.com/PacktPublishing/Hands-On-Automated-Testing-with-Playwright/tree/main/Chapter15`.

Writing clean and readable test code

When tests are cluttered or poorly structured, debugging becomes a chore, and maintaining them feels like unraveling a knot. This section is all about keeping your code easy to follow.

Organizing tests with the describe() block

Let's start by thinking about the structure of your tests. A well-organized test suite is like a well-written story: it has a clear beginning, logical progression, and a satisfying end. Playwright encourages this through its use of `describe()` blocks, which can be used to group related test functions for individual scenarios. Instead of cramming everything into one giant file, break things down into focused files or suites.

For instance, if you're testing a login feature, you might have a `login.spec.ts` file that groups tests under descriptive labels. This not only makes navigation easier but also helps when tests fail because you can quickly pinpoint the context.

Consider this simple example for testing a login page:

```
import { test, expect } from '@playwright/test';

test.describe('Login Functionality', () => {
  test('should allow valid user to log in', async ({ page }) => {
    await page.goto('https://www.saucedemo.com/');
    await page.getByPlaceholder('Username').fill('standard_user');
    await page.getByPlaceholder('Password').fill('secret_sauce');
    await page.getByRole('button', { name: 'Login' }).click();
    await expect(page).toHaveURL('https://www.saucedemo.com/inventory.
html');
  });

  test('should show error for invalid credentials', async ({ page }) => {
    await page.goto('https://www.saucedemo.com/');
    await page.getByPlaceholder('Username').fill('locked_out_user');
    await page.getByPlaceholder('Password').fill('secret_sauce');
    await page.getByRole('button', { name: 'Login' }).click();
    await expect(page.getByText('Epic sadface: Sorry, this user has been
locked out.')).toBeVisible();
  });
});
```

Here, the `describe` block sets the scene, and each test reads like a sentence: `'should allow valid user to log in'`. This conversational naming style makes the intent obvious at a glance, which is important for readability. Compare that to vague names such as `test1` or `loginTest`, which don't really tell a story.

Playwright's docs have a handy page all about best practices for writing tests that are both reliable and resilient. You can check it out here: `https://playwright.dev/docs/best-practices`.

Using fixtures for setup and teardown

Fixtures are another gem in Playwright for setup and teardown. The framework provides out-of-the-box fixtures such as page, `browser`, and `context` that handle browser management automatically. For custom needs, you can define your own fixture.

We explored how to define custom fixtures back in *Chapter 6, Test Parallelization and Performance Optimization*. But just to keep things fresh in our minds, let's take a quick look at them again.

Say you need a logged-in state for multiple tests: you can create a fixture that can be called and logs in at the beginning of each test. Here's an example:

```
import { test as base } from '@playwright/test';

export const test = base.extend({
  login: async ({ page }, use) => {
    await page.goto('https://www.saucedemo.com/');
    const login = async (username, password) => {
      await page.getByPlaceholder('Username').fill(username);
      await page.getByPlaceholder('Password').fill(password);
      await page.getByRole('button', { name: 'Login' }).click();
    };
    await use(login);
  },
});
```

The fixture will take care of navigating to the login page and signing in. The tests now use this fixture to handle the login action, which keeps the code clean:

```
import { test, expect } from './loginFixture';
import { expect } from '@playwright/test';


test.describe('Login Functionality', () => {
  test('should allow valid user to log in', async ({ login, page }) => {
    await login('standard_user', 'secret_sauce');
    await expect(page).toHaveURL('https://www.saucedemo.com/inventory.
html');
  });

  test('should show error for invalid credentials', async ({ login, page
}) => {
    await login('locked_out_user', 'secret_sauce');
    await expect(page.getByText('Epic sadface: Sorry, this user has been
locked out.')).toBeVisible();
  });
});
```

This way, each test can focus on what really matters: checking that valid credentials log in successfully, or that an error message appears for invalid ones without repeating all the navigation and input steps. This keeps your tests **DRY (short for Don't Repeat Yourself)**.

Playwright handles most of the cleanup, but you can use the `afterEach()` or `afterAll()` hooks for any manual teardown, such as closing modals or resetting data (see `https://playwright.dev/docs/api/class-test`).

Keep in mind that this fixture will run the login steps at the start of every test that uses it. If you want to avoid re-logging in for every test, you can use Playwright's `storageState`. We'll cover that in *Chapter 16, Real-World Project – Testing an E-commerce Website.*

> Don't ignore traceability: enable tracing in your config for debugging (`trace: 'on-failure'`).

Another way to give your code a clear structure is by using the **POM**, and that's what we'll cover next.

Implementing page objects for better test organization

POM is one of the key patterns that can transform your code base from a tangled mess of selectors and actions into something clean and maintainable.

Let's look at the problems they solve, and then walk through how to implement POM effectively to create more organized tests.

The pain of test duplication

If you've ever hunted through hundreds of lines of test code just to update a single CSS selector, you already know why POM matters. The idea is simple: you treat each page or any major part of your web app as its own class. That class holds everything about the page's structure (such as element locators) and the actions you can take on it (such as clicking a button or filling in a form). This pattern isn't new: it's been around in tools such as Selenium for a long time, but Playwright's modern API makes it easier to work with.

Without page objects, your tests might look like a series of direct interactions with the browser: navigating to a URL, locating elements by their selectors, and performing actions. That's fine for a quick script, but as your test suite grows, duplication creeps in. Say you're testing an e-commerce site with login, product search, and checkout flows. The same login steps get repeated across multiple tests, and if the UI changes (maybe a button's class name gets updated), you end up fixing it in a dozen places.

Page objects solve this by centralizing that knowledge. Each page class knows its own elements and methods, so your tests become more readable, like reading a story: *Go to the login page, enter credentials, submit.* Plus, it promotes reusability: you can compose complex flows by chaining page methods.

Implementing POM

Imagine you're testing a simple todo app, like the one at `https://demo.playwright.dev/todomvc`, which has a home page for adding and managing todos. To implement a page object, begin by creating a class for the page. Export it from a file such as `pages/TodoPage.ts`.

Here's a basic example for our TodoPage class:

```
import { type Page, type Locator } from '@playwright/test';

export class TodoPage {
  readonly page: Page;
  readonly newTodoInput: Locator;
  readonly todoItems: Locator;
  readonly clearCompletedButton: Locator;

  constructor(page: Page) {
    this.page = page;
    this.newTodoInput = page.locator('input.new-todo');
    this.todoItems = page.locator('ul.todo-list li');
    this.clearCompletedButton = page.locator('button.clear-completed');
  }

  async goto() {
    await this.page.goto('https://demo.playwright.dev/todomvc');
  }

  async addTodo(text: string) {
    await this.newTodoInput.fill(text);
    await this.newTodoInput.press('Enter');
  }

  async toggleTodo(index: number) {
    await this.todoItems.nth(index).locator('input.toggle').check();
  }

  async clearCompleted() {
    await this.clearCompletedButton.click();
  }
}
```

Inside the class, you'll have a constructor that takes a `Page` instance from Playwright. This is your handle to the browser page. Then, define `page.getBy*` or `page.locator()` methods as class properties. These methods are lazy: they don't query the DOM until you use them, which is efficient. For actions, you can add async methods that perform sequences of steps, returning promises so you can await them in tests.

See how this encapsulates everything? The locators are defined once, and methods such as `addTodo` handle the details of filling and submitting. If the input's selector changes, you fix it here, not in every test.

> The `await` keyword is necessary for any actions that Playwright does. For locators themselves, you don't need to add `await`. But when you're calling actions inside your async functions, you do. If you're using locators for assertions or interactions, `await` becomes necessary.

Now, in your test file (say, `tests/todo.spec.ts`), you import this page object and use it like so:

```
import { test, expect } from '@playwright/test';
import { TodoPage } from '../pages/TodoPage';

test('should add and complete a todo', async ({ page }) => {
  const todoPage = new TodoPage(page);
  await todoPage.goto();
  await todoPage.addTodo('Buy groceries');
  await expect(todoPage.todoItems).toHaveCount(1);
  await todoPage.toggleTodo(0);
  await todoPage.clearCompleted();
  await expect(todoPage.todoItems).toHaveCount(0);
});
```

This test reads almost like plain English. You're not cluttering it with low-level details. Instead, you're focusing on the behavior you're verifying. That's the beauty of POM: it separates concerns, making tests easier to understand and maintain.

Let's take a look at another example by refactoring the earlier test in this chapter to use a page object:

```
import { Page, Locator } from '@playwright/test';

export class LoginPage {
  private page: Page;
  private usernameInput: Locator;
  private passwordInput: Locator;
  private submitButton: Locator;
  private errorMessage: Locator;

  constructor(page: Page) {
    this.page = page;
    this.usernameInput = page.getByPlaceholder('Username');
    this.passwordInput = page.getByPlaceholder('Password');
    this.submitButton = page.getByRole('button', { name: 'Login' });
    this.errorMessage = page.locator('[data-test="error"]');
  }

  async navigate() {
    await this.page.goto('https://www.saucedemo.com/');
  }

  async login(username: string, password: string) {
    await this.usernameInput.fill(username);
    await this.passwordInput.fill(password);
    await this.submitButton.click();
  }

  async getErrorMessage() {
    return this.errorMessage.textContent();
  }
}
```

This POM pattern organizes our test code into a reusable class. The class declares private properties to store the locators for key elements on the login page: the username and password input fields, the submit button, and an error message element.

Adding JSDoc comments above your functions makes them easier to understand and use inside editors like VS Code. For example, here's how you can document the login function in your `LoginPage` class:

```
/**
* Logs in with the given username and password.
* @param {string} username - The username to use for login.
* @param {string} password - The password to use for login.
* Logs into the site using the provided credentials.
*/
```

By storing them as class properties, all the element references are in one place, so if the UI changes (say the username field's ID gets updated), you only need to change it in one place.

Now, in your test file, you import this page object like this:

```
import { test, expect } from '@playwright/test';
import { LoginPage } from '../pages/LoginPage';

test.describe('Login Functionality', () => {
  test('should allow valid user to log in', async ({ page }) => {
    const loginPage = new LoginPage(page);
    await loginPage.navigate();
    await loginPage.login('standard_user', 'secret_sauce');
    await expect(page).toHaveURL('https://www.saucedemo.com/inventory.
html');
  });

  test('should show error for invalid credentials', async ({ page }) => {
    const loginPage = new LoginPage(page);
    await loginPage.navigate();
    await loginPage.login('locked_out_user', 'secret_sauce');
    const error = await loginPage.getErrorMessage();
    expect(error).toBe('Epic sadface: Sorry, this user has been locked
out.');
  });
});
```

The tests now read like user stories, and the page object hides the gritty details. This pattern scales beautifully for larger applications with multiple pages.

You may have noticed that the two Playwright tests differ in how they declare their class properties: the `TodoPage` class goes with `readonly` for its properties, such as the page instance and locators, which makes sense because it's signaling that these things are set once in the constructor and won't change afterward. This is a great fit for page objects since they typically hold onto fixed references to a web page and its elements, and `readonly` lets TypeScript enforce that immutability and catches any accidental reassignments.

On the flip side, `LoginPage` uses `private` for its properties, which is more about keeping things under wraps than ensuring they never change. With `private`, the class is saying, "*These properties are mine, and only I can touch them.*" This focuses on encapsulation, making sure no external code can mess with the page or locators directly.

Unlike `readonly`, `private` doesn't stop you from reassigning those properties within the class, though `LoginPage` doesn't actually do that. The difference comes down to style or team preference: `readonly` emphasizes immutability, while `private` prioritizes access control. Both approaches are valid and align with POM principles, but they cater to slightly different needs.

> It's best practice not to include any assertions in your page object file. They belong in the test files.

Experiment with POM on a small scale first, then expand. As you apply this in your projects, you'll likely find your tests becoming more robust and your debugging sessions shorter.

As you build out your Playwright test suite, you'll quickly notice that how you handle test data can make or break its maintainability. Hardcoding values such as usernames or emails might seem like a quick win, but it often leads to brittle tests that fail when environments shift or requirements evolve. The next section dives into managing test data effectively.

Managing test data effectively to reduce maintenance

As we dive deeper into building robust end-to-end tests with Playwright, one aspect that often trips up even experienced developers is how to handle test data. Test data, including the inputs, configurations, and expected outputs that drive your tests, can quickly become a source of fragility if not managed thoughtfully.

The risks of hardcoding test data

Imagine you're testing a user registration form in your web app. You hardcode a username such as `testuser@example.com` directly into your test script. It works fine until the app's validation rules change, or you need to run the test in a different environment where that email is already taken. Suddenly, you're debugging failures that have nothing to do with the actual functionality. This is where poor test data management rears its head, leading to flaky tests, duplicated code, and hours wasted on updates.

Hardcoding data right into test files is quick to start with, but as your suite grows, updating hard-coded values across dozens of tests becomes a nightmare. Dynamic data, such as timestamps or app-generated IDs, are also tricky to deal with. If your tests expect exact matches and don't allow for that natural variability, you might end up with failures that seem to come out of nowhere.

Environmental dependencies are another culprit. Tests might work in development but bomb in staging because the database seed is different or an API returns something unexpected. And if you lean too heavily on production-like data, you risk exposing sensitive info or breaking compliance rules. These issues don't just make tests harder to maintain; they can chip away at your trust in the whole test suite.

Good management means keeping your test logic separate from the data it runs on, so it's easier to adjust when things change. A few smart strategies can help you avoid all of this.

Centralizing data with configuration files

One of the easiest and surprisingly powerful ways to level up your tests is to move your test data out of the code and into external configuration files. These could be JSON, YAML, or even environment variables loaded with a tool such as **dotenv** (as we saw in *Chapter 14, Security and Authentication*). This gives you a single, easy-to-update source of truth, so you can tweak your data without ever touching the test code.

For example, if you're testing a login flow, skip hardcoding those credentials in the script. Instead, keep them in a config file and let your test load them from there.

First, create a `config.json` file:

```
{
  "baseUrl": "https://www.saucedemo.com/",
  "users": {
    "standard": {
      "username": "standard_user",
```

```
      "password": "secret_sauce"
    },
    "admin": {
      "username": "problem_user",
      "password": "secret_sauce"
    }
  }
}
```

Then, in your test file (say, `login.test.ts`), import and use it:

```
import { test, expect } from '@playwright/test';
import config from '../config.json';

test('successful login with standard user', async ({ page }) => {
  await page.goto(config.baseUrl);
  await page.getByPlaceholder('Username').fill(config.users.standard.
username);
  await page.getByPlaceholder('Password').fill(config.users.standard.
password);
  await page.getByRole('button', { name: 'Login' }).click();
  await expect(page).toHaveURL('https://www.saucedemo.com/inventory.
html');
  await expect(page.locator('.inventory_list')).toBeVisible();
});
```

This setup means that if credentials change or you need to add a new user type, you edit one file, not every test. It's especially handy for environment-specific data: you could have `config.dev.json` and `config.prod.json` and load the right one based on `process.env.NODE_ENV`. Maintenance drops because changes are localized, and it encourages consistency across tests.

> Another way to load external data in Playwright is to enable TypeScript's `resolveJsonModule` by setting `"compilerOptions": { "resolveJsonModule": true }` in your `tsconfig.json`. This allows you to import `.json` files directly with `import data from './data.json'` and lets the TypeScript compiler infer a type for that JSON so that you get autocompletion and safer code.

Let's extend the login example by building a fixture that logs in for us and returns an authenticated page, ready for testing.

In your fixture, you might define it like this:

```
import { expect, test as baseTest, Page } from '@playwright/test';
import config from '../config.json';

// Define a new type for our custom fixtures.
// This allows for better autocompletion and type safety.
type MyFixtures = {
  loggedInPage: Page;
};

// Extend the base test with our custom fixture.
export const test = baseTest.extend<MyFixtures>({
  loggedInPage: async ({ page }, use) => {
    // This is the setup code for the fixture.
    await page.goto(config.baseUrl);
    await page.getByPlaceholder('Username')
      .fill(config.users.standard.username);
    await page.getByPlaceholder('Password')
      .fill(config.users.standard.password);
    await page.getByRole('button', { name: 'Login' }).click();

    // Use the fixture. This is where the test code runs.
    await use(page);

    // This is the teardown code for the fixture (if any).
    // In this case, there is no specific cleanup needed.
  },
});
```

The `type MyFixtures = { loggedInPage: any; };` part is useful for good practice, but it's not strictly required for the code to function. It defines a TypeScript type that tells Playwright's `test.extend` function what custom fixtures are available.

It helps TypeScript catch errors at compile time. For example, if you accidentally misspelled `loggedInPage` as `loggeddInPage` in your test, TypeScript would alert you to the mistake. Most modern code editors will use this type definition to provide autocompletion suggestions when you are writing your tests. This makes development faster.

Now, in your test file, you can write the following:

```
import { test } from '../fixtures/test-setup';
import { expect } from '@playwright/test';

test('access cart after login', async ({ loggedInPage }) => {
  await loggedInPage.goto('https://www.saucedemo.com/cart.html');

  // Make sure Checkout button is visible
  await expect(loggedInPage.getByRole('button', { name: 'Checkout' })).
toBeVisible();
});
```

Because our fixture takes care of data management behind the scenes, your tests stay clean and simple. If the login process changes, you just update the fixture once, and you're done. This keeps maintenance low by containing all the variability in a single spot. It's always a good thing to keep your code organized and place all fixtures in the `/fixtures/` directory.

Generating dynamic data with libraries

When writing automated tests that involve unique or randomized inputs (such as user registrations, form submissions, or order creation), hardcoding the values quickly becomes a problem. Not only can it cause collisions (such as trying to register the same email twice), but it also fails to simulate the messy, unpredictable nature of real-world data.

One workaround is to use a data generation library such as **Faker.js** (`https://www.npmjs.com/package/@faker-js/faker`). This library produces realistic test data on the fly (names, addresses, passwords, and much more) so your tests mimic how users would actually interact with your app. This makes them less brittle and better at catching edge cases.

You can install Faker using npm like this:

```
npm install @faker-js/faker --save-dev
```

After installing it, you can import it as follows:

```
import { faker } from '@faker-js/faker';
```

Here's a hypothetical example of using Faker:

```
import { test, expect } from '@playwright/test';
import { faker } from '@faker-js/faker';
```

```
test('register new user', async ({ page }) => {
  const username = faker.internet.userName();
  const email = faker.internet.email();
  const password = faker.internet.password();

  await page.goto('/login');

  await page.getByPlaceholder('Username').fill(username);
  await page.getByPlaceholder('Email').fill(email);
  await page.getByPlaceholder('Password').fill(password);
  await page.getByRole('button', { name: 'Submit' }).click();

  await expect(page.locator('#success-message')).toHaveText(`Account
created for ${username}`);
});
```

Here, every test run generates completely fresh data, so there's no risk of reusing usernames or emails from a previous run. And if your app's requirements change (say, passwords must include a symbol or meet a specific length), you can tweak the Faker calls in one place and instantly update all dependent tests.

`${username}` is just a placeholder in a template literal. Template literals are strings wrapped in backticks that let you plug in variables or expressions right inside the string using `${}`. In this case, `${username}` dynamically inserts the username into the text.

This approach also makes large, data-heavy test suites easier to maintain as your tests adapt automatically.

Mocking APIs to control external data

Let's talk about how modern web apps often pull in data from APIs, and why testing that in Playwright can get tricky without some smart tricks up your sleeve. Imagine you're building an e-commerce site like an online bookstore. Your app fetches book recommendations from an API endpoint, say something like `/api/recommendations` that pulls real-time data from a backend server.

In the real world, that API might return different results based on user behavior, time of day, or even server hiccups. Maybe it's slow one day, or it throws an error because the database is being updated. This unpredictability can make your automated tests flaky: one run passes, but the next fails for no reason related to your code.

That's where **route mocking** in Playwright comes in handy. It lets you intercept those API calls right in the browser context and fake the responses, so your tests always get the exact data you expect, without ever touching the real API. This speeds up your tests (no network latency) and isolates your UI testing from backend woes.

The following test verifies that a web page correctly displays blog posts by mocking an API response from `JSONPlaceholder`, which is a popular fake API for testing. It sets up a controlled environment, ensures the page renders the data correctly, and verifies the output with assertions:

```
import { test, expect } from '@playwright/test';

test('displays mocked blog posts from JSONPlaceholder API', async ({ page
}) => {
  // Mock the specific API endpoint
  await page.route('https://jsonplaceholder.typicode.com/posts', async
(route) => {
    await route.fulfill({
      status: 200,
      contentType: 'application/json',
      body: JSON.stringify([
        {
          userId: 1,
          id: 1,
          title: 'Mocked Post Title One',
          body: 'This is the body of the first mocked post. It helps test
rendering without real data.'
        },
        {
          userId: 1,
          id: 2,
          title: 'Mocked Post Title Two',
          body: 'Here\'s the second post body, keeping things consistent
for reliable testing.'
        }
```

```
        ])
      });
    });

    const data = await page.evaluate(() =>
      fetch('https://jsonplaceholder.typicode.com/posts')
        .then(r => r.json())
    );

    await expect(data[0].title).toBe('Mocked Post Title One');
    await expect(data[1].title).toBe('Mocked Post Title Two');
  });
```

The first major part of this test sets up a mock for the API endpoint `https://jsonplaceholder.typicode.com/posts`. Playwright's `page.route()` method intercepts any network requests to this URL. When the page tries to fetch data from this endpoint, instead of hitting the real API, the test provides a fake response.

The `route.fulfill()` method defines this fake response: it returns a status code of `200` (indicating success), sets the content type to `application/json`, and provides a JSON string as the body. This JSON string contains an array of two mocked blog posts, each with a `userId`, `id`, `title`, and `body`. This mocking ensures the test doesn't rely on the real API.

Next, we run a `fetch()` call directly inside the browser using `page.evaluate()`. This simulates what an actual web application might do: it requests data from the `/posts` endpoint. Because we already intercepted that URL pattern, the browser receives the mocked data we defined. The JSON returned by the mocked response is stored in the `data` variable, which allows us to inspect it in the test environment.

Finally, we use `expect()` to assert that the mocked data contains the correct values. The beauty of this approach is how reliable and fast it is. Your tests aren't at the mercy of network flakiness. No more waiting for slow responses or dealing with rate limits. If the real API changes, say it adds a new field such as `'jobTitle'`, you just update the mock payload in your test file, and everything stays in sync without redeploying anything. To make it even more flexible for bigger projects, you could pull the mock data from a separate JSON config file.

For instance, have a `mocks/profile.json` with variations for different test cases: one for a standard user, one for an error state (such as status `404`), or even an empty bio to check edge cases. Then, in your test, load that file dynamically. This way, if your team has multiple developers working on features, everyone can tweak mocks without stepping on each other's toes, and your test suite handles all sorts of scenarios without ever relying on the live backend.

Summary

It's clear that thoughtful organization and strategic design can transform your test suite from a maintenance burden into a reliable asset. By structuring tests with `describe` blocks and descriptive names, you create a narrative that's easy to follow and debug. The POM takes this further, tucking away the messy details of selectors and actions into reusable classes, so your tests read like user stories and stay resilient to UI changes.

Managing test data smartly, whether through centralized config files, custom fixtures, dynamic data generation with tools such as Faker.js, or API mocking, keeps your tests solid no matter the environment or scenario. It also saves you time and helps you feel confident about your application's quality.

As you try out these techniques, don't be afraid to experiment and tweak them so they work best for your team. For deeper insights, the Playwright documentation at `https://playwright.dev/docs/best-practices` is a great resource to keep exploring.

In the next and final chapter, we will put everything into practice by building a hands-on project.

16

Real-World Project – Testing an E-Commerce Website

So far, we've walked through the essentials of Playwright: from setting projects up and writing simple scripts to tackling more advanced topics such as dynamic content and API calls. Now it's time to bring everything together in a hands-on project.

We'll be testing an e-commerce website, which is perfect for practicing **end-to-end** (**E2E**) testing. It covers a variety of common workflows, such as signing up as a user, browsing products, adding items to your cart, and even handling bulk user registrations for load testing.

For this project, we'll use the **Practice Software Testing Toolshop** (available at `practicesoftwaretesting.com`). This is a demo application designed specifically for software testing training. It simulates an e-commerce website in the form of an online tool shop selling tools such as hammers, drills, and screwdrivers, organized into different categories, such as Hand Tools and Power Tools.

We'll be writing the tests in TypeScript for added type safety, though everything we cover will apply to JavaScript too. By the end of this chapter, you'll have a fully organized Playwright project for testing real-world e-commerce flows using best practices such as the **Page Object Model** (**POM**), helper functions, data factories, and smart authentication with storage states.

By the end of this chapter, you'll have a solid understanding of how to create a robust end-to-end testing framework for an e-commerce website.

The chapter is structured into these parts:

- Initializing the project
- Organizing the project structure
- Managing authentication with storage states
- Using data factories
- Bulk user registration for load testing

Technical requirements

The source code for this chapter is available at `https://github.com/PacktPublishing/Hands-On-Automated-Testing-with-Playwright/tree/main/Chapter16`.

Initializing the project

In this section, we'll lay the groundwork for a smooth testing process by initializing the project and managing authentication with storage states.

The first step is to create a dedicated directory for the project and initialize a Playwright project:

```
mkdir ecom-test-project
cd ecom-test-project
npm init playwright@latest
```

This command makes a new folder called `ecom-test-project` and sets up a new Playwright project inside it with a starter template. When running the `npm init playwright@latest` command, you will be presented with a series of questions to build out the initial scaffolding of a project. We'll choose `TypeScript` for our language, we'll set `tests` as our end-to-end tests folder, and skip adding a GitHub Actions file for now. You will also have a chance here to install the Playwright browsers.

You can verify installation by running the `--version` flag to confirm the installed version:

```
npx playwright --version
```

At this point, you should be able to run the default playwright test by running this:

```
npx playwright test
```

This command should execute six tests in total, two unique tests across three different browsers.

Since we'll be working with TypeScript, let's go ahead and install the necessary dependencies. This will give you type safety and smoother support in your IDE:

```
npm install -D typescript ts-node @types/node dotenv
```

The `ts-node` package lets you run TypeScript files directly without having to compile them first. It's useful for quick scripts or testing things out. The `@types/node` package provides the type definitions for Node.js, so everything works smoothly with TypeScript. Finally, we will install `dotenv`, which will allow us to utilize `.env` environment files. By adding the `-D` flag, you're installing these as `devDependencies`, since they're only needed during development and testing, not in production.

Now, let's create a `tsconfig.json` file in the root directory of the project to configure TypeScript:

```
{
  "compilerOptions": {
    "target": "ESNext",
    "module": "commonjs",
    "strict": true,
    "esModuleInterop": true
  }
}
```

In this file, we have options such as `"target": "ESNext"`, which makes sure your code is compiled with the latest ECMAScript features so it runs smoothly in modern JavaScript environments. We'll also set `"module": "commonjs"`, since CommonJS modules are fully supported by Playwright.

Adding `"esModuleInterop": true` makes it easier to work with CommonJS modules and prevents import issues. For new projects, it's a good idea to enable `"strict": true` so you can follow best practices from the start. If you're working with older code, though, you can relax certain rules – for example, turning off `"noImplicitAny"` so that the compiler no longer throws an error whenever it can't infer a variable's type.

Once that's set up, the next step is to configure your `playwright.config.ts` file:

```
// ./playwright.config.ts
import { defineConfig, devices } from "@playwright/test";
import * as dotenv from "dotenv";

dotenv.config({ path: ".env", quiet: true });
```

```
export default defineConfig({
  testDir: "./tests",
  fullyParallel: true,
  forbidOnly: !!process.env.CI, // Prevent `test.only` in CI
  retries: process.env.CI ? 2 : 0, // Retry failed tests in CI
  workers: process.env.CI ? 1 : undefined, // Control parallel workers
  reporter: [["html"], ["list"]], // Generate HTML and list reports
  use: {
    trace: "on", // Capture traces always for now
    baseURL: process.env.BASE_URL || "https://practicesoftwaretesting.
com", // Base URL for navigation
    testIdAttribute: "data-test", // Custom test ID attribute
    headless: true,
    video: "retain-on-failure",
    screenshot: "only-on-failure",
  },
  projects: [
    {
      name: "setup", // Authentication setup project
      testMatch: /.*\.setup\.ts/,
    },
    {
      name: "customer1-chromium",
      dependencies: ["setup"], // Run setup first
      use: {
        ...devices["Desktop Chrome"],
        storageState: ".auth/customer1StorageState.json", // Load auth
state
      },
    },
    // Additional projects for Firefox, WebKit can be added here
  ],
});
```

We have seen most of these properties in the previous chapters, except for `forbidOnly`. Playwright has a handy shortcut called `test.only`, which developers often use when they're debugging. It tells Playwright to ignore all the other tests and just run the one you've marked. That's convenient when you're working locally, because it lets you quickly focus on a single failing or tricky test without waiting for the whole suite.

The problem is, leaving `test.only` in your code by mistake and pushing it to the main branch would be a big issue. In a CI environment, where the full test suite is supposed to run, Playwright would end up running just that one test.

That's where `forbidOnly` comes in. When this setting is `true`, Playwright will fail the test run if it finds `test.only` or `describe.only`. It's basically a guardrail to make sure no one accidentally limits the test run in a place where you need full coverage.

The `!!process.env.CI` part is just a little JavaScript trick to turn the `CI` environment variable into a `true`/`false` value. Most CI systems automatically set `CI` to `true`, so `!!process.env.CI` becomes `true` when you're in CI, and `false` when you're just running tests locally.

> Most popular CI tools (GitHub, GitLab, Azure DevOps) set the CI environment variable to `true`. If using a CI tool that does not, such as Google Cloud Build, be sure to set it manually in the CI script: `'CI=true'`

Keeping a project well-organized is key to making it scalable when working as a team. That leads us to the next section.

Organizing the project structure

When I first started testing, I quickly learned that a well-organized project is the backbone of smooth, maintainable tests. In this section, we'll explore how to structure our e-commerce testing project thoughtfully.

Structuring the project

For our e-commerce tests, we'll go with a modular setup that keeps everything neatly separated:

```
ecom-test-project/
├── .auth/
│   └── customer1StorageState.json  # Generated auth state
├── data/
│   └── factory.ts                  # Data creation methods
```

```
├── fixtures/
│   └── adminAuth.fixture.ts        # Custom fixtures
├── pages/
│   ├── base.page.ts                # Base class for all pages
│   ├── login.page.ts               # Login page object model
│   ├── registration.page.ts        # Registration page object model
│   └── product.page.ts             # Product page object model
├── tests/
│   ├── auth.setup.ts               # Authentication setup script
│   ├── registration.spec.ts        # User registration tests
│   ├── product.spec.ts             # Product browsing tests
│   └── bulk.spec.ts                # Load/performance tests
├── playwright-report/              # Generated test reports
├── test-results/                   # Test execution results
├── node_modules/                   # Dependencies (git-ignored)
├── playwright.config.ts            # Playwright test configuration
├── package.json                    # Project dependencies and scripts
├── package-lock.json               # Locked dependency versions
├── tsconfig.json                   # TypeScript configuration
├── .env                            # Environment variables
├── .gitignore                      # Git ignore rules
└── README.md                       # Project documentation
```

You've already come across these files in earlier chapters. Here's a quick refresher on the important parts of the project structure:

- `.auth/`: Stores the session state
- `data/`: Houses data factories for generating test data
- `fixtures/`: Holds custom Playwright fixtures (such as parameterized `auth`)
- `pages/`: POM implementations
- `tests/`: Actual test specs, grouped by feature

Now that you know your way around the project, let's dive into writing our page objects.

Implementing the POM

The POM is very useful for building maintainable E2E test automation. It simplifies the code by breaking down complex web interactions into clear, reusable modules.

Rather than scattering raw selectors (such as `page.locator('#email')`) and repeated actions throughout your test scripts, POM centralizes them in dedicated page objects. This simplifies maintenance whenever the UI changes.

For our e-commerce site, we'll have pages such as the login page, product details page, and so on. Each page has its own elements and interactions, which makes POM a perfect fit. For example, if you change the ID of the **Add to Cart** button, you'd otherwise have to update every test that uses it. With POM, you only need to update the selector in the relevant page object.

POM also supports the single-responsibility principle. Each page object manages a specific part of the UI. This allows testers to focus on writing meaningful test scenarios, while the page objects handle the details of interacting with the site.

Creating the base page class

A base page class is a way to avoid repeating the same code across multiple page objects for items that exist across all or most of the pages within the app.

Here's our `base.page.ts` file:

```
// ./pages/base.page.ts
import { Page, Locator } from "@playwright/test";

export class BasePage {
  readonly page: Page;
  readonly navMenu: Locator;
  readonly navMenuHome: Locator;
  readonly navMenuCategories: Locator;
  readonly navCategoryList: Locator;
  readonly navMenuContact: Locator;
  readonly navMenuSignIn: Locator;
  readonly navMenuLanguageSelect: Locator;
  readonly navCart: Locator;
  readonly navCartQuantity: Locator;

  constructor(page: Page) {
    this.page = page;
    this.navMenu = page.getByTestId("nav-menu");
    this.navMenuHome = page.getByTestId("nav-home");
    this.navMenuCategories = page.getByTestId("nav-categories");
```

```
    this.navCategoryList = page.getByLabel("nav-categories");
    this.navMenuContact = page.getByTestId("nav-contact");
    this.navMenuSignIn = page.getByTestId("nav-sign-in");
    this.navMenuLanguageSelect = page.getByTestId("language-select");
    this.navCart = page.getByTestId("nav-cart");
    this.navCartQuantity = page.getByTestId("cart-quantity");
  }

  async gotoHome() {
    await this.page.goto("/");
  }

  async selectCategory(category: string) {
    await this.navMenuCategories.click();
    await this.navCategoryList.getByText(`${category}`).click();
  }

  async clearStorage(page: Page) {
    await page.evaluate(() => {
      localStorage.clear();
      sessionStorage.clear();
    });
    await page.reload();
  }
}
```

We start by importing the necessary components from Playwright's test module: `Page` and `Locator`. Then, we define the `BasePage` class with read-only properties: `'page'` to store the Playwright Page instance, and `'nav...'` element locators we will define on the base page.

The constructor takes a required `Page` object. It simply assigns these to the class properties, which sets up the foundation for any `Page` object that extends this class. This way, every `Page` object will have access to the same browser context without needing to recreate it each time.

We also define all locators within the constructor. By doing this, we create a user-friendly name that we can use when interacting with the locators in our spec files.

For the locators we've added to the base page, we focused on adding any elements that are shared across most, if not all, of the pages within the web application. As you will see with the next `Page` object we add, this page will be extended by the other `Page` objects we create.

After the constructor, we have included three additional async functions, which can be called from the class.

In the `gotoHome()` function, we've created an easy way to navigate to the home page from anywhere within the test or at the start of a test.

We've also included a `selectCategory()` function that accepts a string parameter named `category` when called. The function starts by clicking the category link, which opens a dropdown list, and then selects the category whose name you pass in:

```
async selectCategory(category: string) {
   await this.navMenuCategories.click();
   await this.navCategoryList.getByText(`${category}`).click();
 }
```

> Creating functions within a `Page` object can be a useful way to abstract away common actions that your tests repeat over and over, or for locators that may be dynamic in nature.

The third function that we've written provides a way to reset the browser state to an unauthenticated state. This function wasn't needed when writing the first test, but when we realized we wanted to complete a new registration, we needed a way to have the test start in a logged-out state, without losing the `storageState` authentication:

```
async clearStorage(page: Page) {
   await page.evaluate(() => {
     localStorage.clear();
     sessionStorage.clear();
   });
   await page.context().clearCookies();
   await page.reload();
 }
```

The `clearStorage()` function uses `page.evaluate()` in order to execute JavaScript within the browser, clearing the local storage and session storage. Outside of the `page.evaluate()` method, we use the `page.context().clearCookies()` function, which clears the cookies for the current page. The function then reloads the page to ensure that the website is loaded in a fresh state.

So, with this base class, we abstract the UI interactions into classes. By extending `BasePage` in your specific pages (say, a `LoginPage` class), you inherit these methods automatically, which allows you to add page-specific locators and actions while using the shared ones.

Developing page-specific classes

Page-specific classes are the heart of the POM pattern. Each class represents a single page or a significant component of the application's UI. Each page-specific class typically inherits common functionality (such as interacting with `navMenu` or clearing browser storage) from a `BasePage` class.

Let's create a `LoginPage` class for testing the login functionality:

```
// ./pages/login.page.ts
import { type Locator, type Page } from "@playwright/test";
import { BasePage } from "./base.page";

export class LoginPage extends BasePage {
  readonly emailInput: Locator;
  readonly passwordInput: Locator;
  readonly loginButton: Locator;
  constructor(page: Page) {
    super(page);
    this.emailInput = page.getByTestId("email");
    this.passwordInput = page.getByTestId("password");
    this.loginButton = page.getByTestId("login-submit");
  }

  async goto() {
    await this.page.goto("/auth/login");
  }

  async login(email: string, password: string) {
    await this.emailInput.fill(email);
    await this.passwordInput.fill(password);
```

```
    await this.loginButton.click();
  }
}
```

The `goto()` function is available to navigate directly to the login page when called. In a test, this would look like `loginPage.goto()`, making it clear to read and follow. We typically like to include a `goto()` function on each page object we create for two reasons. First, it serves as an easy way to navigate to the page from within your test, and second, it serves as documentation for where the locators in the class exist within the website being tested.

The `login` function combines multiple steps: navigating to the sign-in page (using the inherited `navigate` method), filling the email and password fields, and clicking the submit button. This method abstracts the entire login process into a single, reusable call, so your tests can just call `await loginPage.login('user@example.com', 'password')` without needing to worry about the underlying selectors or step sequence.

In the same way, the `ProductPage` class (`./pages/product.page.ts`) is designed specifically to handle the product browsing experience on the Toolshop site:

```
// ./pages/product.page.ts
import { Locator, Page } from "@playwright/test";
import { BasePage } from "./base.page";

export class ProductPage extends BasePage {
  readonly productCards: Locator;
  readonly addedToCartMessage: Locator;
  readonly productName: Locator;
  readonly addToCartButton: Locator;

  constructor(page: Page) {
    super(page);
    this.productCards = page.locator(".card");
    this.addedToCartMessage = page.getByLabel(
      "Product added to shopping cart."
    );
    this.productName = page.getByTestId("product-name");
    this.addToCartButton = page.getByTestId("add-to-cart");
  }
```

```
  async goto(productId?: string) {
    await this.page.goto(`/product/${productId}`);
  }

  async clickProductByIndex(index: number) {
    const product = this.productCards.nth(index);
    await product.click();
  }
}
```

The `clickProductByIndex()` method makes it easy for tests to click on a specific product card by simply pointing to it using its index.

We are also exposing the `productName` and `addToCartButton` locators. Rather than creating functions for actions, when the elements are easy to interact with, we favor adding a bit more verbosity to our spec files for both interactions with the page and assertions.

Avoid over-abstraction. Don't create page objects for trivial pages or single-use components. For Toolshop, a **Contact Us** page with one form might not need a full-page object if it's only tested once.

Applying POM in tests

Now that we have created the page objects we need, let's see how we can use them in a test by checking if a product was successfully added to the shopping card:

```
// ./tests/product.spec.ts
import { test, expect } from "@playwright/test";
import { ProductPage } from "../pages/product.page";

test("Add product to cart", async ({ page }) => {
  const productPage = new ProductPage(page);
  await productPage.gotoHome();
  await productPage.selectCategory("Hand Tools");
  await productPage.clickProductByIndex(0);

  await expect(productPage.productName).toHaveText("Combination Pliers");
```

```
    await productPage.addToCartButton.click();
    await expect(productPage.addedToCartMessage).toHaveText(
      "Product added to shopping cart."
    );

    // wait for the message to disappear (up to 10 seconds)
    await expect(productPage.addedToCartMessage).not.toBeVisible({
      timeout: 10000,
    });
    await expect(productPage.navCartQuantity).toHaveText("1");
  });
```

We begin by importing the required modules along with the custom page object: `ProductPage`. The test starts from a logged-in state (which we will cover in the next section), with the first step being creating a `productPage` variable that we can reference in our test.

The test visits the home page, which includes a list of tools. We narrow down the list using the `selectCategory` function to view only the `"Hand Tools"` category. From there, it clicks the first product in the list (index 0). Once on the product page, we make an assertion that the product name is `"Combination Pliers"`, and we click to add the item to the cart.

Figure 16.1: The test asserts that the pop-up message shows up with the proper text

We then have three more assertions that we make after the add to cart action. The first is ensuring the pop-up message shows up with the proper text. We then wait up to 10 seconds for the add to cart message to disappear. We do this by making the assertion by using `not.toBeVisible({ timeout: 10000 })`. We wanted to do this because, in the web application, the pop-up message covers up the cart button in the next assertion, and we want to match our tests as close to the user's journey as well. The final step confirms the cart is updated correctly by using the web first assertion, using the `navCartQuality` locator, which lives on the `base.page.ts` file. This quick assertion ensures the product was successfully added without the need to switch over to a dedicated `CartPage` object.

This test is readable and maintainable. If the **Add to Cart** button's selector changes, you update only the `ProductPage` class. By encapsulating the Toolshop site's pages (login, product, base, etc.) into classes, you create a clear separation between test logic and UI interaction.

So, with the POM pattern, we've organized our test code into reusable classes. Now, let's look at how to take advantage of the storage state feature to make our tests more efficient.

Managing authentication with storage states

In e-commerce applications, many test scenarios, such as adding items to a cart, proceeding to checkout, or viewing order history, require a logged-in user. Running a full login for every single test isn't the most efficient approach: it slows down your test runs and can even trigger problems such as rate limits or CAPTCHA challenges.

Playwright makes this easier with its **storage state** feature. Instead of logging in each time, you can log in once, save the session data (such as cookies and local storage), and then reuse it across your tests.

Using Playwright test projects for authentication

To get this set up, we create a setup project in `playwright.config.ts` and create an `auth.setup.ts` test in our tests folder that takes care of logging in and saving the session state for us. First, we launch a Chromium browser and open a new page. Then, we head over to Toolshop's login page (`auth/login`), enter our test credentials (`customer@practicesoftwaretesting.com` and `welcome01`), which are being stored in our `.env` file, and submit the login form. The setup script utilizes the `loginPage` page object for the locators and the login function:

```
// ./tests/auth.setup.ts
import { test as setup, expect } from "@playwright/test";
import { LoginPage } from "../pages/login.page";

setup("Create Customer 1 Authentication", async ({ page, context }) => {
  const email = process.env.CUSTOMER_1_EMAIL || "";
  const password = process.env.CUSTOMER_1_PASSWORD || "";
  const customer1AuthFile = ".auth/customer1StorageState.json";
```

```
    const loginPage = new LoginPage(page);
    await loginPage.gotoHome();
    await loginPage.navMenuSignIn.click();
    await loginPage.login(email, password);

    // Verify login was successful
    await expect(loginPage.navMenu).toContainText("Jane Doe");

    // Save storage state into the file.
    await context.storageState({ path: customer1AuthFile });
  });
```

The last step in the script calls `page.context().storageState({ path: customer1AuthFile })` to save the browser context's session data, including cookies, local storage, and other session-related information, into a JSON file.

> The `storageState.json` file should be added to `.gitignore` to prevent committing potentially sensitive session data to version control.

This storage state is built into our Playwright configuration (`playwright.config.ts`) through a dedicated `setup` project. That project runs the `auth.setup.ts` script before any tests begin. The `customer1-chromium` project, which runs the main test suite, depends on `['setup']` to make sure the setup runs first. It then uses `storageState: 'storageState.json.auth/customer1StorageState.json'` to load the saved session data. Thanks to this setup, every test in the `customer1-chromium` project starts with the specific user already logged in, so the login step is no longer needed before every test run.

If the site's authentication sessions time out after a certain period of time or if a logout test clears the authentication that is saved, you will have to come up with a different solution. One approach may be to create a separate project that doesn't have the `setup` project dependency.

For more advanced cases, such as testing different user roles (customer versus admin), you can either create additional steps in the setup files, saving different storage states, or utilize custom fixtures to generate the appropriate storage states during a test.

Using playwright test fixtures for authentication

Fixtures have lots of customization options. In `adminAuth.fixture.ts`, we create a fixture named `adminAuthPage`, which can be used within a test to utilize a page that already has the saved storage state for the admin login:

```
// ./fixtures/adminAuth.fixture.ts
import { test as base, expect, Page } from "@playwright/test";
import { LoginPage } from "../pages/login.page";

// Simple fixture that provides an authenticated page
export const test = base.extend<{ adminAuthPage: Page }>({
  adminAuthPage: async ({ browser }, use) => {
    const storageStatePath = ".auth/adminStorageState.json";

    const setupContext = await browser.newContext();
    const setupPage = await setupContext.newPage();
    const loginPage = new LoginPage(setupPage);
    await loginPage.goto();
    await loginPage.login(
      process.env.ADMIN_EMAIL!,
      process.env.ADMIN_PASSWORD!
    );
     await expect(loginPage.navMenu).toContainText("John Doe");


    await setupContext.storageState({ path: storageStatePath });
    await setupContext.close();

    // Create new context with saved auth state
    const context = await browser.newContext({
      storageState: storageStatePath,
    });
    const page = await context.newPage();

    await use(page);

    await context.close();
```

```
  },
});

export { expect } from "@playwright/test";
```

The fixture starts by extending the base test framework with a custom `adminAuthPage` fixture. The fixture performs the login process using environment variables for credentials, saves the authentication state to a JSON file (`adminStorageState.json`), and then provides each test with a fresh, pre-authenticated page context. This pattern centralizes the login operations across tests, much like our setup project, and ensures proper isolation by giving each test its own session. This approach is very useful when you have a short-lived authentication, and you want to create a new authentication every time the fixture is used.

To use this fixture in a test, we will use the `product.spec.ts` test and duplicate the test, but from the perspective of an admin user:

```
// ./tests/product.spec.ts
import { ProductPage } from "../pages/product.page";
import { test, expect } from "../fixtures/adminAuth.fixture";

test("Add product to cart with admin auth fixture", async ({ adminAuthPage
}) => {
  // Use the authenticated page created by fixture for all interactions
  const productPage = new ProductPage(adminAuthPage);
  await productPage.gotoHome();
  await productPage.selectCategory("Hand Tools");
  await productPage.clickProductByIndex(0);

  await expect(productPage.productName).toHaveText("Combination Pliers");

  await productPage.addToCartButton.click();
  await expect(productPage.addedToCartMessage).toHaveText(
    "Product added to shopping cart."
  );

  // wait for the message to disappear (up to 10 seconds)
  await expect(productPage.addedToCartMessage).not.toBeVisible({
    timeout: 10000,
  });
```

```
  await expect(productPage.navCartQuantity).toHaveText("1");
});
```

You will notice that we are importing `test` and `expect` from the fixture that we've created. Since we extended the base `test` class and exported `expect`, all the default functions that are available on `test` are also available to use with this fixture. This is similar to how we extended the `base.page.ts` file in our page objects. The next thing that is done is using `adminAuthPage` in place of where we would typically use page. This is where the magic happens because `adminAuthPage` already has `adminStorageState` saved from the code in the fixture file, granting you a page and browser context that is already logged in as an admin.

> Sensitive data, such as credentials, should never be hardcoded in production environments. While Toolshop provides test credentials for this demo, real projects should use environment variables (such as `process.env.CUSTOMER_1_EMAIL`) or a secrets manager to secure credentials. See *Chapter 14, Security and Authentication.*

Now, to make our testing process smoother and more efficient, it's useful to have a set of test utilities.

Using data factories

When working on a fast-moving project such as an e-commerce site, one of the challenges is avoiding hardcoded data in your test scripts. Using the same email address or password over and over might seem harmless, but it often leads to unpredictable failures such as duplicate account errors or conflicts with evolving validation rules.

That's where data creation methods, often called **data factories**, come in. A data factory is essentially a set of reusable functions that generate fresh, realistic test data on demand. This makes your tests more reliable, gives you broader coverage (including edge cases with unusual characters or lengths), and ensures each test run feels independent and closer to real-world use.

For our Playwright project, we'll use a well-known library called **Faker.js**. It's built specifically to generate believable fake data across a wide range of categories. It's lightweight, simple to integrate, and you may remember we got a first look at it back in *Chapter 15, Best Practices for Test Maintainability*.

Setting up Faker.js

Start by installing it as a development dependency with this command:

```
npm install -D @faker-js/faker
```

Once that's done, you can create a dedicated file, say `/data/factory.ts`, as shown in the project structure. This is where you'll define your factory functions:

```
// ./data/factory.ts
import { faker } from "@faker-js/faker";

export function createUser(_overrides = {}) {
  return {
    firstName: faker.person.firstName(),
    lastName: faker.person.lastName(),
    email: faker.internet.email(),
    password: faker.internet.password({ length: 10, prefix: "#1Aa" }),
    streetAddress: faker.location.streetAddress(),
    city: faker.location.city(),
    state: faker.location.state(),
    zip: faker.location.zipCode("#####"),
    country: "United States of America (the)", // Toolshop requires
specific countries
    phone: faker.string.numeric(10),
    dob: createDOB({ min: 18, max: 80 }),
  };
}

/**
 * Creates an array of user objects.
 * @param {number} count - Number of users to generate
 * @returns {Array<object>} Array of user objects
 */
export function createUsers(count: number): Array<object>
 {
  return Array.from({ length: count }, () => createUser());
}
```

```
export function createInvalidUser() {
  return {
    firstName: "", // Empty name
    dob: "1900", // Invalid format
    password: "123", // Too short
  };
}

export function createDOB(ageRange: { min: number; max: number }) {
  return faker.date
    .birthdate({ min: ageRange.min, max: ageRange.max, mode: "age" })
    .toISOString()
    .split("T")[0];
}
```

If you'd like to set certain values yourself, the `_overrides` parameter lets you do just that. For instance, `createUser({ email: 'specific@example.com' })` locks in that email address while `Faker.js` fills in the rest of the details for you.

> In TypeScript, prefixing a parameter with a leading underscore, such as `_overrides`, is a convention to signal to linters and developers that "I know this parameter exists and isn't being used, and that's intentional."

For testing error scenarios, you can use `createInvalidUser()`. It returns intentionally incorrect data, such as a malformed email or a too-short password, so you can verify that your system properly handles invalid inputs. For this function, I've also included some JSDoc to make it clear what's generated and why, so future contributors know exactly how to extend or adjust the invalid cases without guesswork.

The `createUser()` function is a great fit for e-commerce scenarios where you need user profiles, shipping details, or registration data. Methods such as `faker.person.firstName()` and `faker.person.lastName()` use locale-specific datasets, so you'll see natural results such as **John** or **Elena**. If your tests require gender-specific variations, you can also pass a sex parameter such as `'male'` or `'female'` to guide the output.

For email addresses, Faker's internet module is especially useful. A call to `faker.internet.email()` gives you results such as `john.smith@example.com`, and you can customize it further: whether that's choosing a specific domain or tying the address to the generated name for consistency.

Address details, which are often essential for checkout flows, come from the location module. The `faker.location.streetAddress()` method creates a realistic street line, such as `'123 Main St'`, while `faker.location.city()` and `faker.location.zipCode()` generate cities and postal codes that follow familiar patterns. In this example, the country is set to `"United States of America (the)"`, but you could make it dynamic with `faker.location.country()` for broader international testing.

As for passwords, `faker.internet.password({ length: 10, prefix: "#1Aa" })` produces secure-looking strings, which are good enough for testing, though not meant for real security. Specifically for the fake password, we want to ensure that the password will always meet the criteria of the website, having a special character, a number, and an uppercase and a lowercase character. Using the `prefix` option allows us to ensure this.

By wrapping all of these pieces into a single object from `createUser()`, you end up with a complete, unique profile every time.

Integrating the data factory

Let's look at an example of how we can apply the data factory to our user registration. First, we import all the essentials:

```
// ./tests/registration.spec.ts
import { test, expect } from "@playwright/test";
import { createUser, createInvalidUser, createDOB } from "../data/
factory";
import { RegistrationPage } from "../pages/registration.page";
```

The `RegistrationPage` class contains all the selectors and actions related to the registration page.

Next, we group our tests with `test.describe()`. Before each test runs, we generate two types of user data:

- A valid user for testing successful registration
- An invalid user to test error handling

Setting the storage state to undefined ensures each test runs in a logged-out browser context.

```
test.describe("Practice Software Testing Site Tests", async () => {
  let user: any;
  let invalidUser: any;

  test.use({ storageState: undefined });
```

```
  test.beforeEach(async () => {
    invalidUser = createInvalidUser();
    user = createUser();
  });
```

This first test verifies that a new user can register successfully and is redirected to the login page afterward:

```
  test("Successful user registration", async ({ page }) => {
    const registrationPage = new RegistrationPage(page);

    await registrationPage.goto();
    await registrationPage.clearStorage(page);

    await registrationPage.firstNameInput.fill(user.firstName);
    await registrationPage.lastNameInput.fill(user.lastName);
    await registrationPage.dobInput.fill(user.dob);
    await registrationPage.streetInput.fill(user.streetAddress);
    await registrationPage.postalCodeInput.fill(user.zip);
    await registrationPage.cityInput.fill(user.city);
    await registrationPage.stateInput.fill(user.state);
    await registrationPage.countrySelect.selectOption({ label: user.
country });
    await registrationPage.phoneInput.fill(user.phone);
    await registrationPage.emailInput.fill(user.email);
    await registrationPage.passwordInput.fill(user.password);

    const responsePromise = page.waitForResponse(
      (response) =>
        response.url().includes("/users/register") && response.status()
=== 201
    );

    await registrationPage.registerSubmitButton.click();
    await responsePromise;

    await expect(page).toHaveURL(/auth\/login/);
  });
```

Here, we head over to the registration page, clear out any old data, and fill in all the required fields using the valid `user` object. Then we wait for the network response to confirm that the `/users/register` API call went through successfully. Once that's done, we check that the page redirects to the login screen, which confirms the registration flow completed as expected.

> In our example, we call both `test.use({ storageState: undefined })` and a custom `.clearStorage(page)` helper. This is redundant; we're doing it purely for demonstration. Use `test.use()` when you want a fresh context before the browser context is created, and use `.clearStorage(page)` when you need to reset an already-running context mid-test. Pick one approach based on your needs.

This second test checks how the site handles invalid or incomplete user data and shows appropriate validation messages:

```
  test("Negative registration with invalid data", async ({ page }) => {
    const registrationPage = new RegistrationPage(page);
    await registrationPage.goto();

    await registrationPage.clearStorage(page);

    await registrationPage.firstNameInput.fill(invalidUser.firstName);
    await registrationPage.dobInput.fill(invalidUser.dob);
    await registrationPage.passwordInput.fill(invalidUser.password);

    await registrationPage.submitRegistration();

    await expect(page.getByText("First name is required")).toBeVisible();
    await expect(page.getByText("Please enter a valid date")).
toBeVisible();
    await expect(
      page.getByText("Password must be minimal 6 characters long.")
    ).toBeVisible();
  });
});
```

We intentionally submit incomplete or invalid data from the `invalidUser` object. Then, we confirm that the correct validation messages appear on the page.

With this approach, every time we create a new test, we'll automatically have fresh user data available for it.

> If the web application you are testing has i18n (internationalization), it's usually best to abstract away your test strings for easy maintenance, or even better, utilize the same data source for the text strings for your assertions.

Covering edge cases

Don't forget about edge cases: you can add methods to cover boundary conditions, such as maximum-length names or extreme price values. Here's an example:

```
export function createEdgeCaseUser() {
  return {
    ...createUser(),
    firstName: faker.string.alpha({ length: 50 }),
    email: `test+${faker.string.alphanumeric(100)}@test.com`,
  };
}
```

The `createEdgeCaseUser()` function goes in our `factory.ts` script and builds on `createUser()`, but modifies certain fields specifically to push these limits to test how the application handles tricky or unusual inputs. These are inputs that sit right on the boundaries of what the system should allow, such as names at the maximum character limit, emails with unusual formatting, or entries containing special characters.

For an e-commerce site such as Toolshop, testing these scenarios is especially important. User input happens frequently during tasks such as registration or checkout, and if it isn't validated properly, it could lead to errors, security risks, or even database issues.

An email field might allow long addresses but should reject those that exceed length limits or contain invalid symbols. By testing with these kinds of inputs, the application can respond gracefully: showing helpful error messages instead of crashing or accepting bad data.

As we have seen, you can use Faker's randomization to keep your data varied, but make sure to allow overrides when you need more control.

One thing to keep in mind is localization: Faker supports multiple locales, so if your e-commerce site is multilingual, you can set `faker.locale = 'de';` at the top of your factory file to generate German-specific data, for instance. Also, while Faker is powerful, it's not meant for production data. Keep it strictly in your test environment.

Over time, as your project grows, you might add more factory methods for product creation or customer reviews, turning this into a central hub for all test data generation.

> Keep all data generation in the `./data/` directory to avoid duplication and ensure consistency. This also makes your data creation methods easy to maintain if the application changes, where new fields are needed.

When preparing your website for real-world traffic, it's important to test how it performs when multiple users interact with it at once (especially during common actions such as signups). That's where load testing comes in.

Bulk user registration for load testing

Automating bulk user registration can be a handy way to add light load testing to your website. The following test uses the `registrationPage` object and a new data factory function, `createUsers(3)`, to create test data for three users, fills out registration forms on multiple browser pages at the same time, submits them, and then checks for success by confirming the redirect to the login page.

This is useful for spotting potential performance bottlenecks:

```
// ./tests/bulk.spec.ts
import { test, expect } from "@playwright/test";
import { createUsers } from "../data/factory";
import { RegistrationPage } from "../pages/registration.page";

test.describe("Load test", () => {
  test("bulk user registration", async ({ browser }) => {
    // Generate 3 users for simulation. Adjust as needed.
    const users = createUsers(3);

    const registrations = users.map(async (user) => {
      let context;
      try {
        context = await browser.newContext();
```

```
        const page = await context.newPage();
        const registrationPage = new RegistrationPage(page);
        await registrationPage.goto();
        await registrationPage.firstNameInput.fill(user.firstName);
        await registrationPage.lastNameInput.fill(user.lastName);
        await registrationPage.dobInput.fill(user.dob);
        await registrationPage.streetInput.fill(user.streetAddress);
        await registrationPage.postalCodeInput.fill(user.zip);
        await registrationPage.cityInput.fill(user.city);
        await registrationPage.stateInput.fill(user.state);
        await registrationPage.countrySelect.selectOption({
          label: user.country,
        });
        await registrationPage.phoneInput.fill(user.phone);
        await registrationPage.emailInput.fill(user.email);
        await registrationPage.passwordInput.fill(user.password);

        await registrationPage.submitRegistration();
        console.log(
          `Registering ${user.firstName} ${user.lastName} concurrently...`
        );

        // Expect success
        await expect(page).toHaveURL(/auth\/login/);
      } finally {
        await context.close();
      }
    });

    await Promise.all(registrations);
  });
});
```

For real load testing, though, you'll probably want to bump that number up to something bigger.

> If you want to test heavy traffic with thousands of users, you can use dedicated load-testing tools such as **Locust, K6, Artillery,** or **JMeter**.

From there, the script simulates multiple people registering at the same time. It loops through each user, spins up an asynchronous task for them, and opens a fresh browser page with `await context.newPage()`. Each page then navigates to the registration form, fills it out, and once the user is validated, the page is closed to save resources.

All of these registration tasks run side by side with the `Promise.all()` method, so the script waits until everything is done. This way, you're effectively simulating a small crowd of users signing up at once and testing whether the system can keep up and process each registration properly.

This approach gives you a sneak peek into how the site handles concurrent activity, such as API calls and database writes. It's also useful for spotting potential issues such as rate limiting or performance slowdowns.

Summary

This chapter has walked you through creating a solid and adaptable end-to-end testing framework for an e-commerce website. We used Toolshop as our example, diving into practical ways to test features such as user registration, product browsing, cart functionality, and more. By applying the **Page Object Model** (**POM**), we kept our test code organized and easy to update, even when the website's design changes.

Using storage states helped speed up tests by reusing login sessions, and data factories with Faker.js ensured our tests used fresh, realistic data for better reliability. Helper functions simplified repetitive tasks, and a clear project structure made everything scalable and team-friendly. Together, these techniques create a testing setup that's ready to grow with your application and help you maintain a high-quality website with confidence.

A note from the authors

Thank you for spending this time with us and exploring the world of testing with Playwright. Our hope is that the lessons, examples, and practices we've shared help you build more confidence in your testing and bring a bit more ease to your development process.

Writing this book has been a journey of discovery for us as well, and knowing it may now become part of your own journey is truly rewarding. If these pages sparked new ideas or gave you a clearer path forward, then we've accomplished what we set out to do.

If you found this book helpful, we'd be grateful if you could share a brief comment on Amazon or Goodreads. Your feedback not only helps other readers, but it also encourages us as authors to keep creating and improving.

With gratitude,

Faraz K. Kelhini and Butch Mayhew

17

Unlock Your Exclusive Benefits

Your copy of this book includes the following exclusive benefits:

- Next-gen Packt Reader
- DRM-free PDF/ePub downloads

Follow the guide below to unlock them. The process takes only a few minutes and needs to be completed once.

Unlock this Book's Free Benefits in 3 Easy Steps

Step 1

Keep your purchase invoice ready for *Step 3*. If you have a physical copy, scan it using your phone and save it as a PDF, JPG, or PNG.

For more help on finding your invoice, visit `https://www.packtpub.com/unlock-benefits/help`.

Note: If you bought this book directly from Packt, no invoice is required. After *Step 2*, you can access your exclusive content right away.

Step 2

Scan the QR code or go to `packtpub.com/unlock`.

On the page that opens (similar to *Figure 17.1* on desktop), search for this book by name and select the correct edition.

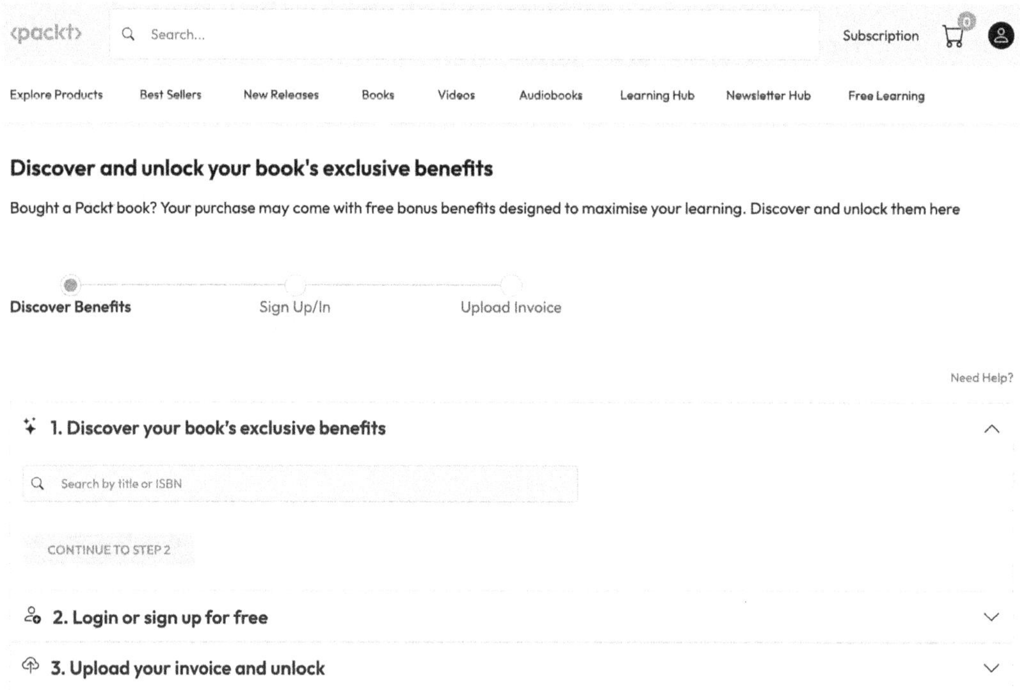

Figure 17.1: Packt unlock landing page on desktop

Step 3

After selecting your book, sign in to your Packt account or create one for free. Then upload your invoice (PDF, PNG, or JPG, up to 10 MB). Follow the on-screen instructions to finish the process.

Need help?

If you get stuck and need help, visit `https://www.packtpub.com/unlock-benefits/help` for a detailed FAQ on how to find your invoices and more. This QR code will take you to the help page.

Note: If you are still facing issues, reach out to `customercare@packt.com`.

Appendix A

Streamlining Playwright in Modern Development Workflows

Throughout the book, we've explored how to use Playwright to write, organize, and run reliable tests. But there are always extra details that don't quite fit neatly into the flow of the main text. That's what this appendix is for. This appendix dives into how Playwright can fit into today's development practices, such as Agile, DevOps, and different CI/CD pipelines.

Using cloud testing services for scalability and cross-environment testing

Running a large suite of automated tests locally is often impractical. You are limited by your machine's hardware (CPU and RAM) for running tests in parallel, and it's difficult to maintain all the different browser, operating system, and device combinations you need to test.

Cloud testing platforms solve these problems by providing on-demand access to a massive grid of virtual machines and real devices. This allows for massive parallelism (running hundreds of tests simultaneously) and comprehensive cross-environment coverage without any infrastructure management on your part.

Microsoft Playwright Testing (part of **Azure App Testing**) is a cloud service designed for Playwright and offers massive parallelism across Chromium, Firefox, and WebKit on Windows, Linux, and macOS. It supports sharding for distributed test runs, unified reporting, and integrates with Azure Pipelines for CI/CD. This service lets you run thousands of tests in minutes and provides shared workspaces for smooth transitions from local to cloud testing.

Other great options include the following:

- **BrowserStack:** Works with Playwright's API and gives you access to real devices and browsers. It's a great fit for mobile web testing through BrowserStack capabilities (`https://www.browserstack.com/docs/automate/playwright`).
- **Sauce Labs**: Lets you run Playwright tests in the cloud using the `saucectl` CLI, with support for both emulators and real devices (`https://docs.saucelabs.com/web-apps/automated-testing/playwright/`).
- **LambdaTest**: Provides WebSocket connections for live testing, along with Playwright-focused features such as AI-powered test orchestration (`https://www.lambdatest.com/playwright-testing`).

These platforms make it easier to test across a wide range of environments, such as different operating system and browser combinations, and scale efficiently with parallel test execution. You can configure them in `playwright.config.ts` using environment variables for credentials and integrate runs directly into your CI pipeline.

Deciding when to use Playwright in Agile workflows

The **Agile** methodology focuses on rapid progress and frequently releasing functional software. Playwright fits right in with its speedy, cross-browser testing capabilities. The key is knowing when to use it based on your testing needs.

In sprint-based workflows, Playwright shines for validating user stories at the end of a sprint. For instance, running **end-to-end** (**E2E**) tests during sprint reviews helps confirm that new features work smoothly with existing ones. To keep things moving, integrate Playwright into your CI/CD pipeline to run tests on every commit or pull request, which gives instant feedback within the sprint. This lines up nicely with the Agile methodology's goal of delivering working software, since Playwright's auto-waiting and reliable locators make handling dynamic UIs smoother and less flaky.

For **test-driven development** (**TDD**), Playwright is better for higher-level tests than traditional unit-level TDD. While unit tests (for example, with Jest) focus on component logic, Playwright can drive **UI TDD** by writing E2E tests for key user flows first, then building features to pass them. It's especially useful in **behavior-driven development** (**BDD**) with tools such as Cucumber, where Playwright automates Gherkin scenarios.

Here's when to lean on Playwright:

- **Early in the Sprint**: Run smoke tests on early frontend builds, such as initial clickable prototypes, to confirm basic navigation and rendering
- **Mid-Sprint**: Use API mocking or route interception to validate frontend behavior before backend services are fully ready
- **Sprint end**: Run comprehensive regression tests to ensure that the sprint's work is ready for demo or release

Since E2E tests are slower, don't overuse Playwright for every small change: save it for integration points and rely on faster unit tests for TDD cycles. In mature Agile teams, parallel execution using workers or sharding can make daily test runs practical and keep your sprints on track.

Aligning Playwright testing with DevOps principles

When you treat testing as a continuous, automated practice instead of a final hurdle, Playwright becomes a great sidekick. It gives you earlier feedback and helps your team move quickly without giving up any reliability. Playwright aligns with the core principles that keep modern DevOps teams shipping smoothly:

- **Continuous testing**: Back in *Chapter 7, Integrating Workflows with CI/CD Pipelines*, we saw how Playwright plugs into CI/CD pipelines to run tests automatically. For example, in GitHub Actions or Jenkins, you can set up a workflow to install dependencies, run `npx playwright test`, and share reports. This catches issues early. Parallel execution through sharding can cut test times from hours to minutes, even for large suites. You can also use tools such as **Allure** to enhance reporting within pipelines for better insights.
- **Shift-left testing**: This DevOps principle pushes testing earlier in the development cycle to catch defects sooner. Playwright supports this through component testing (for example, with `@playwright/experimental-ct-react`), which lets you test UI elements in isolation without a full app. You can run these tests locally while coding.

Here's how to make it work:

- Include tests in code reviews via CI checks
- Use mocks and fixtures to test without relying on external services
- Pair with shift-right monitoring to catch issues in production

So, by embedding Playwright in DevOps pipelines, you enable faster releases and reduce costs.

Building effective feedback loops with Playwright

When a test fails, you want your team to know right away and have clear steps to figure out what went wrong. Playwright makes this easy with its reporting tools and integrations with CI/CD systems.

If a test fails in a CI/CD pipeline, such as GitHub Actions, for example, the system can highlight the issue directly in the pull request and point to the exact line or test that failed. In Azure Pipelines, using the JUnit reporter, you can publish results and set up alerts through email or tools such as Microsoft Teams or Slack for instant notifications. Many teams also use webhooks to send failure summaries to collaboration platforms, so developers don't have to dig through CI dashboards.

To dive into the details of a failure, Playwright gives you a few handy reporting tools (in this book, we've already taken a look at the HTML reporter and Trace Viewer):

- **JSON or JUnit reporters**: These generate structured files for CI tools to parse, enabling custom dashboards or integration with systems such as Jira. For example, JUnit XML files work well with Jenkins or CircleCI to provide detailed failure insights.
- **HTML reporter**: This creates a user-friendly, web-based report saved in the `playwright-report` folder with test results, screenshots, videos, and traces. You can set it to open automatically on failure or upload it as a CI artifact, such as using `actions/upload-artifact` in GitHub Actions. Teams can view it with `npx playwright show-report` or download it from CI builds for a clear, visual breakdown of what happened.
- **Trace Viewer**: Playwright's traces let you replay a test step by step, showing network requests, DOM snapshots, and console logs. These are accessible in the HTML report or standalone, which makes it simple to spot issues such as network delays or UI glitches.

In your `playwright.config.ts` file, you can set up multiple reporters, such as `reporter: [['dot'], ['html'], ['json']]`, to get concise CI output while keeping rich diagnostics for local debugging.

For large test suites running in parallel using sharding, the Blob reporter (see `https://playwright.dev/docs/test-reporters`) combines results into a single, unified report. This setup keeps feedback loops tight: failures block CI merges, alerts reach the right team members, and detailed diagnostics help resolve issues quickly.

Appendix B

References and Resources

As you continue your journey with Playwright, you may want to dive deeper into official documentation, community resources, and complementary tools. Here's a curated list to guide your further exploration.

Official documentation and guides

- **Playwright documentation**

  `https://playwright.dev/docs`

  The official and most comprehensive source for setup, configuration, and API details.

- **Playwright API reference**

  `https://playwright.dev/docs/api/class-playwright`

  In-depth technical reference for all Playwright classes, methods, and options.

- **Playwright test runner**

  `https://playwright.dev/docs/test-intro`

  A guide to using the built-in test runner, with examples for structuring tests and using fixtures.

- **Playwright GitHub repo**

  `https://github.com/microsoft/playwright`

  Official home of the Playwright code base.

- **Playwright MCP GitHub repo**

  `https://github.com/microsoft/playwright-mcp`

  Official home of the Playwright MCP Server for AI agents.

- **Playwright YouTube channel**

  `https://www.youtube.com/@playwrightdev`

  Tutorials, release highlights, and walkthroughs from the Playwright team.

- **Playwright Slack/Discord communities**

  `https://aka.ms/playwright/discord`

  Join the Playwright community Discord server to connect with other developers. Also search for `Playwright Community Slack/Discord`. Active chat groups share tips and help troubleshoot issues.

Community and learning resources

- **Playwright solutions**

  `https://playwrightsolutions.com`

  A blog focused on providing solutions to problems faced when using Playwright.

- **Debbie Codes**

  `https://debbie.codes`

  A series of blog posts on Playwright created by Debbie O'Brien.

- **Stack Overflow**

  `https://stackoverflow.com/questions/tagged/playwright`

  A growing knowledge base of real-world issues and solutions.

- **Third-party plugins**

  Search `npm` for `playwright` to discover plugins for reporting, test management, and extended functionality.

Broader testing and automation resources

- **Awesome Sites to Test On**

  `https://github.com/BMayhew/awesome-sites-to-test-on`

  A curated list of sites to practice testing on.

- **Testing library**

  `https://testing-library.com/docs`

  Can be used in combination with Playwright for testing UI behavior.

- **Cypress versus Playwright comparisons**

  `https://www.reddit.com/r/QualityAssurance/comments/srhafv/cypress_vs_playwright/`

  Reading about differences can give insight into Playwright's strengths and trade-offs.

- **General software testing books:**

  - *Continuous Testing for DevOps Professionals* by Eran Kinsbruner: `https://www.amazon.com/-/en/Continuous-Testing-DevOps-Professionals-Practical/dp/1727132173`
  - *Agile Testing* by Lisa Crispin and Janet Gregory: `https://www.amazon.com/Agile-Testing-Condensed-Brief-Introduction/dp/199922051X`

  These provide a broader context for testing strategies.

packtpub.com

Subscribe to our online digital library for full access to over 7,000 books and videos, as well as industry leading tools to help you plan your personal development and advance your career. For more information, please visit our website.

Why subscribe?

- Spend less time learning and more time coding with practical eBooks and Videos from over 4,000 industry professionals
- Improve your learning with Skill Plans built especially for you
- Get a free eBook or video every month
- Fully searchable for easy access to vital information
- Copy and paste, print, and bookmark content

At `www.packt.com`, you can also read a collection of free technical articles, sign up for a range of free newsletters, and receive exclusive discounts and offers on Packt books and eBooks.

Other Books You May Enjoy

If you enjoyed this book, you may be interested in these other books by Packt:

Learn Model Context Protocol with TypeScript

Christoffer Noring

ISBN: 978-1-80666-139-8

- Understand the MCP protocol and its core components
- Build MCP servers that expose tools and resources to a variety of clients
- Test and debug servers using the interactive inspector tools
- Consume servers using Claude for desktop and Visual Studio Code agents
- Secure MCP apps, as well as managing and mitigating common threats
- Build and deploy MCP apps using cloud-based strategies

Node.js Design Patterns

Luciano Mammino, Mario Casciaro

ISBN: 978-1-80323-894-4

- Understand Node.js basics and its async event-driven architecture
- Write correct async code using callbacks, promises, and async/await
- Harness Node.js streams to create data-driven processing pipelines
- Implement trusted software design patterns for production-grade applications
- Write testable code and automated tests (unit, integration, E2E)
- Use advanced recipes: caching, batching, async init, offload CPU-bound work
- Build and scale microservices and distributed systems powered by Node.js

Packt is searching for authors like you

If you're interested in becoming an author for Packt, please visit `authors.packtpub.com` and apply today. We have worked with thousands of developers and tech professionals, just like you, to help them share their insight with the global tech community. You can make a general application, apply for a specific hot topic that we are recruiting an author for, or submit your own idea.

Share your thoughts

Now you've finished *Hands-On Automated Testing with Playwright*, we'd love to hear your thoughts! Scan the QR code below to go straight to the Amazon review page for this book and share your feedback or leave a review on the site that you purchased it from.

`https://packt.link/r/1806106477`

Your review is important to us and the tech community and will help us make sure we're delivering excellent quality content.

Playwright Events

If you're looking to put your learning into practice and discover hidden tips and tricks to make the most of Playwright, you might want to check out our events. Scan the QR code to register your interest via the landing page and be among the first to hear about upcoming events, including exclusive related offers.

`https://landing.packtpub.com/automated-testing-with-playwright/`

Index

A

D

K

L

M

N

O

P

U

V

W

X

www.ingramcontent.com/pod-product-compliance
Lightning Source LLC
LaVergne TN
LVHW080528210926
848481LV00023B/3753
9781806106479